WORKPLACE VIOLENCE
Planning for Prevention and Response

KIM M. KERR

ELSEVIER

AMSTERDAM • BOSTON • HEIDELBERG • LONDON • NEW YORK • OXFORD
PARIS • SAN DIEGO • SAN FRANCISCO • SINGAPORE • SYDNEY • TOKYO

Butterworth-Heinemann is an imprint of Elsevier

Butterworth-Heinemann is an imprint of Elsevier
30 Corporate Drive, Suite 400, Burlington, MA 01803, USA
The Boulevard, Langford Lane, Kidlington, Oxford, OX5 1GB, UK

Notices

Knowledge and best practice in this field are constantly changing. As new research and experience
broaden our understanding, changes in research methods, professional practices, or medical
treatment may become necessary.

Practitioners and researchers must always rely on their own experience and knowledge in evaluating
and using any information, methods, compounds, or experiments described herein. In using such
information or methods they should be mindful of their own safety and the safety of others, including
parties for whom they have a professional responsibility.

To the fullest extent of the law, neither the Publisher nor the authors, contributors, or editors, assume
any liability for any injury and/or damage to persons or property as a matter of products liability,
negligence or otherwise, or from any use or operation of any methods, products, instructions, or
ideas contained in the material herein.

Library of Congress Cataloging-in-Publication Data
Kerr, Kim M.
 Workplace violence : planning for prevention and response / Kim Kerr.
    p. cm.
 Includes bibliographical references and index.
 ISBN 978-1-85617-698-9 (alk. paper)
 1. Violence in the workplace—United States. 2. Violence in the workplace—United States—Prevention.   I. Title.
 HF5549.5.E43K48 2010
 658.3'8—dc22   2010001435

British Library Cataloguing-in-Publication Data
A catalogue record for this book is available from the British Library.

ISBN: 978-1-85617-698-9

For information on all Butterworth-Heinemann publications
visit our web site at www.elsevierdirect.com

Printed in United States of America

10 11 12 13   10 9 8 7 6 5 4 3 2 1

Dedication

This book is dedicated to my mother, Colleen H. Kerr, and grandmother, Lenora Riding Haycock. Both women instilled in me the need to grow up strong and stand for something.

And, to my loving wife, Cheryle, and my children, Sean, Joseph, Chelsey, and Erin, and their families who help make my life fuller than I ever dreamed possible. And lastly to my spiritual fellowship family who is too large to name but too special to forget.

TABLE OF CONTENTS

About the Author

Kim M. Kerr, CPP, CHS-III, is the Chief Information Officer for Verisys Corporation. He is also the principal for KC Kerr and Associates. He is a former vice president and general manager for LexisNexis, a director of product management, and director of security services for LexisNexis. Currently, Kim assists clients with security consulting solutions, project management for data fabrication, and custom software and screening solutions. He is the coauthor of *Background Screening and Investigations: Managing Hiring Risk from a HR and Security Perspective* (Butterworth-Heinemann, 2008). He is also a security veteran of three Olympic Games; Kim was the security project manager for AT&T's Olympic efforts at the 1996 Summer Olympic Games in Atlanta, a member of the technical security team at the 2000 Summer Olympic Games in Sydney, Australia, and deputy director of security support for the 2002 Salt Lake City Winter Olympic Games.

Kim retired from AT&T after a 28-year career in corporate security and investigations. A graduate of Westminster College in Salt Lake City, Kim performed major investigations, including violence in the workplace, of incidents and threats while managing all members of the investigations staff in the Georgia, Tennessee, and North and South Carolina area. After the 1996 Summer Games in Atlanta, Kim was recruited back to his hometown of Salt Lake City to assist with security in the 2002 Winter Games.

While a member of the Salt Lake Organizing Committee (SLOC), Kim managed a wide range of security projects. Most importantly, he directly managed executive protection for SLOC and International Olympic Committee executives, talent security, SLOC headquarters security, Olympic family hotel security, and all other secure sites where law enforcement was not present.

Kerr is a leading expert in background security strategies, corporate security management and investigations, special event security, executive protection, and the creation and implementation of proactive security policy. He frequently lends his expertise in both recognizing and preventing violence in the workplace as he consults with and speaks to businesses around the country. He works directly with HR and security professionals to create disaster recovery action plans.

Kim is a Certified Protection Professional (CPP) with the American Society of Industrial Security (ASIS international) and has a Certification in Homeland Security (CHS-III) from the American Board of Certification in Homeland Security.

Contributors' Biographies

David Goldman, Esquire

Mr. Goldman has advised management in all areas of employment and labor law in over a decade of practice. He now focuses his practice on helping employers prevent employee-related problems before they become lawsuits.

Mr. Goldman is currently the managing attorney of the Littler Learning Group, the division of Littler Mendelson devoted to meeting clients' employment law training needs. In this position, he helps ensure that all training programs contain Littler's best legal practices and cutting edge learning techniques and meet clients' individual needs. Mr. Goldman has also trained management and industry leaders and published articles on numerous employment law, management, and training topics.

Mr. Goldman has also developed and reviewed employee handbooks, policies, and contracts. He has implemented alternative dispute resolution programs involving both arbitration and mediation of employment issues. When disputes do arise, Mr. Goldman has represented management in federal and state court and before government agencies. Mr. Goldman has counseled employers on traditional labor law as well, defending them against charges of unfair labor practices before the NLRB and state and federal courts.

Prior to his legal career, Mr. Goldman was an assistant vice president at Bank of Boston. In this position, he dealt with many of the legal issues relevant to the clients he now advises and trains.

Mr. Goldman received his JD degree, *magna cum laude*, from the Boston University School of Law in 1992. During law school, Mr. Goldman received the Edward F. Henessey Distinguished Scholar Award in 1992, the Paul J. Liacos Scholar Award in 1991, and was a semi-finalist with Boston University's NYU Moot Court Competition Team. He also received the Book Award for professional responsibility. Mr. Goldman received his BA degree, *magna cum laude*, from Clark University in Worcester, Massachusetts, in 1986. He has also completed accredited coursework on instructional design and online learning.

Mr. Goldman is a member of both the California and Georgia bars, as well as the American Bar Association.

John P. Benson, J.D., AHFI, CIFI, CFE

Mr. Benson is Chief Operating Officer of Government Management Services, Inc. (GMS), soon to be re-branded as Verisys Corporation. Verisys is an aggregator and electronic publisher of objective primary source provider data (sanctions, disciplinary actions, licensure, NPI, and other data sets). Verisys helps health care companies maintain compliance, manage risk, and protect their trust-based reputation. GMS is both NCQA certified and URAC accredited as a CVO.

Prior to GMS, Mr. Benson was with LexisNexis Risk & Information Analytics Group serving as vice president. Mr. Benson drove market strategy, planning and product development, provided management leadership, and held P&L accountability for the health care and insurance sectors. Mr. Benson was responsible for the SIRIS (Special Investigation Resource and Intelligence System) application hosted by LexisNexis in partnership with NHCAA to provide suspected fraud and abuse information sharing across the health care industry membership.

Previously Mr. Benson was VP, Electronic Claim Solutions, for Concentra Inc. (originally NHR, Inc., which was later acquired by Concentra) and was responsible for product development, management, support, and sales of payer solutions for insurers (auto, workers' compensation and health) and third-party administrators. The payer solutions focused on provider reimbursement, electronic document imaging and management, management of care delivery/utilization, utilization and medical necessity rule development, health care data analysis, and decision support and fraud detection and prevention. The products were designed to drive intelligent and integrated claim handling. Mr. Benson's responsibilities also included management of engineering and quality assurance teams, implementation team management, regulatory compliance (including HIPAA), data management (rule, edit, flag development, and fee schedule and UCR data sets), data security, and software quality assurance for his division's line of products.

Prior to Concentra, Mr. Benson was senior vice president for Axios Data Analysis Systems Corp., a Blue Shield of California company, responsible for product design and development and client relationship management and project implementation. Axios was a provider of Internet application solutions delivering web-hosted analytic data marts to clients, primarily in the field of health care informatics. The solutions were focused on cost-of-health-care, profitability and waste/abuse/fraud issues for health and property/casualty insurers. Mr. Benson effectively managed large client engagements to deliver value-added analytical output, intervention design, and outcome tracking.

Mr. Benson has over 20 years of multiline insurance experience, both strategically and tactically (life and health, disability, and personal and commercial lines, including auto and workers' compensation). Mr. Benson developed his management and leadership skills by leading large operational units for established carriers and by owning his own businesses. Prior to joining Axios, Mr. Benson was a manager with DT Health Systems, a health care data analytics consulting practice of Deloitte and Touche, where he held responsibilities for fraud and abuse detection product development, marketing and sales. Formerly, as corporate vice president with Zenith National Insurance Group, he managed a national Special Investigations Unit (SIU) and a specialized litigation unit. Mr. Benson also held a director's position at Fireman's Fund where he developed an integrated workers' compensation SIU and claims program. Mr. Benson started out in the insurance industry as a home office representative for MONY (Mutual of New York) Financial Services. Prior to entering the insurance industry, Mr. Benson owned and managed investigative firms serving the insurance, legal, and business markets.

Mr. Benson has served on editorial boards for insurance industry publications, and chaired committees for industry organizations and for a state Department of Insurance. He has had significant leadership involvement with industry associations including the California Workers' Compensation Institute (CWCI) (committee chairperson), NHCAA, IASIU, AISG/ISO Insurance Fraud Management Committee, and the Antifraud Sub-Committee of the California Department of Insurance (cochairperson). Mr. Benson is frequently sought out for public speaking opportunities on fraud, technology, and insurance issues. His certifications are from the Association of Certified Fraud Examiners, Certified Fraud Examiner (CFE), National Health Care Anti-Fraud Association, Accredited Health Care Fraud Investigator (AHFI), the International Association of Special Investigation Units, Certified Insurance Fraud Investigator (CIFI), and he was the qualifying agent for LexisNexis' Nevada Private Investigator's license. Mr. Benson and GMS's affiliate company, CSI, Inc., is licensed as a private investigations entity in Connecticut, New Jersey, New York, and Virginia with licensure pending in Massachusetts, Nevada, and Pennsylvania. Mr. Benson holds a bachelor's degree in journalism and a juris doctorate form Loyola University of Los Angeles.

Bonnie S. Michelman, CPP, CHPA

Bonnie S. Michelman has extensive security management and leadership experience in diverse industries. Currently, she is the Director of Police, Security and Outside Services at Massachusetts General Hospital, Boston, Massachusetts. She also serves as the security consultant for Partners Healthcare, which is comprised of nine hospitals. She was formerly district manager at First Security Services overseeing 60 diverse operations and 1,200 people, Boston, Massachusetts; assistant vice president for General Services at Newton-Wellesley Hospital, Newton, Massachusetts, managing 16 departments; and in corporate security management at Data General Corporation, Westboro, Massachusetts.

Bonnie currently serves as chairman of the board of the International Association for Healthcare Security and Safety (IAHSS). She served as president of IAHSS in 2008 and 1995. IAHSS awarded the Massachusetts General Hospital's Police, Security and Outside Services Department under Bonnie's direction the Lindberg Bell Award in 1999 and 2007. This is awarded to the finest health care security program nationally. Bonnie served as president in 2001 of ASIS International, a 38,000-person organization, chairman of the board in 2002, and foundation president from 2003 to 2005. She has been an instructor at Northeastern University, College of Criminal Justice, in both graduate and undergraduate programs since 1988. Bonnie is on the regional board of directors for the Anti-Defamation League (ADL). She was the 2007 award recipient of "Campus Safety Director of the Year."

Bonnie is a Certified Protection Professional (CPP) and a Certified Healthcare Protection Administrator (CHPA). Bonnie has an MBA from Bentley College, an MS in Criminal Justice from Northeastern University, and a BA in Government and Sociology from Clark University. She is an international certified instructor in "Management of Aggressive Behavior" (MOAB) and does significant work in the areas of security management, workplace violence, hate crimes, domestic violence, cultural diversity, and risk assessment. She also serves as an expert in negligent or inadequate security litigation. She lectures and consults internationally and has over 60 publications in various journals on safety, security, and management.

Acknowledgments

The author would like to acknowledge Staci A. Cannady for her amazing hard work and editing skills in the completion of this work. Without her focus, this project could have never been completed. A special thanks to Kristen J. Overton for her final review of this book and extraordinary attention to detail. You are a true professional. The author also extends a hearty "well done" to Kelly Grace Harris, for keeping him moving forward and the overall coordination of this work. And lastly, a thank you goes to Pam Chester for her professionalism and guidance in the process from proposal to printing. You are terrific.

Preface

As a young corporate security investigator, I was often sent out of town for investigative assignments or to meet with managers to discuss security of the various in-house AT&T organizations. My territory at that time was primarily the Midwest. In my recollection, violence prevention from internal sources was not one of the topics typically discussed. Physical security, however, was a central topic focused largely to prevent asset loss, both external and internal. That all changed for me on August 20, 1986, when an incident occurred in Edmond, Oklahoma, that would bring a new reality to the emerging problem of violence in the workplace. I was in Oklahoma City that fateful day when Patrick Henry Sherrill, a troubled U.S. postal worker, came into his workplace and shot 21 coworkers and supervisors, killing 14 and wounding 7.

This incident at the post office shifted the ground beneath us all. It shed light on a new threat, a new security, and safety concern into our work and social consciousness. Prior mass killings had been, primarily, between strangers. The post office killing involved people who knew and worked with the killer. This incident crossed an invisible line dispelling the belief that we are generally safe in the workplace from deliberate acts of violence. It created the term "postal," which is essentially undeserved as the post office has seen no more violence than other workplaces. In fact, between 1992 and 1998, only 16 of the 6,719 workplace homicides took place in a post office.

As a practitioner in the field of security, and specifically focused on workplace security, this brutal act of workplace violence was a tremendous shock. It was outside my conscious threat realm. I had considered theft of assets, trade secrets, and proprietary information in the scope of my primary responsibility. I sat in my car stunned as the breaking news came flooding into my car through the radio airwaves. This type of incident seemed, somehow, out of context. But like the Oklahoma City bombing of the Murrah Federal Building in 1995 and the tragic events of September 11, 2001, these types of incidents pierced the hearts of Americans everywhere. They broke a barrier of risk that had previously been theoretical, and created a new reality in the workplace. The workplace, like home or church, had been a place that was considered, by most, to be pretty safe. The work environment was seen as a place where inappropriate behavior was unacceptable and certain lines were not crossed. Our professions were and are centrally tied to who we were as individuals and members of society. The workplace is an environment in which we are expected to be productive, creative, and respectful, and certainly not a place to be violent and vicious.

Since these life-altering events, I have been fascinated by the crossing of the barrier between violence being a rare and nonoccurrence to violence becoming more commonplace. But violence has many faces and these types of attacks, as well as external attacks, must be viewed from many perspectives. It involves more than just killing or attempted killings. It involves acts of intimidation, threats of all types, vandalism, cyber threats and stalking, and assault. The reality of these daily events is that most do not make the United States 24/7 news cycles. In fact, because of the frequency of these incidents, most go unnoticed as workplace violence and get lumped into the street violence we have come to accept as a part of our culture. Unless there are multiple deaths, these incidents may never be widely publicized. Chances are these acts of workplace violence are reported only in local newspapers, buried beneath more interesting headlines.

Electronic news media has helped tremendously to bring more awareness to these stories via blogs and news web services. For those of us who are interested in the twists and turns of this problem, we can have the various news and blog articles captured for daily review through numerous search engines. But, for the most part, the rank and file employees still depend on security, human resources (HR), and management to keep them informed and protected.

Another noteworthy dimension of violence in the workplace is the indirect and often overlooked victims—the family and friends of the people who experienced the act of violence. Family and friends are often forced to watch their loved ones go through the depression, anxiety, anger, and even suicidal behavior that can be the result of workplace violence. Also, the coworkers who watch incidents occur in silence only to berate themselves for not reporting their suspicions or concerns for fear of making waves or being labeled a "whistle blower." Another indirect victim is the business owner who may watch his or her bottom line evaporate due to poor employee productivity, higher turnover, absenteeism, and workers' compensation claims all as a result of acts of violence at work.

Countless books and articles have been published claiming to offer new approaches to violence prevention, and new ways to deal with the complexity of human emotions. This is a human problem that links the depth of human emotions to acts of frustration as a last resort to fix the unfixable or to regain some sort of control of a situation that the perpetrator feels is out of their control. Each occupation has a degree of risk of violence in the workplace. However, there are occupations that are more susceptible to violence. Jobs such as taxi drivers, bartenders, police officers, and military personnel all have special concerns. Of late, our schools have become a receptacle where violence has been spilling its venom. School and college campuses, like Columbine and Virginia Tech, have become prime locations for acts of violence.

On a more positive note, homicides have been declining in recent years. This may have something to do with corporations providing outlets for stress reduction through Employee Assistance Programs (EAPs), gun control policies on company premises, and better physical security. Or the decrease in workplace homicides may have more to do with awareness and prevention strategies taken by HR and security professionals in concert with managers, union leaders, and business owners.

The information presented in this book will draw conclusions that may be used as a minimal list of action items that a company can put into place. However, the key to a successful prevention program may require the infusion of prevention and action into the organizational culture, and the ability to maintain these efforts. Like sexual harassment prevention and awareness, workplace violence is a series of actions or threat of actions that need to be addressed when witnessed or reported. Feedback should be given to reporters to encourage them to report issues in the future.

Good record keeping of events that include a description of how situations were resolved, the individuals involved and how they were impacted, and the overall lessons learned is crucial. If we intend to improve the work environment by fostering an organizational fabric that acknowledges the realities of violence in the workplace, the elements that make up a solid program need to be a part of our daily lives. This should not be just another program we roll out once a year for the sake of due diligence at the request of our general counsel. Openness, candor, and inclusion of this issue must be part of the DNA of business life. I know this all too well as I got a little too close to the flame early in my career. It occurred during my tenure as a corporate security manager and overall project manager of AT&T's security efforts for the 1996 Summer Olympic Games held in Atlanta, Georgia. I am referring to the bombing of the Centennial Olympic Park where I was in charge of the security for the AT&T Global Olympic Village. Although this was considered an act of a domestic terrorist, it was still my workplace as well as the workplace of a thousand or so corporate employees and volunteers. For 30 days I reported to work and led a team of security professionals. I would like to relay my experience to show how this violent act changed my life—forever and always.

It was 1:30 a.m. on July 9, 1996. I was asleep in my hotel room when I heard the phone ringing in the other room. I came out of a deep and long overdue sleep leaping across the room to answer the ringing, flashing hotel phone. It was the command center at the AT&T corporate security headquarters set up for the coordination of security for the games. The voice on the other end was excited, shouting the unbelievable information. A bomb had gone off just outside of the AT&T Global Olympic Village located in the Olympic Centennial Park. The command center attendant gave me a quick summary of the report she had received only seconds earlier. There was a bomb; people were down, maybe dead; exact numbers were unknown. The park was in chaos. A car was on the way to pick me up. I was instructed to be downstairs, and then the line went dead.

My wife asked what was going on. I relayed the contents of the call to her as I turned on the TV. CNN came on with a screen of red flashing lights and people running. The camera was swinging from scene to scene. The banner at the bottom of the screen said bomb explosion in Olympic Park. I dressed quickly in my Olympic uniform consisting of a golf shirt and khaki shorts. I grabbed my radio and cell phone and ran for the door. I staggered to the elevator and pushed the call button. It seemed like an eternity until the door opened. I stepped inside and pushed the lobby key. As the elevator descended my mind raced. This seemed so surreal. This couldn't be happening! Things had been running like clockwork up until now; smooth as silk. It was day nine of the Olympics, and the security had been so fine-tuned that I had decided to take the night off. It was my first night off in days. I agreed to let my wife take me to an early dinner and get a good night's sleep. I was so exhausted I don't even remember falling asleep; I remember only lying down for what seemed like only a second and then the phone ringing almost five hours later.

The elevator door opened and I stepped into the lobby. My boss was coming toward me through the door. He had his game face on. "What happened?" I asked quickly. He gave me the same basic information the control center had given me. Fortunately, the driver was experienced and knew the fastest way to the park. We called him "Van Man." He lived in a company van taking people and supplies throughout the Olympic theater on the company's behalf. He had us there in seconds. The barricades were open. The streets were strangely deserted en route. We rounded just north of the park, and then we could see the confusion. We were only two blocks away.

"This is as close as we can get," Van Man said. "You'll have to walk from here."

We were out and running. I headed for the back gate. I was inside the gate in an instant. I lost my boss in the shuffle. He had been stopped by one of the project managers who was standing just outside the park. I could hear them yelling for me. I turned and looked back. The police had stopped them from following me. I kept going. The officer at the back gate recognized me. He waved me in. I ran to the control room, which was already filled with Atlanta police and very confused security officers from the guard detail.

I asked for a briefing from the shift supervisor. The shift supervisor, who looked dazed, blurted out the bare bones of the event. He received a call from the guard at the mix/light tower. Richard Jewell, security officer, reported a suspicious backpack under a bench. The ATF responded. They looked in the bag using a probe. It was a bomb. As the Georgia State Police cleared the crowd back, the bomb went off. A lot of people were hurt and maybe even dead. I ran to the front of the venue looking for my friend, Tom Dailey. Tom was the guard commander that night. Where was Tom?

I used the radio, "Tom, Tom, this is Kim."

"Go for Tom," was the response. I felt a sigh of relief within me. He was my best friend in the world.

"What's your 20," I asked (20 is radio jargon for what is your location).

"Just south of the stage," he responded.

"Wait for me. I'm on my way—Kim out." I replied.

I ran down a deserted hall and went directly where I thought Tom would be. I got to the patio that was just southeast of the stage. Police officers were everywhere. I could see Tom. He was talking to a police officer. Tom looked back, saw me, and started to walk toward me. A Major from the Atlanta Police Department was there. The venue was under the jurisdiction of the Georgia State Police; white hats and black shirts with the word POLICE in bold white letters across their back—they were moving like a stream across the grass.

I could see a portable light near what appeared to be an off-white tarp lying on the ground. It looked like a body. I later learned it was the body of Alice Hawthorne. Hers was the only direct death as a result of the bombing. It was later learned that a Turkish cameraman died as a result of a heart attack running to cover the crime scene. Crime scene tape was going up. I knew we only had a few minutes before we would be asked to evacuate. Tom filled me in with some additional details.

Just before the bomb was found, a band was on the stage and there were several hundreds of spectators. The Global Olympic Village, or GOV, as we called it, was full of Olympic athletes and guests of AT&T enjoying the summer night's festivities. All was going as planned.

Some men were sitting on benches they had moved against the East light/mix tower. They had been drinking and pushing empty beer cans through a hole in the corrugated metal apron that acted as an outer barrier of the mix tower, creating a mess. In this mix tower were the technicians who ran the light and sound for the stage. They had complained to Richard Jewell, a contract security officer, about the beer cans, and he had responded. Jewell confronted the group of three individuals, and then the group decided to move off. As they began to walk away, Richard noticed the backpack. He called to the group and one of the departing drinkers responded that the bag did not belong to anyone in their group.

Richard Jewell did his job perfectly. He asked adjacent spectators if the bag was theirs. All responded negatively. Jewell called his supervisor on the radio and asked a Georgia Bureau of Investigation (GBI) agent, who was near the tower, to call in a suspicious bag report. Two ATF agents responded to that call. They approached the bag and one of the agents used a probe to, gingerly, open the bag. The agent observed the contents of the bag well enough to call it a bomb and directed the police to start an evacuation. The crowd had been moved back approximately 100 yards when the bomb went off. One spectator was killed instantly. Somehow she had slipped through the evacuators' path. Approximately 200 others were injured—many of them police officers. Fortunately, somehow the blast went upward and not directionally as the bomber had probably planned.

The remnants of the AT&T security force, of which Tom and I were a part, were asked to leave the park. All civilians out! We were unable to reenter the park for four days. Eventually, the park was reopened with great fanfare. The good news for AT&T was that none of the guests, volunteers, or workers of the GOV whom I was charged with protecting were physically injured. However, some of my charges were very much traumatized by the event. Some of these people went home just after the bombing and never returned to work. Others came back reluctantly and worked the rest of the event but were noticeably affected by the traumatic events.

The Olympics came to an end with a cloud of suspicion hovering over Richard Jewell, who was later cleared of any involvement or wrongdoing. During the 1984 Olympics, a police officer planted a bomb under a team bus and reported it to gain hero status. He later confessed to the hoax. It is my belief that the investigators, who initially questioned Richard's involvement, may have been influenced by what happened in 1984. After three subsequent bombings in and around Atlanta after the games, a new suspect, Eric Robert Rudolph, emerged. He was made famous, not only because of the bombings, but also because of his ability to elude capture by living off the land (and eventually garbage can raiding!) in the Appalachian Mountains until May 31, 2003. He was arrested by a local police officer who had been in junior high at the time of the Centennial Park bombing.

The real point I want to make is how this senseless act of violence changed my life. After the bombing I made sure that everyone on my team and anyone connected to the event was part of the company initiative to debrief all employees, volunteers, contractors, and guests who had been there that night. I had not been there, but I was devastated. I had spent two years planning the security for this venue and the coordination of the security for the entire AT&T sponsorship of the 1996 Olympic Games. Anyone who has been involved in something like this knows that your stress level goes up when the event starts and doesn't come back down until the event is over. It was a zero-sum game for me. I had failed. It had especially become painful when Richard Jewell came under suspicion. I felt I should have done something different or something more to vet him. My thinking was not rational. I internalized these thoughts, and they festered in my mind. I took time off after the games, but the emotional pain only got worse. My wife became concerned. When I returned to work, my relationship with my boss became strained. A depression set in. I eventually sought professional help which broke the spell. The pain lifted, and I returned to my normal self with a little more wisdom. I came to know, for myself, the far-reaching effects of violence in the workplace on everyone involved—the witnesses, the witnesses' families, and those who feel a sense of responsibility for their inability to prevent the violent act.

In this process I started to study the effects of violence in the workplace with a new interest and, as I looked back on all the threats I had investigated, I identified the problem using new lenses. I came to understand that addressing the, now common, problem of violence in the workplace should be attacked holistically. Such an approach should not just focus on prevention via policy, training, background checks, physical security strategies, or through reactive means of investigation and mitigation tactics or incident response and crisis management. All of these factors must be engaged, but through a process of understanding the overall impact to the organization, the security professional responsible for the coordination of all security efforts for the site or series of sites, and business can break new ground in effecting culture. It might be in understanding the role of the HR professional who talks on the phone line with an employee who is concerned about bullying in the workplace, or the manager who is so under pressure to perform that she misses the warning signs of an employee who is moving closer to acting out. It could be the business owner or a senior manager who watches their strategy turn to mush after years of hard work and sacrifice. Regardless of who, what, when, where, and why, violence is a theft of dreams and has serious ramifications that must be addressed.

As I mentioned earlier, there have been many articles and books written on the subject of violence in the workplace, and the theories, strategies, and tactics to prevent, deter, detect, and react to such acts. But the land on which most of those works are standing is shifting. Many of the theories of the underpinnings have evolved and new threats are emerging. Old ideas and attitudes need to be reviewed, revisited, revised, or even revived.

Some of the tried and true methodologies still apply. Many of those will be outlined and discussed in this book. However, some false assumptions and planning pitfalls still exist on the baseline, and these assumptions, which were once true or partly true, need to be reviewed for accuracy in the current environment and possibly tossed out. It is my contention that if you start your process of addressing violence in the workplace from a false premise, you are risking missing the key points altogether. Let's look at a few false assumptions.

False assumption #1: Most of the perpetrators of violence in the workplace are men between the ages of 35 and 50, white, and tenured service employees.

A review of the first documented acts of violence in the workplace that involved employees found this premise to be basically correct. Consider the case mentioned earlier involving the postal worker, Patrick Henry Sherrill. He was a white male, 45 years of age. However, a strong word of caution is needed here. Profiling is a dangerous practice when it comes to violence prediction. This is especially true when those acts of violence involve individuals known to the organization, like employees, contractors, or vendors. Watching for documented, well-researched, and patterned behavioral warning signs, along with a number of adjacent factors, is a much better indicator. These patterns should be based on behavior that can be linked to predictable progression. Disregarding gender or age will allow you the freedom to assess acts as precursors to a progressive condition. Like alcoholism, violence is often progressive in nature with increasing severity. Mark Braverman concludes in his book *Preventing Workplace Violence: A Guide for Employers and Practitioners*, "Focusing on the individuals who may be at risk for violence on the basis of lists of characteristics alone is useless as a predictive tool and illegal in almost all cases from an employment law standpoint. Most important, however, limiting the focus to a search for predictive tools is a dangerous distraction from the crucial issue raised when we take a look at the real causes of the workplace violence problem." I wholeheartedly agree. Especially if any form of profiling is used as a starting point for addressing or planning an organizational response to the problem.

False assumption #2: Violence in the workplace is male dominated. Most of the violence is between males and directed at males, especially homicide, assaults, threats, and fighting. Men are normally the perpetrator.

In the book *Understanding Workplace Violence*, the authors, Michele Paludi, Rudy Nydegger, and Carmen Paludi, do an excellent job clarifying the effects of profiling based on gender. They write, "Certainly, men are statistically more likely to be victims of violence at work but this finding clouds the important point—women are not safer at work because of their sex" (2006). The truth is that domestic violence is often played out tragically at work locations. Also, cyber stalking has entered the mix as an emerging threat along with rape, sexual assault, and traditional stalking focusing. Cyber stalking will be discussed more thoroughly in Chapter 15. Homicide is still the number one cause of death for women in the workplace. Also, women are now perpetrators of workplace homicide. Let's look at the case involving a former postal worker, Jennifer San Marco. On January 30, 2006, San Marco shot and killed seven people. Her first victim was a former neighbor, Beverly Graham, and six at the post office where San Marco used to work. San Marco had a history of mental illness, and the consensus was that she also had difficulty dealing with a multicultural workforce. Of her seven victims, six were minority employees, three being African-American. This is another emerging issue that needs to be factored into discussions and strategies regarding violence prevention.

False assumption #3: Post offices are violence-prone organizations that continue to be a lightning rod for violence in the workplace.

My last two examples might give the impression that post offices are full of violence and individuals prone to violence. But the truth is post offices are no more prone to violence than any other organization. In fact, according to the Society of Human Resource Management (SHRM), the post office is now a safer workplace when compared to other organizations of similar size. But the term "postal" is now a popular word used to describe bizarre and spontaneous emotional outbursts and has replaced terms like "crazy" or "nuts" as synonyms for individuals who "go off" on people who can't fight back. Maybe a sign of emotional security is not picking on people who can't fight back. But the reality is, this term, "postal," is destined to stay with us for the foreseeable future. It is true, however, that most experts agree that the shooting by Patrick Henry Sherrill triggered the term.

False assumption #4: Most organizations have violence in the workforce policies. Violence in the workplace must be dropping substantially because of this inclusion.

Is having a policy is not better than not having a policy? In reality, just having a policy gives a false sense of security and might actually work against any forward movement to counter workplace violence. Effective strategies must start at the point of hiring with effective employment application vetting. Background screening that is commensurate with the risk of the organization by function, business sector, and location must be conducted. All of the strategies to prevent or mitigate violence must be interlaced with solid security and best practices in root cause investigations, record keeping, and trend analysis.

The phrase "holistic approach" is overused in business. But the challenge of a multilayered approach converging on this problem from all angles is paramount if an organization is committed to reducing the risk in a 360 degree manner.

False assumption #5: Physical security devices, databasing of key elements and evidence, and security processes have never been better. Camera systems, entry systems, and security processes are keeping violence from external sources at bay.

For those of us who are active members of the American Society of Industrial Security (ASIS international) and attend the annual international ASIS events, we are often overwhelmed by the available number of physical security solutions for the workplace. The span of approaches to external and internal access control, electronic surveillance, data linking of public records and instant retrieval of relevant data, and information and computer system security advances are truly remarkable. The unfortunate and unforgettable events of September 11, 2001, brought an almost fever pitch of focus to finding the silver bullet that would not only address terrorist threats, but also prevent violence from ending up on the doorstep of businesses and government entities.

But the truth is, many of the solutions are expensive and require a nonrevenue generating cost that is not always fully understood and often perceived as cutting into profit margins. Not only is there an initial investment, but there is an ongoing cost of staff and administration of the solutions. The cost to integrate people, systems, and procedures should be layered in a logical and efficient manner. In other words, the best strategy is to layer different prevention, detection, and response and recovery strategies that may solve a myriad of security risks individually, but, when implemented together, net out violence in an organization.

In her book *The Design and Evaluation of Physical Protection Systems* Mary Lynn Garcia makes the point much better than I can when she writes, "A physical protection system (PPS) integrates people, procedures and equipment for the protection of assets or facilities against theft, sabotage or other malevolent human attacks." When violence is the case, these systems must be added to the discussion. But the reality is that physical solutions cannot peer into the mind of an employee or view the off-premise behavior of the vendor who visits each day, nor can it see into the home life of a contractor who has been recently assigned to a project at the facility. Therefore, the primary takeaway here is that we must understand the importance of physical security, technical security, and investigative security, and to note the need for a layering of a series of strategies which include engaging security, senior management, human resources, and line management. Also, health and safety personnel, union representation, legal, chief finance office representation, and even EAPs should be included in any effective program. However, it is vitally important that an owner of the program is named, and an executive sponsor is established. Without senior management buy-in, prevention of violence in the workplace and response to it can be lost in a series of "flavor of the month" programs that get pushed aside to make room for whatever is hot.

False assumption #6: We pay a lot of money for safety and security, and so it will never happen to us.

Let's hope you are right! But the overall outcome is really dependent on your ability to ingrain prevention of violence into the DNA of every senior manager, manager, employee, contractor, vendor, and visitor, stressing that prevention of violence is a top priority of your organization. Everything from the words used to the hiring models to the training provided is key. Tactics as straightforward as effective use of signage, tightly managed access control, and proactivity in reporting incidences, no matter how small, can be critical to deterring, detecting, and resolving violence issues. These layers have to be interwoven into the fabric of the organization. Violence prevention programs should not be defined by delegation but rather in cooperation. We must recognize that violence can happen anywhere and in any organization but is preventable in most cases. In the event that a violent act does occur, we must also know how to appropriately respond.

False assumption #7: We live in a violent society. This is primarily a problem found in the United States and not seen as predominantly in other parts of the world.

As recently as October 2008, conferences and efforts are being focused on the challenges surrounding the problem of violence in the workplace on a global scale. These efforts are taking hold. The first international conference was held in Amsterdam, the Netherlands. ASIS is attempting to drive awareness throughout the world via the organization's efforts to proactively make the prevention of violence in the workplace an international challenge. The October conference was focused on the health care field, but the centralization of the concept is a vital first step because, for many years, violence in the workplace in the United States was not really separated from street violence—making the analysis fuzzy and, ultimately, a misrepresentation of data.

The underlying issue could be as simple as this: homicide in the workplace is more prevalent in the United States because we as a society have crossed a line where the workplace can no longer be considered a safe place universally. Organizations have taken proactive steps to contain gun violence but still have violence growing in other ways. The real growth in violence in the United States and around the world is in the area of threats, assaults (including sexual assault), and bullying. I will attempt to address these issues in the following chapters.

The concepts and conclusions around the issue of violence in the workplace may be a matter of perspective. Where you fit into an organization, where your organization stands on the violence issue and its associated risks, may be where you stand with regard to how you perceive this issue. I will tackle this topic by looking at it from different perspectives, including the perspectives of the perpetrators, victims, witnesses, and the families and friends of the people and organizations who are impacted. I will also relate experiences and suggestions in response to everything from simple acts of intimidation to mind-numbing explosions of events that create full-blown crises. This will require a discussion on how practitioners should respond, including the components of a response plan and the array of possible outcomes.

References

Braverman, M. (1999). *Preventing workplace violence: A guide for employers and practitioners*. Thousand oaks: Sage Publications.

Lynn Garcia, M. (2001). *The design and evaluation of physical protection systems*. Boston, MA: Butterworth-Heinemann.

Paludi, M., Nydegger, R., & Paludi, C. (2006). *Understanding Workplace Violence*. Westport, CT: Praeger Publishers.

Foreword

Pay attention to what you see. In my 30 plus years of work in law enforcement, I have worked in every aspect of the field and collaborated, on numerous endeavors, with both private and corporate security.

In one of my assignments, we developed a counterterrorism law enforcement patrol strategy. This strategy was based on case studies of past attacks that were planned, but not carried out, because intervention was successful. The strategy also included information learned from acts of terrorism that were actually carried out and the subsequent evaluations of how those acts could have been prevented. Additionally, the expertise of officers who experienced success in every aspect of policing from investigations, patrol, gangs, crime prevention, community policing, analysis, and a host of others was used to determine the commonalities of success in the deterrence and prevention of crime.

In short, the result of the development of such a strategy is having a basic understanding of the threat and knowing what indicators, or suspicious activities, should be reported, analyzed, and acted upon. Individuals involved in a specific act will engage in observable behaviors, indicators, and steps that lead up to the commission of an act. A common understanding of what those behaviors, indicators, and steps are is also very important in the prevention and deterrence of violent acts. The partnership between law enforcement, businesses, and private security is critical to successful prevention or intervention. Hardening the workplace, identifying and reporting indicators to the appropriate authorities, are an integral part of prevention. This is preferable to "overlooking" the problem and taking the path of least resistance, which, many times, is just trying to remove the problem rather than preventing it. After evaluating many violent incidents, we find past and present associates who reveal that they had observed troubling indicators but did not say anything about them or report them. Although a behavior, in and of itself, may be harmless, patterns or multiple indicators may come from several sources, enabling employers and authorities to act prior to tragedy striking.

Kim Kerr has composed an essential handbook that provides insights into the understanding and prevention of violence in the workplace. Violence in the workplace is a growing phenomenon that has moved into shadowy areas that do not fit into a neatly defined box. Kim describes his experience with a bombing that many defined as an act of terrorism. For Kim, it wasn't just an act of terrorism, but also an experience of workplace violence. His personal and professional experience makes Kim highly qualified to go beyond just the academic research and theory that many authors offer in this arena. He walks the reader through practical strategies and tactics that have real-life application. Kim realizes that determining the root causes of violence is critical and that, for those practitioners responsible for the workplace, prevention application and solutions are needed. His experience includes giving hands-on training of prevention activities that focus on individual customer needs and he now presents years of actual application in a book.

In my experience in working closely with security professionals in very high-profile businesses that rely on favorable public perception, it is obvious that these businesses realize that just one act of violence may cause irreparable harm. These security professionals also understand the importance of securing their employees and businesses through prevention and deterrence. While I believe that, in a democratic society, it is impossible to completely secure any facility, it is critical to have an understanding of the threat and a known, visible security process is essential to create deterrence. The ideas and solutions outlined in this book will help companies develop a comprehensive prevention and response plan.

Chief Tom Dailey,
Independence Missouri Police Department

VIOLENCE—A MATTER OF PERSPECTIVE?

It has been said that the only constant in this world of ours is change. In the realm of violence and violence prevention, this statement is also true to some extent. However, it is important to incorporate the principles of asset protection, which have been tried and true for many years, as a baseline for action. The key is to establish a strategy that is flexible enough to adapt to emerging and ongoing threats. It is vital that the tools to combat violence in your organization are adaptable that they might properly address changes in the violence climate as they come to bear. Hopefully, your point person(s) in this effort is plugged in to the pertinent intelligence and news sources to gather and trend data in an attempt to correctly forecast the likelihood and severity of violent behavior within your organization.

When the phenomenon of violence in the workplace came into our collective conscience in the mid-1980s, we were rocked by the number of mass murders that blazed across the headlines. However, in all fairness, there have been changes in how we view the problem as well as notable improvement, especially in the homicide rates. According to the U.S. Department of Labor, Bureau of Labor Statistics, there has been a steady decline in the number of murders directly linked to violence in the workplace. In the mid-1990s, the year-over-year murder totals exceeded 1,000. In 2006, there were less than 550. This is a drop of nearly 50 percent over the previous decade.

In Figure 1-1, you will note that death in the workplace shows the workplace homicide trend is counter to the

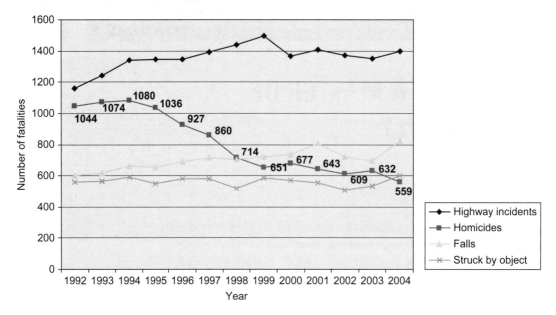

Figure 1-1. The four most frequent fatal work-related events, 1992–2004. *Note*: Data from 2001 exclude fatalities resulting from the September 2001 terrorist attacks. *Source*: U.S. Department of Labor, Bureau of Labor Statistics, Census of Fatal Occupational Injuries, 2004.

overall numbers of deaths by other causes. For example, highway accidents, falls, and being hit by objects have risen or stayed relatively flat although homicides have dropped significantly. Does this mean that we, as a society, are winning the war against violence in the workplace? It would seem that in this one category there has been vast improvement. Clearly, the efforts of security, HR, and management have been working in this area to some degree. But, counter to that statistic, we've seen an increase in reports of threats, assaults, bullying, and domestic violence spilling into the workplace.

Still, violence in the workplace is the fourth leading cause of death in the workplace and the leading cause of death for women. Workplace violence is an evil and corrosive poison that can rob an organization of its focus, resources, and, in extreme cases, its ability to operate entirely. So, it is still a serious threat to our commerce and way of life. But the real point is that the face of workplace violence may be changing ever so slightly. This year alone there will be approximately

1.5–2 million incidences of violence in the workplace that will undoubtedly affect these organizations. These acts can be measured in violent terms such as threats, acts of intimidation, bullying, and physical assault including sexual assault, rape, and sexual battery. According to the Bureau of Labor Statistics, murder is still the fourth largest reason people die on the job; however, over the last decade, there has been some improvement. Experts speculate about why this is the case, but in general, the impact may be a combination of factors. Currently, larger organizations have violence in the workplace prevention policies and programs. This may influence the statistics in a couple of ways. The first effect that corporate workplace prevention policies and programs may have on the statistics is the reduction in the more serious incidents like murder. Secondly, these programs may also account for the increase in reports of assaults and threats.

To further scope this issue, the National Institute of Occupational Safety and Health (NIOSH) (http://www .cdc.gov/niosh/) has compiled an overwhelming amount of data, surveys, and studies to shed light on the problem. To proceed with this discussion, it would only seem appropriate to define the type of violence that is discussed in this work in the typology table produced by CAL/OSHA 1995.

It is important to note that 85 percent of all violence in the workplace falls into category I. Therefore, excluding any discussion around the prevention of external issues is incomplete. However, a deep dive into all the physical security nuances is not the main purpose of this work even though a rigorous overview and suggested strategy will be discussed referencing other sources for even greater clarity. The best practice is to interlace the principles and processes of both internal and external risks that should be considered for the individual reader's particular situation and organization. This topic will be covered in a subsequent chapter.

There is a significant rise in bullying incidences reported by businesses today. According to the Employment Law Alliance, a staggering 50 percent of all workers reportedly complained that they were abused in some way at work. Whether this perception is a new phenomenon or HR and security organizations have had an impact on getting workers to report such abuse is unclear. Regardless, this is a troubling statistic and area of violence in the workplace which will be addressed in a later chapter.

Reviewing the current works on this subject reveals a litany of statistics that help demonstrate the size of the problem, which can cause a loss in perspective for individual incidents. Having been involved in investigations of violent behavior in organizations—both large and small—this author has observed a consistency in how this subject is approached by professionals who have published on the subject. In this macro approach, which seems to be the most frequently taken in other books on this topic, all organizations are synthesized into trends and numbers. However, the real issues boil down to whether or not the members of an organization believe, with every fiber of their beings, that an incident could happen or is happening within their organization or place of business. For those of us who have been a victim, witness, or family member affected by workplace violence—the question is moot. Of course it might happen. We need to stay alert and focused on the issue. We need to ask questions, engage, communicate, and be vigilant.

It appears that one of the biggest symptoms of this problem is denial—denial that an incident is happening or could happen. This "it won't happen here" perspective is the greatest enemy to a successful prevention and reaction strategy. If a business is lulled into a sense that WPV does not apply to their business or that the stronger threat is external, then the chances that an incident is teeing up as you read this page are better than you think. You are putting your business or organization at risk by denying the reality that it can happen to you.

Operating in denial of the possibility of Workplace Violence (WPV) is especially true for small businesses. According to the Bureau of Labor Statistics, approximately 70 percent of businesses do not have a violence prevention policy or program. The issue of WPV may be included in broad base language as "disruptive behavior" or "violation of law," but it is not attacked directly. In other words, the problem and policy are not called out as a subset of an overall need for the business. Most experts agree that organizations need to draw universal attention to the issue by communicating what the policy is and what each team member or employee is responsible to report, respond to, and avoid. One of the most pressing issues is simply understanding how to report a concern. This is especially true in company cultures where reporting is considered a heavy "no-no," resulting in the reporting employee becoming persona non grata with the rest of the workforce. A facet of reporting should consider anonymity and confidentiality wherever or whenever possible.

Awareness of WPV goes beyond making policy decisions to address violence. There should be a clear strategy to introduce any new employee to a thorough understanding of the policy and procedures, and his or her reporting responsibility. The general employee body should review these policies and procedures annually to keep the issue ever green in their minds. The message should be, "Yes, it can happen here."

Also, after an incident has occurred, there should be disclosure of what has happened and what changes are being implemented in response to the event. These changes very well could include stricter access control. By explaining the experience in a generic way and discussing the need to adjust the security approach, you will add to the credibility of your program and allow employees to ask questions and offer feedback.

Policies should include some creative solutions for communicating and reporting violent events. These methodologies should be clearly understood by the entire universe of constituents in your organization and tested routinely. Contractors and vendors should be fully educated as well. Conduct surveys and Q and A sessions with the workforce to make sure they understand what their role is with regard to violence reporting and response.

If there are hotlines or other ways to anonymously report events or suspicious activity, the number of reports would, logically, go up. Therefore, the statistics surrounding incidences or suspicion and concerns would better reflect what is really going on under the hood of everyday interaction within an organization. Email, text messaging, and other tools might also have an impact by allowing the witnesses to report what is going on before they rationalize why it would be better to keep quiet. Responses also tend to be quicker.

However, if you establish hotlines or other communication protocols and you do not receive reports, you may want to revisit the culture that exists within your organization. There may be some trust factors that are preventing the reporting of incidences, or the training may be saying one thing while supervisors or union representatives are saying another. Employee surveys may hold the key to understanding the perception of confidentiality within your organization.

The press also impacts the perspectives and understandings of the underpinnings of WPV. Walter Cronkite, the famous news anchor for CBS, used to end his nightly news by saying, "And that's the way it is." The advent of more and more news outlets and mediums really contradicts that statement. Not only are our local and national news media able to report events in almost real time, but the more sensational events are magnified to give the appearance that we are in the midst of an explosion of violence in the workplace. If there is a relationship angle, like domestic violence, the story can take on an even larger, more reportable twist. Often-times, web news, blogs, and 24/7 news cycles bring awareness to events, and sometimes even sensationalize the story, but offer very little follow-up on the causes and conditions. From a practitioner's perspective, most reports create more questions and perpetuate more false assumptions than answers. In fact, it is fascinating that there is language that even extended myths about workplace violence of the Types II, III, and IV of violence discussed in Table 1-1. Further, if you drill down on the various reports, key issues emerge as to what is being reported and where the root cause may lie, giving some allowance to the use of entertaining language and the lack of a full investigation of all extenuating factors that may not have been addressed by the reporter; these reports raise issues that may frame the discussion.

So the questions here are obvious: Why wasn't something done long before this incident went south—ending in a homicide? What was the culture like at this particular place of business that allowed employees to engage in long-standing arguments that may have been common knowledge to at least the coworkers? What was the management style like here that allowed this to happen? Or, did the

Table 1-1. Typology of Workplace Violence

Type	Description
I: Criminal intent	The perpetrator has no legitimate relationship to the business or its employee, and is usually committing a crime in conjunction with the violence. These crimes can include robbery, shoplifting, trespassing, and terrorism. The vast majority of workplace homicides (85%) fall into this category.
II: Customer/client	The perpetrator has a legitimate relationship with the business and becomes violent while being served by the business. This category includes customers, clients, patients, students, inmates, and any other group for which the business provides services. It is believed that a large portion of customer/client incidents occur in the health care industry, in settings such as nursing homes or psychiatric facilities; the victims are often patient caregivers. Police officers, prison staff, flight attendants, and teachers are some other examples of workers who may be exposed to this kind of WPV, which accounts for approximately 3% of all workplace homicides.
III: Worker-on-worker	The perpetrator is an employee or past employee of the business who attacks or threatens another employee(s) or past employee(s) in the workplace. Worker-on-worker fatalities account for approximately 7% of all workplace homicides.
IV: Personal relationship	The perpetrator usually does not have a relationship with the business but has a personal relationship with the intended victim. This category includes victims of domestic violence assaulted or threatened while at work, and accounts for about 5% of all workplace homicides.

Source: CAL/OSHA, 1995; Howard, 1996; IPRC, 2001.

Cambridge Police Arrest Suspect in Workplace Shooting

The first line of the report read: "The coworkers had been arguing for months." The article went on to explain that two coworkers of a local pool supply company had their final argument "inside and outside" the business, resulting in one employee shooting the other several times in the "head and torso." A comment made by a reader at the bottom of the article read: "They'd been arguing for months? In the workplace? Where was HR? Counseling after the fact. Nice." (Abel, 2009) management even know? Were the disputes ever reported to anyone or relayed to HR or security? A deeper read into the article tells the reader that bystanders tried to break up the fight. What were the company incident response plans, or did such a plan exist? This is no mom and pop shop. This company has locations in eight states!

The commenter of the article makes the common and erroneous assumption that HR is in the loop. With the rising cost of administration, HR departments are often not on site. More and more, the HR function is not only remote—it is even outsourced. Like security, HR is a cost center, and centralization of HR leaves the day-to-day discipline response requirements to the local managers. Is there a union here? Were they involved in forming a solution or alternatives to reporting a potential incident? The many questions this short article generated illustrate the many misconceptions around violence in the workplace. It also demonstrates that many individuals who may know about conflict do not report what they know. They may not know how to report such an issue, or they may assume the issue is none of their business or not worthy of reporting. Was the culture at this workplace one that tried to ignore conflict? Unaddressed conflict, over time, can, and almost always will, grow and morphs into rage and hatred causing the participants to see no way out or no solution for resolution that doesn't involve threats, assault, and revengeful acts or, as in this case, murder.

So the reader should be asking him- or herself some systemic questions: what is the culture of my workplace? What is the level of tolerance for acts of violence or sexual harassment before a report is made? Is there a difference in tolerance between sexual harassment and violence or threats of violence? What is the attitude of the person or persons who routinely receive the report? Is your culture one of making sure you complete your due diligence while not addressing the morality of how we should treat each other in the workplace? Are you reluctant to speak out because your voice would fall on deaf ears for the sake of maintaining status quo?

It is imperative to be honest with the collective conscience of the organization as to what is going to have to be overcome to really have the organization buy into the idea that there are issues of culture to address before an effective WPV prevention program can be rolled out or changes implemented to the existing one. If the overall thinking is that "it could never happen here," then the business may be, inadvertently, teeing up an incident.

This attitude of underestimating the daily threats can extend to access control. Lax access control to the workplace by unknown or unauthorized parties before establishing their business purposes poses a real threat. Most security professionals agree that access control is key to mitigating both external and internal threats to the organization on many fronts including violence prevention. The next example is a shocking illustration of how crucial proper access control really is. This story involves an incident at a day care in Dendermonde, Belgium, reported by the Associated Press on January 3, 2009. In this case, three deaths were reported including two children. Ten others were wounded in the assault. Here, the perpetrator arrived on a bike and "was let in" where he immediately starting slashing people. He had no known prior connection to this business. The key question here is the circumstances around the "was let in" comment. What was the access control process and perimeter security at this day care? Access to children by unauthorized persons takes on many dimensions including child abduction and sexual abuse. But in this case, the perpetrator was focused on harm. So, a strong access control process can potentially prove highly effective, even life saving.

A large part of dealing with violence is physical security processes, procedures, and devices. How we deal with controlling the movement and access of employees, vendors, contractors, and visitors is critical to effective prevention of WPV. If violence is seemingly random, without warning signs when coming from outside the organization, how do you deal with the day-to-day business? What is the risk associated with your particular type of business or function within your facility? These questions need to be asked about not only your business but also the businesses in adjacent facilities. If you are in a condominium arrangement, what are the businesses of your neighbors?

Risk analysis, as it relates to violence in the workplace, is a key activity that every business and organization should embrace. Risk factors should be listed and compared to the business or activity of the organization involved. This activity, which will be discussed later, will be the precursor to access control. What was the access control at this day care?

Six Killed in Factory Shooting, Including Gunman

The article leads with the statement, "A factory worker with a reputation for not getting along with coworkers went on a shooting spree at a Kentucky plastics plant early today after getting into an argument with his supervisor, police told ABC News" (Goldman, 2008).

The article goes on to give the details of the shooting. In total, six were killed—five fellow employees and the gunman's supervisor. Beyond the supervisor, the killings appeared to be random. Further into the article, the reporter quotes CEO Bud Philbrook who advised, "As far as any other motivation may be, we know that he's had some problems with other employees in the past." Apparently this man had the gun on his person at the time of the argument. As he was being escorted from the building he produced the gun and shot his supervisor charging back into the break room shooting fellow employees before shooting himself.

Former Security Guard Held in Office Stabbings

A guard is fired after he requests more work hours. He was instructed to return his uniform to the headquarters but instead came in and stabbed his boss and a coworker. The boss, who was carrying a gun, shot the former employee potentially saving his life and the life of the other victim. Witnesses said he was a "mellow" guy who was always friendly and polite. This type of report gives credence to the belief that people just snap. People who have no history of violence or threatening behavior get fired and come back to take revenge. There is no real understanding as to how the termination was handled or the on-the-job history of the employee. However, the question raises the issue of varying levels of aggression and aggression triggers. There has always been a signal or signals of potential violence in every case that was reviewed in detail. The report gives rise to the myth by including the comment of a casual observer that he just snapped (Llanos, 2009).

Long-time troubled employee with a gun on the premises. Did anyone know he brought or was bringing a gun to work? Is this a new incident or did management turn a blind eye to gun control? Was he a troublemaker with a history of conflict? Did the supervisors and managers know how to deal with troubled employees? What role, if any, did HR play? What is the culture at this workplace relating to reporting acts of conflict, threats, and assaults? Again, more questions than answers, but it does appear there was some history that was not viewed as extreme enough to deal with this employee prior to his deadly rampage. Was any prevention of violence in the workplace training conducted prior to this event to raise awareness in both the managers and employees?

A recent ruling in Denver allows Oklahoman workers to have guns in their locked vehicles. Although most security practitioners agree that guns and workplaces are a bad mix, the Oklahoma legislature passed a law allowing citizens to have guns in locked vehicles in company parking lots. This occurred after the National Rifle Association took issue with the firing of eight employees at Weyerhauser who had violated company policy by having guns in their vehicles. This raises concerns for proximity of guns to potentially agitated employees. This may require a different strategy coupled with access control.

S. Anthony Baron, PhD, PsyD, wrote the book *Violence in the Workplace*. It's a concise and easy read for the practitioner or manager who needs a basic understanding of the levels of progression of violence in the workplace. Baron delves into the warning signs that would red flag the first indicators that call for some action by the organization. It has been my personal experience that these signs are real and often missed by coworkers, managers, and HR and security professionals.

The key point is that workers, vendors, and contractors do not just snap. There are patterns and indicators that, if known and reported to the appropriate parties, can potentially stave off an employee acting out. The key link goes back to an earlier statement. What is the culture at your place of business? How is the reporting of concerns viewed, received, and responded to? Is there feedback to the reporters to make sure they are not left feeling that they should have never gotten involved?

The land of instant messaging, blogs, and emails has brought a new dimension to threats, intimidation, and menacing in the workplace. Later in the book, a contributor, John Benson, will address this technological phenomenon and demonstrate how it is a dimension of WPV that needs to

South Salt Lake Community Stunned by Murder–Suicide

In this murder/suicide case, a new employee of a local business, Kimberly Marvin, was shot to death in the parking lot by her on again/off again boyfriend, Jeremy Scott Taylor. The victim, a mother of two, was gunned down in the parking lot after receiving several text messages from the perpetrator/suicide victim. After reviewing all of the available news reports and blogs, no one noted that the cyber stalking may have been a cause. Marvin was new on the job and may have been concerned about the shooter causing a problem for her. Was she lured outside to her death? (2009)

be included in all prevention strategies. Needless to say, the ability to get information to someone who you need or want to communicate with on an instant, or nearly instant, basis is enormous. However, like many of our electronic conveniences, there is misuse and even abuse that can result in tragedy or, at a minimum, disruption, and conflict.

As a result the story involving the South Salt Lake shooting (see insert), comments left by readers to the electronic report were, at first, very conciliatory to the event. The comments quickly took the opposing views of gun control and the use of guns for protection. Often, shootings such as this one spark the debate around guns in the workplace or at least available in unsecured areas of the workplace. In the case mentioned above, the incident occurred in a parking lot outside the South Salt Lake Courts and Administration Building. There were plenty of people who were authorized to carry weapons within a few feet of the victim. She was lured into the parking lot and shot to death by the boyfriend who, to commit the act, had to get her out in the open. Therefore, the security in parking lots is a real issue. This was a municipal parking lot open to the public.

So, again, there are some questions to consider. Had there been threats? Was Ms. Marvin's employer notified of a potential threat? Had the perpetrator ever threatened to commit suicide? How secure are the parking lots that are used by this workforce? Domestic violence and violence in the workplace—how bad is it? Do home offices and the ability for field workers to have full access to computer and communication systems pose any new threats to workers from customers or suppliers?

Needless to say, this case raises several questions as to the perspective of a worker who has domestic problems and how these problems interface with the job. In the case of a breakup that results in a protective order of some sort, there are things that can be done, if the employer is made aware of the situation. This article leaves more questions than answers. As we separate the various subjects into subsets, we will drill down into specific strategies and reactive tools to help answer the multitude of questions.

We should look forward as well as in the rearview mirror as we develop strategies for the future. The advent of new technologies and remote reporting and offices has been mentioned. But, in 2008–2009 recessionary-type economic climates, other factors need to be considered. If unemployment is skyrocketing and bankruptcy laws are tightening, employees, vendors, and contractors are feeling the added frustration of difficulties in just getting by. Although fuel prices have moderated currently, fuel station attendants and owners have seen customers act out their frustrations at climbing prices. Few believe that gas prices will stay affordable long term. It is estimated that the problems of Bernie Madoff and the $50 billion fraud case may only be the tip of the iceberg. Investors who have lost some or all of their savings may decide that current difficulties should be dealt with more directly through the use of threats or violence as a form of revenge or acting out their frustration.

As an example of economic pressures driving violence, Michael McDermott, 42, an Edgewater Technology employee, had been notified his company was required to garnish his wages by the IRS back in 2000. In response to this difficulty, he shot and killed seven of his coworkers. Another example of an individual known to the company as a customer was a day trader, Mark Barton, 44, who killed 12 people including his wife and two children after losing hundreds of thousands of dollars in the 1998–1999 stock market drop which set off the 2000 recession. Barton stormed into two brokerage offices in the downtown Atlanta area opening fire with three handguns, killing nine of his 12 victims.

Economic downturns should be a factor in identifying current risks of violence.

A more recent incident in California involves the murder/suicide of an upper middle class family in Sorrento Pointe, California. Karthik Rajaram, a recently laid-off accounting industry worker from PricewaterhouseCoopers, shot and killed his wife, mother-in-law, and three children before killing himself, in their upscale neighborhood. Rajaram had been dealing with his layoff and the tanking stock market. Mr. Rajaram, an immigrant from India with an MBA from UCLA, was considered an American success story due to years of hard work in a new land of promise. This tragedy may mark a relatively new frustration that is painfully festering in this current economy. This could affect not only the United States but many other economies around the world. While considering emerging threats, could these types of frustrations move from internal to external reactions focused on former employers or the investment industry (*Source*: time.com). The economy is a factor and practitioners should take downturns seriously.

After the Vietnam War, there was an increased problem with delayed stress and drug addiction. As with any military conflict, the casualties of the war are often the heroes who fought the conflict and are now returning to their homes. These heroes are changed in ways that are largely unknown at this point. Rotation after rotation can have effects we cannot completely understand or appreciate. Up-and-coming risks will develop over time and strategies to mitigate these risks should be discussed and vetted now before the problems accelerate, and we are, again, forced to look in the rearview mirror.

Campuses have seen a tremendous rise in mass shootings and violence that culminated in the unfortunate events at Columbine and Virginia Tech. This book won't delve deeply into the educational arena but will offer information that is particularly pertinent to campuses in a later chapter.

The use of controlled substances, both legally and illegally, is a rising concern. Several of the drugs that are prescribed for various legitimate medical reasons may be abused and/or cause unexpected side effects where anger or violence may result.

Food for Thought

1. What is the culture of your business or organization when it comes to bullying, threats, or intimidation? Is there a milieu of tolerance for aggressive or abusive behavior?
2. Has there been any kind of violence policy, awareness training, or reporting protocol in your facility, business, or organization?
3. Is there a policy regarding violence in your organization?
4. If you have a program to help prevent violence in the workplace, are contractors and vendors a part of that strategy?

References

Abel, D. (2009, January 28). Cambridge police arrest suspect in workplace shooting. *Boston Globe*. Retrieved from http://www.boston.com/news/local/breaking_news/2009/01/police_probe_ca.html.

Goldman, R. (2008, June 28). Six killed in factory shooting, including gunman. *ABC News*. Retrieved from http://abcnews.go.com/US/story?id=5242853&page=1.

Llanos, C. (2009, February 9). Former security guard held in office stabbings. *Los Angeles Times*. Retrieved from http://www.thespec.com/article/510422.

South Salt Lake community stunned by murder–suicide (2009, Jan 30). KSL.com. Retrieved from http://www.ksl.com/?sid=5463469&nid=148.

US Department of Labour Statistics, Census of Fatal Occupational Injuries (2004).

2

THE NEAR MISS

INTRODUCTION

The stereotypical, dark, and sinister mental image of a killer may not always fit the description of a person who would enter a workplace and open fire on coworkers, friends, and associates. Likewise, the person who assaults or threatens a coworker or a customer won't always look the part. Often-times, the physical description of a troubled coworker is vastly different than what a person might think. In many cases, the troubled coworkers who have lashed out were, at one time, hard working and even successful in their careers. Such employees may have had glowing performance appraisals and even high marks for their notable contributions to the organization's success over the years. However, before the act of violence, the perpetrator's on-the-job performance will slip. Sometimes, the evidence is more subtle and sometimes more dramatic. Let's begin this discussion with the internal threat, which is often the type of incident we don't read about in the news.

Coworkers and supervisors will notice differences in an employee's behavior and instinctively, or as the supervisor is trained to do, use traditional motivation techniques to address the behavior. But all too often, the supervisor just leaves the employee alone thinking the situation is temporary and will somehow work itself out. "We all have bad days," the supervisor may say to rationalize away the problem. But, in the end, if someone doesn't step up and address the issue, it very well could escalate into a form of violence—harassment, bullying, acts of intimidation or threats, and even homicide. In almost every case of violence in the workplace this author has investigated, there were patterns of violence that were not dealt with until a final act triggered a major incident that resulted in a call to the police or security.

In the world of safety and accident prevention, oftentimes the Safety Director or Human Resources Manager, who might wear the safety cap as part of his or her overall responsibilities, will be made aware of a near miss. A *near miss* is an accident or event that could have resulted in a reportable accident to OSHA. The incident may result in lost time off the job, workers' compensation claims, grievances, and even lawsuits. However, although the incidences of this nature are unfortunate, they could be worse as they don't involve permanently altered or even lost human life. It is often considered best practice to bring the leadership team together with the work team to discuss what could have been handled differently in a nonconfrontational, constructive environment. This "near miss" review is critical to prevention.

Near Misses and Tabletop Discussions

A near miss review is critical in preventing violence in the workplace. It is vitally important to look in the rearview mirror after an investigation of a threat, bullying, or violent behavior to accurately understand the circumstances from all perspectives. It's equally important to formulate what could have been done differently to prevent not only the near miss, but also possible full-blown incidences that very well could have been the outcome. This process should bring together a number of disciplines, in a *tabletop discussion*, to review the event and offer possible prevention strategies for the future. Tabletop discussions are scenario based. Therefore, by having a discussion, you can ask in a *what-if* format. What would the participants sitting around the conference table do or should they do in a similar situation? This technique can also be relevant when using recent violent events that have taken place at other facilities or businesses. Organization, contract or corporate security, HR professionals, senior and line management, union leadership (if appropriate), and Employee Assistance Program

(EAP) counselors are excellent choices for participation in a near miss review. In some organizations, this group could include floor wardens and first-aid trained employees who have been designated as first responders. It might even be appropriate to ask local law enforcement to sit in or even facilitate the review.

The tabletop discussion was one of the techniques used during Olympic planning, including everything from medical emergencies to social disruption like demonstrations to violence and even to terrorism. This technique uses a trained facilitator who has experience in keeping the group focused, organized, and on topic. This exercise calmly determines accountability in a nonaccusatory or punitive way and identifies critical paths to corrective and preventative measures. These discussions drive awareness to a directional stream of actions leading to prevention.

Tabletop discussions begin with the facilitator simply throwing out a scenario that might occur. Such scenarios might include things such as how to handle everything from a broken water pipe to a report of a weapon seen in the workplace. The scenario may also be an actual incident that recently occurred, and, after learning the basic facts, the discussion could be focused around interdiction points where corrective action could have made a difference. Corrective action may be as simple as making a call to security to creating a response team designated to assess next steps in a compromising situation.

Near misses are often the impetus that establishes violence prevention strategies and policies, in addition to news reports and stories that appear in trade journals. A devout security or HR professional might read an article or attend a webinar or seminar that outlines an event that disrupted the workplace on any level. This exercise will bring some of the systemic issues to light. Remember, a critical factor that is often overlooked is the culture that allowed the deeds or behavior of potentially violent individuals to go unrecognized or unnoticed. A near miss might be at the end of many interdiction points that were squandered because of an organizational culture that is ripe with opportunities for violence. The following is an example of a near miss that actually happened.

Case Study

Background

To maintain confidentiality, an alias will be used to discuss a case this author investigated several years ago. To begin, it's important to understand the culture, management style, and social dynamic of this particular organization—all of which may have contributed to the event.

The move by management looked good on paper. It saved millions of dollars long term, and moved the business in a more technology-based direction. This effort demanded consolidating and streamlining the management. Two large existing centers in rural areas of major cities, one East and one West, were retrofitted and expanded to accommodate the new technology hub. There was plenty of excitement and a lot of money spent on the centers. "This is a workplace of the future," was the overarching mantra of the organization.

We will focus on the Eastern center, where there was a team of corporate security investigators who investigated events and incidences of interest to the company for the protection of assets and employees. There were tons of committees and working groups divided logically from technology to facility and process to people.

Work teams were formed on paper, and the employees were scheduled to report to work. Looking back, it reminds me of football coaches filling a line up and creating a bunch of "X's and O's" that represent how the teams should play. Many of the upper and middle management personnel were local to the area and were told to report to the new rural center commuting from the downtown metropolitan area. Additionally, large portions of the rank and file personnel also came from the downtown area and were assigned to this rural site, almost 35 miles away from the old worksite. Some employees were required to commute over 1 hour or more. However, the bulk of the workforce was relocated from the Northeast and upper Midwest. The culture of this rural center was also very Southern in an area where if you weren't from the South you were from the North, even if you came from California! Many of the employees were urban African-Americans relocated to a predominantly white suburb in deep South. In fact, some of the employees, who were close to retirement, even decided to leave their families and take up temporary living near the center.

So the stage was set with many employees who could be described as fish out of water. The centers were opened with great fanfare and high praise from the great towers of headquarters which were a long way away. It turned out, this Eastern center was a test tube for conflict created by well-meaning corporate planners and executives.

Conflict

So the conflict began with union complaints of favoritism and mismanagement. Absenteeism began to skyrocket, drug and alcohol problems were reported, and divorce and office romances began to crop up in all areas of the new center. Production plummeted throughout the center and fingers were pointed in all directions. The number of requests for EAP assistance became so high that a full-time counselor was placed on-site. HR doubled its presence and union membership dramatically increased. A new district manager (DM), with a reputation of fixing troubled business units, was assigned to reduce the number of grievances and to improve production. It was like changing deck chairs on the Titanic. Things only continued to get worse.

Eventually, an anonymous call was made to corporate security about the "management style" that, if not changed, would mean trouble. There were allegations of veiled threats from management in an attempt to illicit compliance to team goals. The allegations seemed like a stretch but investigations were attempted. Often-times, these calls were too vague to investigate but names of people to talk to "if you really wanted the scoop" were provided by the callers. So with no more than a flimsy frame of facts, an investigation, which was nothing more than an inquiry, began.

The DM seemed well meaning. An investigator was dispatched to ask if there were any issues or concerns that needed security's attention. The DM was viewed, by both employees and the union, as the ultimate leadership at the center. His tone was echoed throughout the center. He had a management team and frequent meetings with the Union Vice President who had unlimited access to him. Every issue, large and small, was escalated to the top management of the business center. Lower-level managers, both first and second tier, were called on the carpet after each of these meetings creating undue pressure to keep the lid on problems. It was apparent that the DM was working hard to keep all the issues held inside the center. There seemed to be a philosophy of nothing should go up or outside. Calling corporate security was definitely going outside the center. So, when initially interviewed, the DM could not think of any incidents or problems that would warrant any investigation. He gave the investigator names of a few managers who would substantiate his belief that any rumors of problems were just that—rumors.

"Carol" was a technician. She had worked for the company for over 15 years. She had been considered a stellar employee for the first 10 years of her tenure. She worked in the same office as her ex-husband, "Bob." He was not her "ex" when Carol was moved to this center. Due to policy restrictions, Carol and Bob worked for different managers but ultimately reported up to the same DM mentioned previously. Bob was a supervisor. This particular office was one of the divisions that brought in employees from several offices from around the country. Most of the employees in Carol's department were tenured and had agreed to the relocation to this center to maintain their tenure in the hopes that, eventually, the company would sweeten a separation payout allowing them to retire and move back to the place from where they came. Some of the employees had over 20 years invested with the company and would have jumped at the offer of an early out. However, the company determined that offering early retirement to these employees was too expensive in the initial planning stages of the organizational changes. There were also training and loss of expertise concerns that losing these employees might cause. So, employees moved or left the business with a diminished retirement or nothing. For Carol and Bob, moving was the second chance to fix a troubled marriage.

But like most second chances there would be no third. Within months of the move, the couple's marital troubles intensified and divorce ensued. They saw each other every day through the months of legal proceedings. And office drama ensued. Bob soon found another relationship within the same office. His new romantic companion, Sally, was a fellow supervisor. In fact, Sally had been Carol's supervisor at one point. Carol was moved under a different supervisor when the romance between Bob and Sally became common knowledge. It was certainly not an ideal arrangement. It would have been interesting to see the outcome had the DM run this reporting problem by someone other than his subordinates. The situation was a recipe for disaster.

One day Carol came into her cube visibly upset. Her moods had been erratic of late, and those who worked near her knew enough to keep their distances when she was visibly disheveled. During these episodes, which were becoming more frequent, Carol was viewed as unapproachable by coworkers and even by her immediate supervisor. In the midst of her downward spiral, Carol's on-the-job performance went from excellent to mediocre to poor. In an attempt to be sensitive, Carol's new supervisor, Beth, tried to avoid any form of confrontation. She moved Carol onto special projects that weren't driven by deadlines. In essence, Beth tried harder to be Carol's friend rather than her supervisor.

On one particular day, one of the unsuspecting gossips made a crack about Bob and Sally's recent engagement. Carol stood up abruptly and grabbed her chair, pushing it across the tile floor with enough force to slam it into the other side of the, fortunately vacant, adjacent cubicle. It rattled the shared wall in a line of cubicals so intensely that heads popped up like gophers looking up from their holes. Carol ran from the office crying. The incident was never investigated or documented by anyone but was remembered by everyone.

A few months passed without any major incidences, but even still, the employees were basically on "Carol alert." So when Carol came into the office with little or no makeup on, and a scowl on her face, employees knew to simply keep their distance. So, instead of dealing with the problem, the employees chose to ignore Carol's behavior and work performance, which was rapidly deteriorating, until the whole mess became an elephant in the room.

In A. Anthony Baron's (2001) book, *Violence in the Workplace*, Mr. Baron discusses early warning signs that are often precursors to acts of violence. It is during the early phases of the progression of this condition that intervention can prevent the catastrophic result of violence or threats of violence. Over the years, other authors and practitioners have tried to improve upon or segment these red flags, but it's my experience that Baron's list is an excellent guidepost of key factors that are systemic to this issue of violence in the workplace.

Within weeks prior to the final report made involving Carol, this author had just finished reading Baron's book as part of a project to create a violence in the workplace prevention program that had been started by our corporate security region. The warning signs provided by Baron can be used to evaluate Carol's behavior, and map out and analyze the progression of activities, actions, and/or attitudes that might result in a violent outcome. Let's run what we have seen with our troubled employee thus far using Mr. Baron's list as a starting point.

Early Warning Signs

1. *Attendance problems*—Monday was always a challenge for Carol. She was consistently late, which was ignored and even covered by her immediate supervisor.
2. *Impact on supervisor/manager's time*—Notwithstanding the ultimate investigation, which took several days, the supervisor was either coaching or encouraging other employees to "understand" Carol's problems and pressures. He avoided talking to Carol herself but spent much of his workday fielding complaints.
3. *Decreased productivity*—"On her particularly bad days," Carol would work at half steam to say the least. She would be on the phone talking loudly, complaining about everything and everybody. Her cube neighbors would find ways to move to vacant cubes away from her when they became available.

4. *Inconsistent work patterns*—On the days where she seemed in normal or good spirits, her productivity would soar in comparison to down days. It would sometimes come in strings of days that would renew the supervisors' hopes that some miracle of healing had occurred. But it was always short lived, and a bad day would soon wipe out any hope of the old Carol being back.

5. *Poor on-the-job relationships*—Carol was liked by few, ignored by most, and feared by many. Most people in her work group stayed away and tolerated her bizarre behavior. In other words, they avoided her.

6. *Concentration problems*—One of the complaints of the various supervisors to whom Carol had been assigned was her inability to stay on task. She was often found wandering around the office popping into others' cubes just to chat. This behavior was disruptive and often resulted in confrontations in which she was encouraged to return to her workstation and go back to work.

7. *Safety issues*—No clear violations of safety policy were uncovered or reported. But, keep in mind, this is a cubical/computer terminal environment of technicians who worked with proprietary software applications.

8. *Poor health and hygiene*—As previously mentioned, Carol had days where she would show up to work in disarray. She was described as looking like "she just got out of bed."

9. *Unusual/changed behavior*—Her behavior was very unpredictable. She was up then she was down then she was up and so on. As actual violence was considered out of the question, Carol's behavior was seen as bizarre at best and disruptive at worst.

10. *Fascination with guns or firearms*—Interestingly enough, there was never any evidence found that this was an issue. A more likely scenario at the time of the investigation would be that Carol may have started to show signs of revengeful behavior like sabotage or character assassination, threats, or vandalism.

11. *Evidence of possible drug or alcohol use or abuse*—Several of the witnesses and interviewees indicated that Carol loved to party. She had, at one point, been

invited to functions with the Friday after-work crowd. But those days were long gone. There was conjecture by some that her coming to work in less than business-ready condition might be linked to substance abuse.

12. *Evidence of serious stress in the employee's personal life*—One of the biggest stressors in anyone's life is marital breakup and divorce. Carol was not only going through that stress but she was doing so in a very public way with her ex-husband and his new wife in her general workplace every day.

13. *Continual blame and excuses*—When confronted in even the mildest way, Carol would blame the situation on her ex and his new wife as being the reason for her erratic behavior and poor work performance.

14. *Unshakable depression*—It was learned, after the final review, that Carol had been asked to speak with the now on-site EAP counselor. Appointments were made and missed by Carol on at least two occasions.

Resolution

The final incident started on a Wednesday. It was a day like any other day at the office. Carol was late for work. After finally arriving, she complained to a coworker of having an exceptionally bad night, specifically mentioning that she had not slept well because she was thinking about how upset she was at her ex-husband. The coworker tried to change the subject unsuccessfully and then made an excuse to leave the discussion as she knew it would be a long, emotional ramble that she had heard many times before.

Carol's workstation was approximately 15 feet away from the entrance to the conference room where the managers were just finishing a morning staff meeting. It is unclear what was actually said as the management team came out of the conference room laughing about a comment that was made by Bob about, "how good life can be." Carol took it very personally that Bob was apparently happy, and she was so incredibly miserable.

And then Carol finally snapped. She confronted Bob, and after a few colorful adjectives, said she wanted him dead. She was going to go and get a gun and blow his brains all over his "c***" new wife. Carol ran out of the office toward the parking lot. Corporate security was immediately notified this time along with the police. A preventative and exhaustive investigation and threat assessment plan was initiated.

Later in the book, we'll discuss various incident response strategies. However, in this situation, when a certain line is crossed, it should immediately eliminate any chance of salvaging the employee's career. This type of behavior can potentially change lives forever.

As a result of her behavior, Carol was terminated and prosecuted. She pled guilty and was given a delayed adjudication if she sought and completed psychiatric evaluation and treatment. She was required to visit with a probation officer monthly and was ordered to stay away from her ex-husband and his new family. The union filed a grievance on her behalf and eventually took the incident to arbitration with an argument which was quite interesting. They contended that management failed to do their job by not adequately helping her cope with this unprofessional situation in which she was forced to work. The arbitrator found for the company but cited several areas that should have or could have been handled better. Fortunately, Carol eventually moved away and, as of today, is doing better and has moved on with her life.

During the subsequent investigation, all of the personnel records were reviewed. Some supervisors had unofficial files regarding their assigned employees locked in their personal desks. They referred to these personnel files as drop files. In a drop file retained by a previous supervisor another incident was described. Carol had slapped a coworker on the shoulder, which the coworker considered inappropriate. The complaining employee said that she became somewhat fearful when she saw real anger in Carol's eyes. Carol denied any real harmful intent, and as the slap was not hard enough to create an injury to the coworker, the two shook hands and the incident was documented on a small note and dropped in a file. This was a file that didn't follow Carol to a new supervisor to whom she was assigned.

The investigation of Carol's final incident found no real corrective or preventative action by any former supervisor or manager except for the note which was a feeble attempt at documentation of an incident. Instead of dealing with the situation, Carol's former supervisor sidestepped the situation without thinking about the potentially negative, long-term effects. This was due to a lack of training. The incident with the chair was never documented, and the incident involving the slap, though documented, was basically underplayed and forgotten. HR and security were never notified, and the second-level manager was not even apprised of the incident. Therefore, it was clear that the supervisors were never coached on the importance of reporting and documenting incidents in the proper way.

The incident involving Carol and Bob generated a full battery of violence prevention awareness training. The training was rolled out to the employee population at this facility and a risk assessment team was established. After Carol was dismissed, a culture shift slowly began, and the "acting out" by others in the facility began to fade. Each successive year following Carol's outburst, fewer incidents were reported or rumored. The DM was promoted and the replacement asked corporate security to regularly attend the senior leadership team meetings to discuss issues. This incident never made the paper.

Whatever we think we know or suspect about the reality or reasonableness of a deeply held resentment is irrelevant. What matters is the resentment, rage, and even fear. These emotions drive events of this nature, but they have little to do with a person's sense of right or wrong. And, to the person who has these deeply held feelings, justice is demanded. The person has been wronged—just as Carol felt she had been wronged. Ignoring the situation or assuming that time will heal the issue by letting the potential perpetrator act out in small ways will only ultimately result in escalation.

Near Misses and the Prehiring Process

Let's look at the case of Michael McLendon, 28, of Samson, Alabama. In the course of 2 hours, McLendon shot and killed 10 people, many of them relatives. He ended this rampage by taking his own life. As he is not here to interview as to his motive behind his behavior, we may never know all of the demons that drove him to execute this act of insanity and brutality. However, after the shooting, investigators found a list of individuals that McLendon felt had harmed him, including people with whom he had worked at various employers in Samson. We also know he was a job jumper. McLendon would move, without apparent provocation, to another job in the area. According to news reports, coworkers and acquaintances described him as shy, quiet, and laid back (*Source*: www.msn.com/id/29623587/).

The process of hiring should involve ways of spotting troubled employees. During the hiring process, the hiring manager needs to know the questions to ask and the signs to look for that are indicative of a problematic employee. HR professionals should be trained to ask questions about why someone left his or her last job, searching for trends or overt acts or covertly held beliefs that show a pattern of victimization. Although certainly not conclusive, closely held beliefs of being harmed in some way by a previous employer may be identifiable in the form of a pattern of employment where the individual left because of how he was treated or he perceives he was treated. Most of McLendon's employers saw promise in this young man, but he left his various jobs, seemingly without cause.

The prehiring process is a great opportunity to keep potential problems from entering your work environment. Use of applications on *every* employee from the boardroom to the broom closet and thoroughly evaluating comments made by the applicant about prior employment and reasons for leaving past positions may offer up some red flags to employers (Figure 2-1).

In the United States in 2005, it was determined that employers are not mobilized to keep potentially violent persons out of their businesses. Even in the government sector, which has a larger percentage of proactive programs (70 percent+), the real risk lies in the screening of customers, clients, and visitors. This is also true of patients in the health care sector. Only approximately 40 percent of employers screen their potential and current talent. The idea of screening clients or customers may seem a little strange, but it is my experience that vendors, clients, and

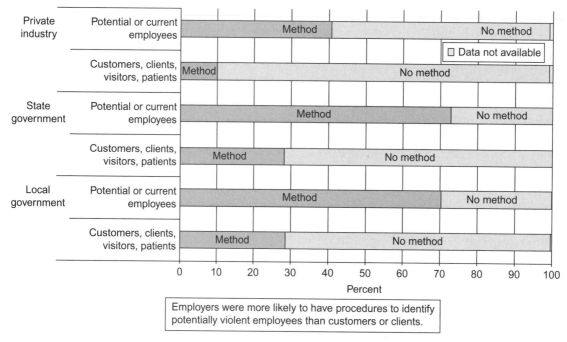

Figure 2-1. The chart indicates the number of employers that have a process in place to identify customers or employees with a history of violence by ownership, United States 2005. *Source*: Bureau of Labor Statistics, Survey of Workplace Prevention, 2005.

contractors are often given the same access or almost the same access to businesses, employees, and other customers and contractors, as permanent employees. Only 10 percent of private industry has a policy or program to address this risk.

Additionally, the smaller the company, the less likely the company will have a violence in the workplace prevention program. Larger companies (1,000+ employees) are over the 80 percent mark, but the smaller companies are closer to 40 percent (see Figure 2-2).

It is reasonable to assume that even if the violence-prone individual is giving warning signs that seem obvious to the trained eye, it is highly likely that most employers are not prepared to recognize the severity of these threats or take the necessary steps to prevent violence in their workplace.

So, it's actually not surprising that Carol's emotional state was able to get to the point that caused her to act out, disrupt the work environment, and eventually make a threat that

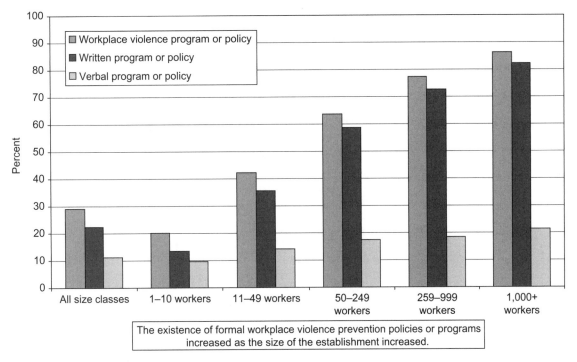

The existence of formal workplace violence prevention policies or programs increased as the size of the establishment increased.

Figure 2-2. Percentage of workplaces that have a program of some sort of addressing violence in the workplace according to the BLS, 2005. *Source*: Bureau of Labor Statistics, Survey of Workplace Prevention, 2005.

ultimately cost her job. Most companies and coworkers are not prepared to effectively identify and address the possible risks that may exist in their workplace. In the case of Michael McLendon, he may have been stopped from going to the former employers by the action of the police who eventually caused the standoff where McLendon took his life.

Key Elements of an Effective Workplace Violence Prevention Program

The key elements of an effective prevention program are:
1. Have an established, written policy and procedure that outlines how the company views, and intends to deal with, potential and real acts of violence in the workplace including threats. A clear understanding of senior

management buy in should be established and reinforced with changes in leadership to make sure the plan has teeth.

2. Have a clear hiring program that includes a rigorous review of the application and interview process (including panel interviews) of potential new hires. This should extend to temporaries, part-time employees, and interns. No class of employee should be excluded from this process.

3. Certain constituent groups should be background checked before being given access without escort or appointment into your facility. This should include employees, contractors, and routine vendors who cannot be physically escorted or segregated from the general population or common work areas.

4. Companies should have orientation training of all new employees. This introduces the new employees to the culture as well as the policies and procedures the new employees will need to know to be successful. This is in addition to their function-based training necessary to do their job. A segment of the training should be focused on prevention of violence in the workplace. Training should also include how to react to weapons or acts of violence that are happening now. The most important of which is to also have a mechanism to report suspicions or incidences while maintaining confidentially or anonymity if necessary.

5. Annual or biannual refresher training for incumbents regarding prevention should be scheduled with mandatory attendance. This could be performed via online training if the medium is interactive and has a testing segment.

6. A risk assessment team or teams, depending on the size or configuration of the business, should be established. This group should be empowered to act in accordance with a clear mission so that they can react quickly to any incident report in a timely manner.

7. If the company does not have a crisis response plan they should create one. Within the crisis scenarios, there should be violence in the workplace examples and scenarios included. If there are annual tests of the crisis management process, WPV should be among both the tabletop or

actual scenarios used for the tests. Make sure the roles of the responders are established and understood.

8. If there are safety or security newsletters that go to the employees, have reinforcement messaging to make sure that the concept of prevention of violence in the workplace is a top priority.

Many of the above concepts will be covered in additional detail in the following chapters. However, if your company lacks an adequate prevention plan, it is critical that you start this process today because you never know when it will be too late.

Food for Thought

1. Does your organization have a "Carol"?
2. What is the senior management of your organization's position on prevention of workplace violence? Is it on their radar?
3. Are you aware of situations of individuals who are tolerated in your work environment and who are protected by cultural fear of intervention?
4. What is your hiring process like? Does your organization use applications and screening strategies?
5. What is the role of security in your business? Where does it reside in the organization? Who would you call right now if you had a concern?
6. Does your company have a crisis management program?
7. If an incident occurred, who would be in charge? Who would liaison with the police and fire department? Who would talk to the press?

Reference

Baron, A. (2001). *Violence in the workplace.* San Francisco: Pathfinder Publishing.

3

VICTIMS OF WORKPLACE VIOLENCE: A LIFE-CHANGING EVENT

INTRODUCTION

When discussing victims of violence, it is important to point out that most violent acts against organizations originate outside of the organization. Therefore, in prevention and response planning, we need to be sure to include all potential victims. In any discussion of high-risk contributing conditions where violence is a factor of performing any particular activity or business, motion starts at the source for violence and moves inward. The focus of an evaluation should not be limited to internal sources of violent acts of persons known to the organization such as employees, vendors, or contractors. With any person or persons known to the organization, there are some additional strategies that should be used. However, once an incident occurs, whether by someone inside or outside the organization, the victim response plan should be similar even though the dimensions of the facts surrounding the event might differ. Both instances have victims that are directly or indirectly affected and must be identified and responded to in a methodical and respectful manner.

While addressing the issue of victim assistance and response planning, consider who within your organization is most likely to experience a deliberate act of violence. Begin your evaluation with possible external sources and move inward to internal sources. In the case of internal violence, there are warning signs that can help identify potential perpetrators. If you have a corporate security or internal security organization, this group should have statistics or reports of incidences that will help map the most likely department or location where internal problems might occur. If the security personnel have records but have not had or taken the time to perform any trend analysis, then this information is essentially worthless. Further analysis is critical as the results of such analyses will expose risk points within your business. In the event that an external source is responsible for the violence, the motivation is often greed or an immediate need for money or property. According to the raw data, the majority of acts of workplace violence occur from external sources.

Robbery continues to be the primary trigger or cause of workplace violence. In instances of robbery, weapons are used to engage in these criminal acts by perpetrators who are at maximum energy levels which leads to the randomness of the violence. If a victim does not act exactly as the perpetrator demands or if a bystander enters the scene, the gun could easily discharge with tragic results. According to the National Victim Assistance Academy (2002), the following activities are common in the milieu that spawns violence (2002).

- *Contact with the public*—Individuals such as retail employees, taxi drivers, bartenders, and convenience store clerks, for example. The close proximity of the money to the door gives the robber the opportunity to get in and out before law enforcement can arrive on the scene.
- *Exchange of money*—Despite the frequency at which credit cards are used in purchase transactions, significant amounts of cash are often on hand at places like bars, convenience stores, and gas stations. Hotel front desk clerks and fast-food restaurants are easy and frequent targets.
- *Deliveries of passengers, goods, and services*—Pizza and food delivery services as well as the aforementioned taxi drivers have little physical security barriers to deter a robber or aggressor. Delivery drivers are focused on the task at hand and are, often, not trained to assess the surroundings or movement outside of their immediate area.
- *Having a mobile place of business like a police cruiser*—The riskiest jobs continue to be those in law enforcement.
- *Working with unstable persons*—Health care professionals are increasingly becoming a target of aggressive behavior from patients or family members of patients.

In emergency room settings, even the perpetrator may come to the health care facility to continue to finish the dispute.

- *Working alone or in small numbers*—If the individuals have ready access to the public domain or are close to the street or exits and have no associate to call for assistance, they are subject to increased vulnerability.
- *Working at night or late hours*—There will be fewer witnesses or traffic to slow the perpetrator's escape. Also, the time of day or night may restrict law enforcement's ability to respond in certain areas.
- *Working in a high crime area*—The problem here should be obvious. Awareness of how quickly certain neighborhoods or areas can change from seemingly safe to not-so-safe is important. Businesses should stay on top of criminal trends in areas where they have outlets, stores, or a physical presence.
- *Guarding valuable property or items*—There has to be a partnership between private security and law enforcement. This is often not the case with private security personnel who are, typically, lower paid and lack adequate training.
- *Working in a community-based setting*—Being located with other businesses where you can keep a watch on each other will deter violence. Camera systems and security from associated businesses may drive the problem to a solitary location.

All businesses and organizations should have deterrent and physical security plans, coupled with employee training. The training should include making employees aware of the risks associated with the particular type of business and location. Such training should also include information regarding law enforcement limitations. Part of a new employee's orientation training should include dealing with anger and violence in the workplace. This should include a breakdown of both external and internal threats. A growing source of violence in the workplace stems from domestic violence. For example, a study by Body Shop in 1998 advised that 24 percent of domestic violence victims reported that violent incidences at home caused them to be late for work; 15 percent reported that the violence contributed to the victim losing a job; 20 percent reported that they felt the violence limited their ability to advance in their careers.

If the organization is unaware of the violence at home, they will deal with the employee based on the result: tardiness, absenteeism, or poor performance. The children who are supported by the victim are victims themselves. Violence resulting from the loss of a job or curtailed career advancement and, not to mention, the trauma of possibly witnessing the act(s) will have impact on the perpetrator's and victim's families.

The Impact of Violence on the Victims

The most obvious victim is the person or people whom the violence is directed toward, or, in other words, the targets of the physical, emotional, and/or mental abuse, threats, assaults, acts of intimidation, etc. These individuals are often the ones whose names appear in the paper or media or are often associated with the victim in a direct way. In a best-case scenario, victims of workplace violence will be shaken up—physically, mentally, or both. Obviously, in a worst-case scenario, a life or lives can be lost. And, unfortunately, because of the media attention, the perpetrator's name often lives on much longer than the victim's.

In the introduction, the 1996 Centennial Olympic Park bombing is discussed. As mentioned earlier, most people associate the bombing with the falsely accused Security Officer Richard Jewell. Jewell was certainly a victim of media and law enforcement scrutiny. But he was not the perpetrator. Eric Rudolph was the bomber. One of the direct victims of the bombing included Alice Hawthorne, a bystander who was attempting to cross through the park and was within mere feet of the bomb when it exploded. There were 111 others who were wounded by shrapnel—including several police officers who are at the greatest risk of experiencing violence in the workplace. The police officers' workplaces are the mean streets of America. They rush to protect and defend us—the citizens of the United States.

There are long lists of infamous perpetrators whose names will live on much longer than deserved while the victims' names will fade from our consciousness within days of the initial news report. For the surviving victims, their lives require action. Extreme action is often needed to recover from the trauma that accompanies the violence in the workplace. Victims require both immediate and possibly long-term physical and mental medical attention.

The less obvious victims are the witnesses or bystanders who may have seen the incident from a safe distance. These people may have encountered the perpetrator, and, for whatever reason, were bypassed. For instance, in the Royal Oaks Michigan Post Office shooting, the perpetrator Thomas McIlvane bypassed several individuals who were in his path only to kill and wound others. He reportedly looked them in the face. Although the targets in this circumstance appeared to be random, it is suspected that McIlvane had created a mental list of victims. This differs from Patrick Sherrel, the Edmond Oklahoma shooter, who shot every target he could see with deadly accuracy.

Yet another subset of victims is the families of the victims who watch in horror as their wives, husbands, sons, and daughters change before their eyes—often displaying irritability, lack of concentration, angry outbursts, withdrawal from social events, showing little interest or energy. Families very often will see alcohol and/or drug use and abuse begin to take hold as the victim attempts to self-medicate.

There are many films and training aids that have been created to assist in the prevention of violence. A film produced by Littler Mendelesen, the largest law firm specializing in legal matters around employment and hiring, has a dramatic intro showing news footage of police responses to violent incidences. A particularly memorable scene shows a woman standing by herself with her hand up to her mouth visibly shaken. She is frantically looking for something or someone. She was not being interviewed by the police or newscasters. She was by herself in a remote part of a parking lot. She, too, is one of the most random of victims of violence. Was she out to lunch and stopped by police from going into a crime scene? Is she an HR manager who was in an adjacent building attending a meeting and was not there when the incident began, and, for whatever reason, was the real target of the perpetrator?—and the flood of horror is now hitting her mind. This is unknown. What is clear is that she is also a victim of violence in the workplace and the symptoms of her trauma may take weeks, months, or even years to fully manifest.

In 1997, Werner Bergmann identified three basic groups of post-traumatic consequences of violence.

1. Re-experiencing consequences where the victim relives the incident in his or her mind generating fear or anxiety. This includes intrusive thoughts and nightmares.
2. Withdrawal consequences occur when a victim attempts to suppress the negative emotions and memories of a violent event with various strategies and tactics like overworking or not working at all. Depression and drug or alcohol abuse are often behaviors that are used to withdraw from family and friends.
3. Other consequences may include anger, irritability, sleep disorders, loss of concentration, and exaggerated responses to sudden changes or movement.

Some of the darker aspects of the response develop over time. These matters will worsen if the victim initially refuses assistance or denies the need to be debriefed altogether. This path can potentially leave a residual of negative emotions that will be felt long after the wreckage of the violence is cleared and the organization returns to its day-to-day activities. Therefore, it is vital that any WPV program contain a checklist of action items as part of the recovery response. This checklist should include information regarding how to identify and categorize victims, both direct and indirect. The key is to not assume that any particular population, within the organization, is in any way immune to violence in any of its ugly forms and the accompanying aftermath.

For example, the security team should be included. Unlike an incident on the street, there are personal relationships that may be involved. The security team may work closely with the victims as they may feel a sense of responsibility for the event. They may have been working on a complaint of veiled or real threats when the incident, that ultimately brought all kinds of focus, occurred. Therefore, security personnel should be debriefed along with all the other employees, witnesses, and bystanders.

A key stakeholder in this process is the HR professional who may be the administrator of the policies involving violence or threats of violence. Therefore, they should be viewed as a possible victim. Like security, they may also have a personal relationship with the victim(s) or feel some sense of responsibility for the violent act. Many HR professionals enter the field of Human Resources to be of service to an organization's employees or members. So they need to be debriefed as well.

It may be wise to bring in an objective party or parties to assist in these situations. If the incident occurs at a decentralized location, it might be best to send representatives from other locations to assist in the debriefing process. Employees from the corporate headquarters may be a good solution, but be careful not to use individuals as investigators as they may be perceived as blame finders.

Security professionals are trained to gather facts and oftentimes they are the best debriefing body. General counsel or outside counsel can also be a good source for gathering and debriefing. But again, perception is reality; so the use of a group that is perceived as impartial is critical.

Often, an outside resource can be used if there are no appropriate individuals or groups available from within the organization. These individuals, from outside of the organization, should have the ability to ask questions in a nonthreatening and methodical manner. All interviews should be documented and reviewed with relevant stakeholders who have the opportunity to give insight and offer suggestions and historical context regarding the persons involved.

EAPs are a significant resource. This is especially true in the weeks and months following a significant incident. An EAP can help stabilize the workforce by offering confidential sessions with voluntary candidates. Normally, use of an EAP is not required in instances of WPV but is seen as a resource for referral. There is a delicate balance here, and EAP professionals know or should know the limitations of sharing information. Stakeholders can use the EAP resources to run hypotheticals of human response symptoms and advise of different things to look for in the weeks or months following an incident. The services provided by the EAP should also extend to family members of the employees, witnesses, and bystanders, if reasonable. The dollars spent here might pay untold benefits by avoiding excessive workers' compensation claims, higher than normal turnover, absenteeism, and various sorts of legal actions including class actions. Use of an EAP might also reduce the perception of an uncaring corporate response. Be aware that the perception of a corporation, true or false, can quickly find its way to blogs, news articles, and various public web sites.

In a subsequent chapter, we'll discuss a crisis management tool, including effective strategies and tactics. Among many things, this tool will explain the roles that need to be filled by stakeholders. At this juncture, let's suffice it to say that a Crisis Management Team (CMT), which is a critical entity for a crisis management plan, should be the key decision-making team, and should also be the central clearing house for any information that might be of interest for the organization going forward. This extends to the debriefing process. There are many moving parts to be coordinated in the aftermath of an incident. Making sure all victims and potential victims are debriefed and offered assistance, including EAP assistance, is done as a part of the overall CMT plan.

There are specific industries and organizations that are feeling the aftereffects of violent events in the workplace as they seem to be the prime targets. For example, college campuses and hospitals are beginning to feel the overall effects of victims emerging as a group of workers who live in high-risk employee populations. As you can see from Figure 3-1, there

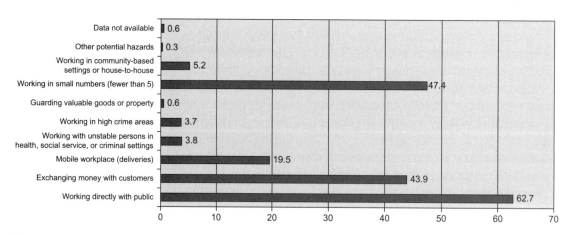

Figure 3-1. Percent of establishments by selected potentially hazardous work environment characteristics. *Source*: Bureau of Labor Statistics, U.S. Department of Labor, 2005.

are several occupational categories that are highly compensated and highly trained, like health care, which was mentioned earlier in this chapter. These sectors are prone to many of the aftereffects of incidences of violence that may have happened elsewhere, and the perpetrators and/or victims arrive on their doorsteps still displaying anger or violent behavior.

For example, in a recent Canadian news article, the health care industry was cited as a particularly risky area. The article estimates a staggering 34 percent of all nurses in the Canadian health system (*Source*: Statistics Canada) had been physically assaulted in 2005. A secondary source, 2005 National Survey of Work and Health of Nurses, cited similar findings after polling 19,000 nurses. They found that more than 25 percent of the polled nurses had been physically assaulted.

Linda Haslam-Stround, a registered nurse and president of the Ontario Nurses Association, reports that violence is probably underreported as some nurses have come to believe violence is part of their job. These statistics do not include the verbal abuse that is a daily occurrence in many areas of the medical facility, especially in the psychiatric wards and emergency rooms.

Dealing with Victims or Potential Victims: A Proactive Approach

Probably the most valuable recommendation for the reader is to surface the issue of violence with their constituent group. Make sure they are made aware of the problem of violence in the workplace today. Make sure the group understands the particular risks in the industry in which they work, keeping in mind the risk categories discussed earlier. For example, if you have a retail outlet in a mall, what risks can be associated from external sources in that environment? Also, the employees should be aware of how to report both internal and external acts, issues, and concerns.

Acknowledge the fact that an event could occur within the wall of your workplace. Don't fall into the trap of thinking it could never happen at your location or within your business. Having a policy regarding violence or threats of violence, bullying, etc. should be openly discussed and covered with all new and current employees on a reoccurring basis prior to a violent outburst. Prevention requires a proactive approach.

In the event an act of violence occurs in your workplace, acknowledge the fact that there will be short- and long-term effects that need to be managed within the emotional framework of the workforce. The effects of the event may surface during a company-facilitated discussion with the victims and bystanders, or it may be seen through the eyes of the family and friends of the victims. Despite what you may believe, talking the problem to death is actually necessary. Issues that remain in the mind can be blown out of proportion and result in mental and emotional challenges down the road. For the business, the result of this is delayed claims of stress-related illnesses, accusations of an uncaring corporate environment, and corporate management that only care about their own bottom line. So, providing a forum or forums to discuss the issues should be part of any response plan.

Discussion of what happened and what could have been done differently, without seeking or assigning blame, is also important. This tactic will mold a more effective program. For example, let's assume there was an incident on the third shift of a manufacturing firm involving a threat or act of intimidation. Let's suppose the supervisor was off duty that particular evening and the relief supervisor was new and had never received the WPV training which would offer the much needed training techniques to deal with the victim(s) of an event. A change in priority in training could be made as a matter of fixing a hole in the program. So, post-event debriefs are essential in a roundtable forum.

Determine what resources will be necessary to deal with the victim(s) when an incident impacts the entire business. If you have only one or two EAP response resources, determine what additional resources would be needed. Also, consider where additional resources would come from if a very serious act or acts of violence were to occur to properly handle the victims' needs.

Don't deny the need of post-event counseling and victim assistance. Regardless of whether or not you believe the trauma is real, your response plan of action should be executed based on worst-case scenarios. If a victim or witness is having a difficult time coping, the difficulty is real. In other words, feelings and perceptions need to be treated as the reality. Employees will have positive feelings toward the company in the aftermath of an incident if they believe the organization is concerned about their short- and long-term care of the victims. Just because management wants to move on, doesn't mean an employee can or will. In the event of violence in the workplace, an organization will either "pay now or pay later." Chances are, if an organization's response is delayed, the outcome could actually become more severe and result in greater long-term losses.

Legal and Ethical Responsibilities to Victims or Potential Victims of WPV

All who work within your organization have a right to a safe work environment. OSHA regulation 29 U.S.C. 654, § 5, states:

Duties:

(a) *Each employer – (1) shall furnish to each of his employees employment and a place of employment which are free from recognized hazards that are causing or are likely to cause death or serious physical harm to his employees; (2) shall comply with occupational safety and health standards promulgated under this Act.*

(b) *Each employee shall comply with occupational safety and health standards and all rules, regulations, and orders issued pursuant to this Act which are applicable to his own actions and conduct.*

Your organization must adhere to these regulations to avoid tremendous liability. The spirit of this regulation is much more difficult to navigate. With that fact in mind, consider what is cost-effective and reasonable and how that will be interpreted within a legal context, potentially by a jury of your peers. However, the real ethical response is much more subtle and telling. Would you want your son or daughter to work at your place of business with the security and concern for victims of threats or incidents or actual violence? Would your organization do what is right and necessary to assist the victim recovering from an incident or, better yet, have adequate policy, security, and response capability to thwart or respond quickly enough to curtail an escalation?

Food for Thought

1. If your organization has a violence deterrence, detection, and reaction program, is it externally or internally focused?
2. What is the biggest risk factor in your particular business? Public facing? Exchange of monies?
3. Do you have a crisis management strategy?
4. If you do, does it include a victim post-event strategy including debriefing of all affected employees, vendors, contractors, and bystanders?
5. Who within your business will lead the debriefing of victims?

References

National Victim Assistance Academy. (2002). *Foundations in victimology and victims' rights and services.* Retrieved August 30, 2009, from http://www.ojp.usdoj.gov/ovc/assist/nvaa2002/.

Bureau of Labor Statistics, U.S. Department of Labor. (2005).

LEGAL OBLIGATIONS AND WORKPLACE VIOLENCE

David Goldman

INTRODUCTION

The weakening of the U.S. economy in 2008 and 2009 amplified the challenges facing American employers. And analysts predict that workplace violence could potentially increase through 2010 as workers attempt to cope with changing work conditions.[1] As the recession in this country continues, and corporations of "all industries and sizes" continue with "unprecedented layoffs," some employees will lose their jobs, homes, retirement savings, benefits, and job security, while other employees will continue working with increased pressure to perform and an overall feeling of day-to-day uncertainty.[2] This "perfect storm of stressful conditions," combined with recently passed legislation in states such as Florida, Georgia, and Louisiana, allowing employees to bring weapons to the workplace, could result in extreme tragedy.[3] More than ever before, employers will increasingly be called upon to implement plans to protect their workforce and workplace.

This chapter delineates the most common types of liability employers face if they fail to adequately prepare for and respond to workplace violence. It also outlines steps employers

---

[1] Ross Arrowsmith, *Stress of weak economy may increase workplace violence*, Workplace Violence News, November 30, 2008, available at http://www.workplaceviolencenews.com/2008/11/12/stress-of-weak-economy-may-increase-workplace-violence/.
[2] Ibid.
[3] Ibid.

should consider to prevent the charges of workplace violence and lessen the chance for liability if such acts do occur.

Liability for Failing to Prevent and Respond to Workplace Violence

Fed-OSH Act Requirements and Guidelines

The Federal Occupational Safety and Health Act ("Fed-OSH Act" or the "Act") contains a general duty clause which requires employers to provide their employees with a place of employment "free from recognized hazards that are causing or are likely to cause death or serious physical harm to ... employees."[4] The Occupational Safety and Health Administration ("Fed-OSHA") has used this General Duty Clause to encourage employers to take steps to prevent injury to employees. Fed-OSHA has also developed guidelines that focus on preventing workplace violence in health care and social service operations, as well as in the late-night retail industry. Fed-OSHA has noted that it will continue to issue citations for workplace violence under the General Duty Clause where criminal activity endangers workers.

Fed-OSHA Fact Sheet: *Workplace Violence*

A brief, two-page Fact Sheet published by OSHA entitled *Workplace Violence* is a helpful resource to employers. Although the information it addresses is discussed in greater detail in other Fed-OSHA publications, the Fact Sheet is a convenient and useful first step for an employer in search of the initial direction needed in creating policies and procedures to prevent or limit violence in the workplace.

The Fact Sheet suggests establishing a zero-tolerance policy toward workplace violence by or against employees. It also recommends that employers ensure that all employees know the policy and understand that claims of workplace violence will be promptly investigated and remedied. The Fact Sheet also provides tips for employees to protect themselves, such as alerting supervisors to concerns about safety or security and carrying a minimal amount of cash.

[4] 29 U.S.C. § 654(a)(1).

Negligence Theories

In addition to the Fed-OSH Act's General Duty Clause, employers may be subjected to liability for acts of workplace violence based on various negligence theories, including *negligent hiring, negligent training, negligent supervision, negligent retention, negligent recommendation or misrepresentation*, and other *general common law duty* theories.

Negligent Hiring

The tort of *negligent hiring* is based on the principle that an employer has a duty to protect his or her employees, customers, and the general public from injuries caused by employees.[5] The duty is breached when an employer fails to exercise reasonable care in ensuring that his or her employees and customers are free from risk of harm from unfit employees. Thus, an employer may be found negligent in selecting an applicant for employment if, for example, the employer failed to contact the applicant's former employers or to check references, and where such an investigation would have demonstrated that the applicant had a violent propensity or was otherwise unfit for the job.

Many state courts have recognized the tort of negligent hiring and have placed the burden on employers to investigate applicants to prevent the risk of violent acts directed at employees and others.[6] Negligent hiring liability can be based on violence that occurred outside the scope of employment.

---

[5] Because negligent hiring is a tort committed by the employer itself, some courts have suggested that an employer may be liable for injuries caused by temporary workers. See *Doe v. Bradley Mem'l Hosp.*, 2003 Conn. Super. LEXIS 2447 (July 24, 2003) (finding issue of fact as to whether hospital was liable for negligently hiring a temporary nurse's aide).

[6] See, for example, *American Multi-Cinema, Inc. v. Walker*, 605 S.E.2d 850, 855 (Ga. Ct. App. 2004) (finding sufficient evidence to support jury finding against employer for negligent hiring); *N.H. v. Presbyterian Church (U.S.A.)*, 998 P.2d 592, 600-01 (Okla. 1999) (discussing facts necessary for plaintiff to show in support of negligent hiring and negligent supervision claim); *Underwriters Ins. Co. v. Purdie*, 145 Cal. App. 3d 57 (1983); *Connes v. Molalla Transp. Sys., Inc.*, 831 P.2d 1316 (Colo. 1992); *Kelley v. Baker Protective Servs., Inc.*, 401 S.E.2d 585 (Ga. Ct. App. 1991) (employer satisfied duty of ordinary care by investigating security guard's criminal and employment records); *Fallon v. Indian Trail Sch.*, 500 N.E.2d 101 (Ill. App. Ct. 1986); *Western Stone Co. v. Whalen*, 38 N.E. 241 (Ill. 1894) (finding that master has a duty to exercise ordinary and reasonable care

The proper focus generally is not whether the employee was acting within the scope of employment, but whether, in view of the employee's known characteristics, his or her violence was reasonably foreseeable by the employer. As a result, negligent hiring and negligent retention liability may exist even where respondent superior liability does not.[7]

Employers should take steps to protect themselves against incurring liability for negligent hiring by incorporating the following practices into their hiring process:

- Carefully review all information on employment applications and resumes prior to hiring an applicant.
- Question applicants about any gaps in employment history (such gaps could be due to the individual's serving time for violent crimes).
- Contact every prior employer to verify dates of employment and positions held. Obtain information on the applicant's reliability, honesty, and tendency to engage in violence from prior employers.

in the employment and careful selection of employees); *Medina v. Graham's Cowboys, Inc.*, 827 P.2d 859 (N.M. Ct. App. 1992); *Fisher v. Carrousel Motor Hotel, Inc.*, 424 S.W.2d 627 (Tex. 1967); *Fort Worth Elevators Co. v. Russell*, 70 S.W.2d 397 (Tex. 1934), *disapproved on other grounds in Wright v. Gifford-Hill & Co.*, 725 S.W.2d 712, 714 (Tex. 1987); *Hays v. Houston & G.N.R. Co.*, 46 Tex. 272 (1876). *But see McDorman v. Texas-Cola Leasing Co., LP, L.L.P.*, 288 F. Supp. 2d 796 (N.D. Tex. 2003) (employer has a duty to the public to employ competent drivers, but such duty does not require an independent investigation into the employee's nonvehicular criminal background); *Mulloy v. United States* 937 F. Supp. 1001, 1008 (D. Mass. 1996) (applying Illinois law, employer does not have a duty to assure all persons that its employees will not injure them at any time, whether on or off the job); *Mendoza v. City of L.A.*, 66 Cal. App. 4th 1333 (1998) (City of Los Angeles was not liable for the shooting of a woman by her fiancé, an intoxicated off-duty police officer); *Roman Catholic Bishop v. Superior Court*, 42 Cal. App. 4th 1556 (1996) (church with no prior knowledge of priest's unfitness was held not liable for his sexual abuse of a female minor); *Peek v. Equipment Servs., Inc.*, 906 S.W.2d 529, 534 (Tex. App.-San Antonio 1995, *no writ*) (perpetrator's employer was not liable, as the violent act was the result of personal animosity brought about by the delusion that the customer's officer and his Mafia associates were out to destroy the perpetrator); *Butler v. Hurlbut*, 826 S.W.2d 90 (Mo. Ct. App. 1992) (imposing duty to search the applicant's past criminal record was unreasonable in the particular circumstances of the case); States have also ratified statues outlining an employer's duty to its own employees and customers with respect to hiring and retention. See, for example, Ga. Code Ann. § 34-7-20.
[7] See *TGM Ashley Lakes, Inc. v. Jennings*, 590 S.E.2d 807 (Ga. App. Ct. 2003).

- Document investigative and screening efforts and all information received from prior employers and references, even if efforts to obtain such evidence have proven unsuccessful.
- Do not offer an applicant employment until the screening process is complete.
- Employment applications should advise the applicant that omissions, misrepresentations, or falsification of information will result in the rejection of the applicant or termination of employment.
- Consider performing background checks, including criminal record checks, on all applicants or on all applicants for particular positions.[8]

Employers should also be cognizant of federal and state laws that severely restrict pre-employment inquiries, investigations, and testing. Specifically, the Fair Credit Reporting Act (FCRA)[9] places restrictions on background checks done by third parties. Also, many states strictly limit the extent to which employers may investigate and use prior criminal records in making hiring decisions. For example, California Government Code, section 6254, prohibits the release of arrest records for commercial purposes.

Negligent Training

Courts in certain circumstances have also recognized a cause of action for employers' *negligent training* of employees that results in the injury of a third person. For example, California courts have recognized that medical universities are responsible for the proper training and supervision of residents as the universities have a duty to patients who are cared for by these residents.

Negligent Supervision and Retention

Some courts may also recognize the theory of *negligent supervision*, under which an employer may be held liable for

---

[8] Some states have enacted statutes creating a presumption that an employer is not liable for injuries to a third party caused by an employee's intentional acts under a negligent hiring theory, if the employer conducted a background check which failed to reveal information calling into question the employee's suitability for employment. See, for example, Fla. Stat. Ann. § 768.096.
[9] 15 U.S.C. § 1681.

failing to exercise reasonable care in supervising an employee who threatens violent conduct.[10] For example, the Texas Supreme Court held that the employer of a visibly intoxicated employee has a duty to restrain the employee from causing harm to third parties.[11] A finding of negligent supervision rests on whether the claimant can establish that the employer failed to exercise ordinary care in supervising the employee and that negligence proximately caused the claimant's injuries.[12] Liability for negligent supervision also may extend to an employer's failure to control the actions of *off-duty* employees while on the employer's premises.[13] Similar to a claim of negligent supervision, an employer may also be exposed to liability for *negligent retention*. This is the case when an employer is aware, or should be aware, that an employee is unfit to perform his or her duties; however, the employer fails to investigate, discharge, or reassign the employee.[14] As with negligent hiring claims, an employer need not have actual knowledge

[10] See, for example, *Dias v. Elique*, 276 Fed. Appx. 596, 598 (9th Cir. 2008) (discussing Nevada law regarding negligent supervision and dismissing claim); *Bradley v. Guess*, 797 P.2d 749 (Colo. Ct. App. 1989), *rev'd on other grounds*, *Seaward Constr. Co., Inc. v. Bradley*, 817 P.2d 971 (Colo. 1991); *Degenhart v. Knights of Columbus*, 420 S.E.2d 495 (S.C. 1992). Maine, for one, does not recognize this tort. *Mahar v. Stonewood Transp.*, 823 A.2d 540 (Me. 2003).
[11] *Otis Eng'g Corp. v. Clark*, 668 S.W.2d 307 (Tex. 1983) (liability based on the fact the employer sent home a visibly intoxicated employee who killed two women in an automobile accident on the way home).
[12] See *Mueller by Math v. Community Consol. Sch. Dist. 54*, 678 N.E.2d 660 (Ill. App. Ct. 1997); *Young v. Lemons*, 639 N.E.2d 610 (Ill. App. Ct. 1994).
[13] See generally *Foradori v. Captain D's, L.L.C.*, 523 F.3d 477 (5th Cir. 2008) (affirming jury finding of negligent supervision where an off-duty restaurant employee physically assaulted a restaurant patron in the parking lot, resulting in the patron's quadriplegia).
[14] See, for example, *Ekokotu v. Boyle*, 2008 U.S. App. LEXIS 20308, at *12 (11th Cir. September 24, 2008) (dismissing negligent retention claim under Georgia law because underlying claim of discrimination and retaliation failed as a matter of law); *Cook v. Greyhound Lines, Inc.*, 847 F. Supp. 725 (D. Minn. 1994); *TGM Ashley Lakes, Inc. v. Jennings*, 590 S.E.2d 807 (Ga. App. Ct. 2003); *Bryant v. Livigni*, 619 N.E.2d 550 (Ill. App. Ct. 1993), *appeal denied*, 631 N.E.2d 705 (1994); *Bates v. Doria*, 502 N.E.2d 454 (Ill. App. Ct. 1986); *Yunker v. Honeywell, Inc.*, 496 N.W.2d 419, 421 (Minn. Ct. App. 1993). But see *Brown v. Brown*, 739 N.W.2d 313 (Mich. 2007) (employer not liable for rape of employee by coworker as coworker's crude comments did not put employer on notice of propensity to commit rape).

of the employee's lack of fitness to be held liable for negligent retention; only constructive knowledge is required for liability to attach.[15]

Negligent Recommendation or Misrepresentation

Courts across the United States have also held that an employer may be liable for *negligent recommendation or misrepresentation* for providing a positive reference for a problem employee. For example, a Pennsylvania court held that a school that previously employed a perpetrator may be liable when it informed another school that the employee's performance was satisfactory, even though the employee had resigned because of sexual misconduct toward a student.[16]

California courts have also noted that, even absent a duty to provide information, the information that is provided by the employer must be true, and the employer must not suppress or misrepresent facts within its knowledge.[17]

Employers should exercise extreme caution in providing references for employees with violent tendencies. Although no court has yet ruled that prior employers must disclose violent tendencies to other employers, this issue has resulted in litigation. Employers who consistently follow a

[15] See *Harvey Freeman & Sons, Inc. v. Stanley*, 378 S.E.2d 857 (Ga. 1989); see also *G.G. v. Yonkers Gen. Hosp.*, 858 N.Y.S.2d 11, 12 (App. Div. 2008) (liability for negligent retention requires that employer be "on notice" of employee's propensity to commit the alleged acts); *Bumpus v. N.Y.C. Transit Auth.*, 951 N.Y.S.2d 591, 591 (App. Div. 2008) (necessary element of negligent retention is that "employer knew or should have known of the employee's propensity for the conduct which caused the injury").

[16] *Doe v. Methacton Sch. Dist.*, 880 F. Supp. 380 (E.D. Pa. 1995). See also *Jerner v. Allstate Ins. Co.*, No. 93-0-9472 (Fla. Cir. Ct. 1995) (unpublished) (punitive damages available against violent perpetrator's prior employer for failure to disclose in a letter of recommendation that perpetrator was terminated for bringing firearm to work). But see *Francioni v. Rault*, 518 So. 2d 1175, 1177 (La. Ct. App. 1988) (when former employer was asked for dates of employment, its duty to furnish accurate employment history of former employee who had embezzled did not encompass the risk that the former employee would murder his coworker at a subsequent job).

[17] *Randi W. v. Muroc Joint Unified Sch. Dist.*, 929 P.2d 582 (Cal. 1997); see also *Davis v. Board of County Comm'rs of Dona Ana County*, 15 Individual Empl. Rts. Cas. (BNA) 740 (1999).

policy of providing no references or neutral references—that is, merely confirming a former employee's name, dates of employment, and position—minimize their risk of future liability.

Special Role of the Civil Court System: Restraining Orders

Purposes of Restraining Orders

Restraining orders serve two major purposes—to prohibit specific conduct by the perpetrator and to order the perpetrator to stay away from the victim. The first purpose typically includes prohibiting the perpetrator from making physical contact with the victim, conducting surveillance of the victim, following the victim, telephoning the victim, and blocking the victim's movement. The second purpose usually includes a requirement that the perpetrator stays a specified distance from the victim, the victim's residence, the victim's workplace, and the victim's children's schools or places of child care.

Types of Restraining Orders

Victims of workplace-related harassment or threats of violence now have two different types of restraining orders that they can pursue in many states. An individual employee may obtain a civil-harassment restraining order that prohibits specified conduct by the perpetrator and orders the perpetrator to maintain a certain distance from the victim. In order to persuade a court to grant a civil harassment temporary restraining order under California law, the victim must show specific facts, including a knowing and willful course of conduct which (1) requires more than one act directed at a specific person; (2) seriously alarms, annoys, or harasses the person; (3) serves no legitimate purpose; (4) would cause a reasonable person to suffer substantial emotional distress; and (5) actually causes emotional distress to the victim.[18]

In some, but not all states, another option is for the employer to seek a temporary restraining order or injunction

---

[18] Cal. Civ. Proc. Code § 527.6.

to protect against threats or harassment at work.[19] In Arizona, an employer may obtain an injunction to protect the company, an employee, or person on the employer's property. Such an injunction may effectively prohibit the defendant from going near the employer's property or contacting the employer or individual employees while they are at work.[20]

As a slightly diverse example, Indiana law allows an employer to obtain an injunction against a person on behalf of an employee to prohibit further violence or threats of violence only if the employee has already suffered violence or threats of violence by the person at work. The Indiana law specifically states that it does not expand, diminish, alter, or modify the duty of an employer to provide a safe workplace.[21]

Steps for Obtaining a Temporary Restraining Order and Injunction

Once the individual victim or the employer has decided to pursue a restraining order, several steps must be completed before the petition seeking the restraining order and other legal papers are filed with the court. Although the particulars for this process vary by state, an employer in California, for example, would follow the process described below.

The employer's first step is to interview the victim and determine the facts surrounding the act(s) of violence and/or harassment. The interviewer should be either a manager experienced in investigating such incidents or legal counsel for the employer. The interviewer should obtain all the facts necessary to support the elements that must be proven to obtain the desired type of restraining order. When interviewing the victim, information regarding the perpetrator should also be gathered, including the perpetrator's home address and home phone number; work address and work

---

[19] See, for example, Ariz. Rev. Stat. § 12-1810; Ark. Code Ann. § 11-5-115; Cal. Civ. Proc. Code § 527.8; Co. Rev. Stat. § 13-14-102; Ga. Code Ann. § 34-1-7; Ind. Code § 34-26-6; Nev. Rev. Stat. §§ 33.200-33.260; N.C. Gen. Stat. § 95-260; R.I. Gen. Laws § 28-52-2; Tenn. Code Ann. §§ 20-14-101 to -109. Similar statutes have been proposed in Florida (S.B. 200 108th Reg. Sess. (Fla. 2006)) and New Jersey (A.B. 1512 212th Legis. (N.J. 2006)).

[20] Ariz. Rev. Stat. § 12-1810.

[21] Ind. Code § 34-26-6.

phone number; typical work hours; physical description; and vehicle description.

The second step is to interview any corroborating witnesses. It is often helpful in convincing the court to issue the temporary restraining order to have other individuals confirm that the incident in fact was as egregious and terrifying as the victim believes it to be. Also, interviewing other witnesses may uncover important facts that negate the need to seek a temporary restraining order.

The third step is to draft the papers that will be filed with the court to persuade the court to issue a temporary restraining order. Because of the sensitive and often highly emotional nature of the event giving rise to the need to obtain a temporary restraining order, it is recommended that legal counsel familiar with this process and with the unique rules of the jurisdiction be used to minimize stress and confusion otherwise inherent within the process. The Judicial Council of California has approved forms to be used when obtaining injunctions prohibiting harassment. Using the proper forms will help to avoid delays in filing the papers with the court clerk.

After the legal papers are drafted, the fourth step is to meet with the victim and other witnesses to review and sign the papers. Because the affidavits or declarations are signed under penalty of perjury, factual accuracy is critical. After obtaining signatures, the documents are taken to the appropriate court to obtain the judge's signature.

After the legal papers are delivered to the victim and to the appropriate police departments, the perpetrator must be served with the legal papers, the signed court order, and other documents as specified by law. Because the protection should be as complete as possible, before the perpetrator is notified that the victim has initiated legal proceedings, the perpetrator should not be served with the documents until after the victim and police have received copies.

Finally, a process server or a sheriff should be hired to serve the perpetrator. A party to the action (the individual or employer seeking the temporary restraining order) cannot serve the perpetrator. Because many perpetrators try to avoid service, attempts to serve the legal papers on the perpetrator should begin as soon as the victim and the police departments have received their copies of the paperwork.

To obtain a long-term injunction (generally three years in California), the victim or other witnesses must testify in court as to the required elements summarized above. Once the judge grants and signs the three-year restraining order,[22] the restraining order must be delivered to the victim and to the appropriate police departments. Some counties have developed abbreviated procedures for notifying the sheriffs' and police departments.

Practical Recommendations for Preventing Workplace Violence: A Seven-Step Practical Plan

In response to the growing frequency of workplace violence and the growing legal obligations imposed on employers to control violence, consider this practical seven-step approach (Seven-Step Plan) for preventing and addressing workplace violence. Although these recommendations are weighted in favor of policy and protection from legal liability, we also include recommendations based on the work of trauma experts and security consultants.[23] The Seven-Step Plan also incorporates some of the guidelines for employers published and compiled by the International Association of Chiefs of Police.[24]

Step One: Develop a Management Team

The first step in the Seven-Step Plan is to make preventing and controlling workplace violence a priority and to form a management team to develop, review, and implement policies dealing with violence in the workplace. The top levels of

[22] Because the court will often sign the injunction immediately after hearing evidence (if the evidence supports granting the order), the injunction should be prepared before the court hearing and should request the same protection as the court granted in the temporary restraining order.

[23] See, for example, C. Hatcher & S. White, Violence & Trauma Response, in *Occupational Medicine: State-of-the-Art Reviews,* Vol. III, No. 4, 677-94 (Handley & Belfus, Inc., Phila. October–December 1988).

[24] See *Combating workplace violence, Guidelines for Employers & Law Enforcement,* report provided by IACP's Private Sector Liaison Committee (1995).

management must be aware that the problem of workplace violence is a real and growing threat and can have devastating effects on individual employees as well as entire organizations. Management must recognize the potential threat and make violence prevention a priority. One of the most tangible methods of establishing this as a priority is to designate a management team and task it with responsibility for: (1) identifying and implementing a preventative plan and (2) being available to deal with issues as they arise.

Step Two: Implement an Education and Training Program

The second step is to conduct an education and training program regarding early warning signs of potentially violent behavior, the steps to follow to deescalate violent situations, and the methods of responding to and investigating incidences of workplace violence. Under the direction of the management team, supervisors should receive education in and guidelines for preventing violence in the workplace. Experts agree that a potential violent felon in the workplace is likely to be a loner, often angry, paranoid, depressed, and fascinated by weaponry. The individual may be undergoing a private stressful situation, such as a death or divorce in the family, which could be compounded by stress at work.

Supervisors and managers should be instructed in how to deal with individuals who exhibit early warning signs of violence. When investigating a complaint, the employer must take threats of violence seriously. Do not assume that a disgruntled employee is merely "venting" or "blowing off steam." The employer should also assure the reporting employee that he or she has acted appropriately and will not be subject to retaliation and that a thorough and prompt investigation will occur.

If possible, prior to discussing the matter with the employee, the management response team should be convened. The possibility of using outside consultants to assist in the interviewing process should be considered.

The employee should be asked for suggestions on how to minimize the risk of a violent behavior. At the conclusion of the investigation, if appropriate, the employer should report back to the complaining party its conclusions as well as any planned affirmative steps to control the situation.

In addition to training supervisors, when it comes to violence in the workplace, employers should have a "zero tolerance" that is distributed to all employees. Employers should also consider training employees regarding the signs of potential workplace violence and how employees should respond to these early warning signs. Both the "zero-tolerance" policy and the training should emphasize the need for employees to report unusual behavior or suspected violence, with assurances that: (1) such reports will be promptly investigated and, if warranted, action taken and (2) the reporting employee will not suffer retaliation for good faith reports.

Step Three: Increase Security Measures

The third step involves increasing security measures and developing a cooperative relationship with local law enforcement authorities. Employers should have in place a comprehensive plan for maintaining security in the workplace. Many employers have developed this as part of an injury and illness prevention program; other employers, based on their location or the nature of their industry, long ago implemented tight security measures to prevent outsiders from having access to the employers' facilities. These plans should be reviewed with special attention to the potential of violent behavior on the part of former employees, current employees, or other individuals who may carry domestic violence into the workplace. In addition to physical changes in the employer's environment designed to increase employee safety, policies should be reviewed to ensure that they are consistent with and promote the employer's basic program for preventing and responding to workplace violence. Finally, the employer should establish a relationship with the local police and sheriff's departments well in advance of any incident. Local law enforcement may prove to be an excellent source of information on experiences that other companies in the area or industry have had and suggestions on how to prevent these situations.

Step Four: Develop Response Procedure

The fourth step entails developing crisis procedures for responding to an incident of workplace violence. No matter how effective the management team is in educating managers and supervisors in detecting early warning signs of possible violent behavior and in defusing threatening situations, there are no guarantees against workplace violence. Some of the nation's most responsible employers, who have implemented highly sophisticated procedures for preventing violence, have still experienced occasional incidences of workplace violence. Accordingly, the planning process demands the development and practice of crisis procedures in preparing for violence in the workplace.

Step Five: Use Judicial Resources

The fifth step is to consider using the courts to prevent and redress incidences of workplace violence. State law may provide a procedure for obtaining a court order that prevents an alleged perpetrator from gaining access to the intended victim. Also, most states provide legal avenues for the detention and psychiatric evaluation of perpetrators of violence if there is probable cause to believe that the perpetrator is dangerous to him- or herself or others.

Although employers often distribute photographs of a dangerous employee after obtaining a restraining order or after threats are made, circulating such photographs creates a risk of potential claims of invasion of privacy and defamation. State statutes may also prohibit circulating photographs. To reduce the risk of liability, an employer should not provide photographs of employees or former employees to third parties without consulting with legal counsel. If photographs are distributed to personnel, those employees receiving photographs should be instructed not to release the photographs to third parties and not to have them in public view.

Step Six: Prescreening and Consistent Enforcement of Workplace Policies

Step six is to prevent workplace violence through the use of proper prescreening, consistent enforcement of workplace rules, and EAPs or other health care resources. Increasingly, employers face an obligation to investigate an employee's propensity for violence prior to offering employment. The case law in this area has been generated under the tort of negligent retention and is discussed in this chapter. Establishing procedures for background investigation and considering the use of screening tests are essential parts of the overall plan to minimize workplace violence.

An employer may even be held liable for failing to perform applicant background checks and employee investigations. As previously discussed, current statutory and common law sources of liability include negligent hiring and retention, negligent failure to warn intended victims, breach of an implied contract or covenant of good faith and fair dealing, occupational safety and health acts, intentional or negligent infliction of emotional distress, assault, and battery, and equal employment opportunity laws. Aside from the liability issues, employers are likely to gain significant benefits from conducting applicant background investigations. The practical benefits of such investigations include verifying abilities, skills, qualifications, reliability, and honesty. Careful screening of applicants through background checks also maximizes the employer's investment of resources in hiring and training new employees and reduces the likelihood of litigation concerning terminations.

Another important element of this step is the need for the employer to inform its employees of what it considers unacceptable behavior. A model policy prohibiting workplace threats and violence should be developed and implemented after careful review by legal counsel. The employer's disciplinary procedures, consistent application, and the willingness to consider alternative solutions, such as EAPs, may decrease the likelihood of workplace violence. Normally, proper and consistent application of effective policies results in an earlier detection of inappropriate behavior and sends a message that such conduct will not be tolerated.

The employer should consider using health care and other resources to provide support for employees. With rising medical care costs, it is increasingly important for employers to be knowledgeable about the resources available to their employees and, where necessary, to guide the employees to make effective use of available health care programs. To cope with the trauma of a crisis situation, employers should consider arranging for trauma specialists to be available to work with the management response team and the occupational physicians in restoring what was damaged or lost due to a violent event. In less threatening situations, employers should consider using the company's EAP, if one is available. Counseling can be obtained from these programs on an individual basis and, by special arrangement, on a group basis. Employees can be assured that the treatment is confidential and will not become a part of an employee's personnel records.

Finally, employers must consider their obligations when asked for recommendations on former employees who were involved in threats and/or who displayed violent conduct at work. Several courts have held that where supervisors do not remain silent when asked for recommendations about their former employees, they owe a duty of reasonable care, to both third parties and prospective employers. Given this precedent, some legislatures are considering the conditions under which employers are immune from liability for providing the employment history of a former or current employee. In 2004, Minnesota enacted such legislation.[25]

Step Seven: Establish Clear Communication Channels

The final step involves establishing clear internal and external lines of communication to avert and respond effectively to crisis situations. In this step, the management team should establish an internal emergency hotline and instruct personnel to report any and all threats of violence or violent behavior. The emergency's hotline should not be a replacement for calling 911. Employees should be instructed to call 911 in the event of a serious emergency. This should be followed by a call to the company's hotline. The person staffing the hotline must have ready access to telephone numbers to contact appropriate representatives in the management team.

The crisis response plan must include the establishment of a corporate command center that will serve as the communication hub. The command center will direct the actions of the

[25] Minn. Stat. § 181.967. Arkansas law also addresses liability for disclosure of employment records. Ark. Code Ann. § 25-19-105(c).

company as they relate to the crisis. The chain of command within and among the management team members must be clearly established and arrangements must be made to ensure unimpeded communication among them. Alternates for each team member should be designated in case the member is injured or is otherwise unavailable to carry out his or her functions. These procedures will facilitate communications among company management, employees, victims' families, vendors, customers, and the public.

Finally, the employer must carefully consider how information is disseminated to the media. A widely publicized corporate crisis can often be detrimental to the reputation and goodwill of a company. Preplanning on the part of the employer can greatly assist in protecting the employer's reputation, can affect how the media understands the crisis, and ultimately will safeguard the company against potential liability. As the Seven-Step Plan indicates, employers should use various measures to combat workplace violence. They should consider the causes of workplace violence and utilize available security and law enforcement resources to prevent it.

Psychological factors are relevant in determining whether particular individuals are more prone to workplace violence than others. For example, psychologists may assist in performing threat assessments to assist an employer in identifying and managing the risks of targeted violence. These assessments are often of the utmost importance for properly evaluating and controlling perpetrators.

Food for Thought

1. Does your organization understand the differences between negligent hiring, negligent retention, and negligent training?
2. Has someone in your business reviewed the Fed-OSHA Fact Sheet: *Workplace Violence?*
3. What is your policy on protective orders on threats against an employee?
4. Are you FCRA compliant in your hiring practices?

WORKPLACE CULTURE THAT MAY BREED VIOLENCE

INTRODUCTION

Much has been written about the early warning signs and corporate complacency that often escalate and result in violence. It's obvious that if an organization believed an incident could happen, the management would take every precaution and make every effort possible to address and diffuse any and all threats of violence and prepare a thorough response plan just in case. So the first symptom of an unhealthy and unprepared organization is denial. Emerson wrote, "What you are, sir, speaks so loudly that I can hardly hear what you say." With regard to the organizational culture, tone, words, phrases, and even gestures have tremendous impact. However, the language used and accepted as part of a business culture should also be considered as it may be systemic to a larger problem.

- "Did you see that news report about that guy who came into the office downtown and shot his ex-girlfriend? That could never happen here. Our employees would let us know if there was a problem at home."
- "I never report anything around here, nothing would change anyway!"
- "Management talks a pretty good game, but I really feel they don't care about the employees."
- "I sat on this committee to get some new policies for our workforce, but we presented our recommendations and no one ever got back to us; what a waste of time."

- "I went into a meeting with the boss and she about bit my head off! There is no respect for the individual around here."
- "This job means everything to me. I don't know what I'd do if they laid me off."

In the ever-changing world in which we live, and the speed at which we are capable of completing tasks, comes tremendous efficiency and tremendous pressure. The organizational culture, the language used by employees to describe the work environment, the style of management, and the ways in which the organization views employee strife and morale are just a few examples of the first tangible pieces of evidence that a problem within the organization may exist. We are all busy, and it is easy to believe that all is well because the "lid is on" today. But what would it take to change the status quo? The following is an anonymous case that demonstrates how a change in government policy affects the culture of a business.

Case Study 1

During a recent conversation with a client, an all-too-common situation was described. A large portion of a particular workforce was being scrutinized by the United States' Immigration Service. Several of the client's employees who had work visas that were about to expire and coming up for review were being required to return to Mexico for a recertification process. Although these employees were not necessarily key to the operation, their inability to work for an extended period of time would create staffing challenges. Also, these absences would spawn a general disruption in the lives of the employees who see recent approaches to curtailing illegal immigration as discriminatory and arbitrary.

This is a highly controversial issue and well outside the scope of this book. However, the point is that an outside force can influence the overall culture of a business. In this case, some of the affected employees began to respond to the situation in a negative way. For example, some began making unflattering remarks about the U.S. government and Americans in general. This, logically, created a backlash toward the non-U.S. employees, and the game was on. Several overt acts were investigated by management ranging from decreased productivity and work quality to veiled threats and disparaging remarks about the ancestry of different employees to crude hand gestures.

There were several facts that were determined during the hour meeting that was held to discuss solutions. The following were determined:

1. This was a family-run business that has gradually grown from a two-person operation to one of over 60 employees.
2. Until recently, the company's founder had been running the business. All decisions of any importance were made entirely by him. The company did not have a real HR department—only an office manager who was responsible for handling I-9 and payroll processes. There were no employment applications, orientation trainings, or any other trainings besides the training that related directly to the job.
3. Supervisors were brought through the ranks and received direction from the founder, who made all the hiring and firing decisions.
4. Recently, the founder's son was placed in the presidential seat and began to oversee the operation as the founder transitioned into semiretirement. The son was a completely different type of manager. He delegated more and more of the day-to-day business decisions to his management team who were, to put it mildly, not trained in the art of decision making.
5. At the urging of some of the new president's more proactive supervisors, an employee handbook was rolled out. This handbook did not include any mention of how to deal with or report threats, violence, acts of intimidation or bullying, or unprofessional behavior of any kind. The handbook did talk about days off, vacation scheduling, and other safety-related issues dealing with the functional aspects of the job.
6. As would logically follow, there was no training for supervisors regarding how they should address, diffuse, or deal with an act of violence in the workplace.

7. There was no plan in place on how to deal with a crisis in the workplace other than to call the founder and ask for direction.

The client was asked what the culture was like at his business, but he was not sure how to answer the question, so he was asked the following questions:

1. When it comes to the workforce, what keeps you up at night?

2. Are you ever fearful that a violent act might occur at your place of business?

3. If you were to reprimand or discipline an employee for unprofessional behavior of any kind, would you be supported by your manager or senior management?

4. Are you aware of any person or persons leaving the business because they were uncomfortable around individuals or groups of individuals at your facility?

5. How is confrontation viewed within your business?

Drilling down into each of the questions listed above could make for a much longer list of questions, but the bottom line was simply that the client was concerned for the safety of his peers, subordinates, and even the people who worked in the office. This person didn't feel supported and felt the management of the business was timid and afraid to discuss the tough issues. This client was quietly networking to find himself a new job.

To clarify, culture is generally defined as the traditions, customs, and mores of a group of people. In the larger sense, it is the philosophy of how people interact in society and ultimately determines a person's way of life. In the workplace, people who come from different cultures are brought together for a common purpose. There are some who believe that the only reason an individual works is for money. Although that is certainly the case for many, the environment within the workplace is often a determining factor in employee production and longevity.

As of today, the economy of the world is in a pretty dire situation. However, there is hope that, in the future, there will never be another economic situation like this one. But because of the cyclical nature of economics, it is important to be aware that economic factors can negatively affect work environments. One such negative side effect is violence against decision makers or perceived decision makers by recipients of a layoff or "resizing" initiatives.

Possible Causes of Workplace Violence

Violence against decision makers or perceived decision makers can also be fueled by negative press that may accompany such occurrences as in the case of the 2009 troubles at American International Group, Inc. (AIG). Edward Liddy, chairman and CEO of AIG, laid out his concerns regarding his managers before the House Financial Services Committee on March 18, 2009. In this testimony, Mr. Liddy provided evidence by citing two graphic examples of threats to his managers and their families. His examples were given in an attempt to not release names of executives who received performance bonuses at the same time the company was conducting layoffs and applying for government bailout money. So, in this case, the threat is from both current or soon-to-be former employees, former employees, and possibly the disgruntled tax payer.

It is logical to assume that a company that learns of such threats would provide additional security around its facilities that house its key managers or even hire bodyguards to enhance executive protection. Partnering with local law enforcement to investigate threats externally or internally with corporate or internal security is also an option. The protection teams need to be fully briefed as to potential suspects, and the nature of any and all known threats if the business wishes to be successful in its reaction to an actual event (*Source*: Kiplinger.com).

As a countermeasure, all decisions to lay off employees for economic reasons have to be communicated. This communication must happen in such a way that all who are or may be effected are given the opportunity to be heard to reduce the feeling of personal powerlessness. The idea that "we are in it together" needs to be understood and communicated frequently. Abnormal or exaggerated reactions to the news of layoffs should be noted. Providing electronic pathways like open 800 telephone numbers for employees to call, even anonymously, is recommended. It is important to diffuse frustration through communication.

Diffusing Frustration in the Workplace

The following are some strategies that might be used to help diffuse frustration in the workplace. All of these may not apply in all situations, but many might be helpful for discussions within your organization.

- Provide email address boxes or internal company blogs where questions can be asked and answered. Post answers to questions back to all in a generic manner so as not to break a confidence with a source.
- Additional EAP resources may be sourced and made known to the workforce.
- Allow for and facilitate company meetings in both large and small forums to discuss the realities of the company's economic dilemmas.
- Try not to hide from the tough discussions or appear defensive. Avoidance or defensiveness will only confirm the appearance of uncaring corporate executives who are lining their pockets at the expense of the rank and file.
- Remember to communicate. If there is one area that is relatively inexpensive yet often overlooked, it is this simple courtesy. Communication will be absolutely critical to changing or improving a corporate culture.

Workplace Culture and Its Effect on Violence

Another common dilemma is the concept or belief that a violent incident could never happen at your organization or place of business. The belief that the workforce is part of an artificially created family and that no one in this family who would commit such a stupid or careless act—to actually threaten or bully another employee, customer, or vendor—is very naive. This belief is especially prevalent when a company is ramping up a new location to the business. In this case, all of the associates are brought on together and experience a camaraderie and closeness that often is lost in larger more established environments.

A family-like culture may become a factor that will boomerang on a business when it is faced with downsizing or when one of the "family members" is asked to leave. This is the stark reality of business because, in a real-life family, you are in for good whether you like it or not or the family likes it or not. The old adage that "you can pick your friends but you can't pick your family" is not true in the workforce. A business chooses its workers, and there can certainly be bad hires who slip through whatever application, interview, and/or background screening process is used. The intrinsic qualities that might negatively affect your work culture are not often seen in the hiring process. So the expectation that an employer will always pick an employee who fits seamlessly into the current work fabric is unrealistic.

The truth is that the culture of the organization is set at the very top of the business through actions, not words or policies. The real culture is set only if the actions match and support the words and polices of the business.

Case Study 2

A real-life example of what is meant here can be demonstrated by a real-life situation relating to the wearing of identification badges and having to produce them for a security officer. This scenario seems pretty straightforward—if you don't have an ID, you don't get in. The company represented by this story was a large communications firm. This firm had in excess of a million employees with thousands of facilities in all 50 states and over 100 countries. This company had a culture of promoting from within. Employees were hired right out of high school and would often sweep floors while going to college. Once the employees graduated, they would be given a job as a first-level supervisor and moved up through the business. The culture was seen as internally focused for any advancement especially at the executive levels where the CEO came from a leadership position in one of the company's many divisions. The CEO always wore his ID. He wore it with pride. In every picture that was taken of him, whether he was in a suit or sport shirt, he always had his ID badge on. The security department appreciated the CEO's eagerness to wear his badge as it made the enforcement of this policy straightforward and understood. When employees took exception to the badge system because the facility was small or simply out of desire to buck the trend, the corporate security representative could show the offender a copy of the company magazine with the CEO and Chairman of the Board wearing their ID badges with obvious pride. The culture of this business was to adhere to the security system that included a strong ID policy and established entry policies to its facilities. Visitors, contractors, and customers were required to be signed in and escorted while on the premises. Employees routinely reported violations of the ID policy to facility managers and, if such a violation persisted, to corporate security. It was an image that was communicated to the company's customers. This policy gave customers the peace of mind needed to hand over sensitive information.

Then, a major restructuring occurred. The company was divided into large segments. New facilities were opened to great fanfare. New names of business units were formed. A new headquarters was opened and, for the first time, new senior-level managers were brought from outside the business into the newly formed business units. One of these new executives had never been required to wear an ID since everybody at his former company knew who he was.

As a matter of course, the building security force was provided pictures of the senior executives to give them a heads up. All of the security officers had established security post-orders. In these post-orders, all employees were required to show and wear their ID badges at all times while on company premises. The senior executive pictures were placed in a manila folder next to the post-orders. The security officers were new to this building, and so they studied the pictures diligently.

One senior executive carried the lofty title of Senior Vice President of Marketing and Sales. He came to work the first day and was ushered into a room where his picture was taken. The HR director saw him come in and ushered him to the front of the line. His card was specially processed and delivered to his assistant. It was clear that he wasn't too thrilled about being required to wear a badge at all times. He complied for the first week.

During his second week on the job, he "forgot" his ID. The security officer stopped him and advised him that he would have to be signed in. He was with a group of his direct reports and within earshot of ten or so employees coming into work.

The executive asked the security officer in a loud and arrogant tone, "Do you know who I am?"

The security officer replied with what he felt was the correct response, "Yes sir, I have your picture here. I know who you are."

The executive responded, "Then you don't need to see any ID, I am a busy man, and I don't have time for this nonsense!"

The security officer was staggered. He allowed passage, and called his superior who called the building manager. The building manager called Corporate Security who escalated the issue to the Director of Security for the company. Meetings were held, and it was decided the Director would make an appointment with this Executive to, hopefully, garner his cooperation.

Unfortunately, however, the damage had been done. The junior executives who were now walking with the senior executive would just walk alongside and when asked where their IDs were, they would respond, "I'm with him," pointing at the Senior Executive. The incident cascaded through the facility.

In one fell swoop, the culture changed at this facility, and the Director could not convince the Senior Executive to change his position. The point here is simple. A security policy has to be understood and internalized at all levels of the business.

It is common for security policies and procedures to be established and signed off on by senior managers and even CEOs and Chairpersons of Boards. To have effective security and HR processes that effectively and proactively prevent cultural breeding grounds for violence, senior management must understand the risks and strategies to prevent external and internal challenges associated with violence. Facility management, contract security, and corporate security are typically the front line of the preventative plan. HR professionals should also be players in violence prevention via the hiring process. A fatal error in prevention occurs when enforcement is delegated to a low-level manager or supervisor who has little or no authority to impose compliance.

To confront an executive who perceives himself or herself as "above the law" can be detrimental to any effective security and violence prevention strategies within the workplace. And treating an executive as "above the law" can extend to the overall respect in how people at all levels within the company are treated. Bullying in the boardroom can be seen as a green light for heavy-handed or even hostile actions that may be seen as acceptable.

When this kind of behavior is witnessed by the rank and file, finding a strategy for establishing or changing an existing, unhealthy culture will be difficult, to say the least. This is especially true if the personalities of the real leadership are combative or disrespectful. Confronting the CEO or senior-level manager with news that he or she is setting a bad example could be career ending for the messenger in many organizations. So for any author to sit on an intellectual hilltop preaching love and tolerance may appear to be condescending and worthless in practice. However, in addition to writing this book, this author also served as Vice President and General Manager for a division of LexisNexis which provided insight into a workplace culture from a boardroom perspective. From either perspective, security or boardroom, experience has shown that a culture that seems to be less defined by contention promotes a spirit of openness within an organization.

CLEAR

Let's step away from violence or the behavior that can lead to violence and look at a strategy not only to improve the company prone to violence but the operational efficiency as well. It is recommended that your organization adopts a process of being CLEAR.

C—Communication is critical in every organization to reduce frustration, develop trust, and create a culture of transparency. To this day, there is a belief that knowledge is the source of real power in any business or organization. Therefore, by withholding information, the persons "in-the-know" are often seen as separate and become targets of criticism. A certain amount of belief and lore will always remain. However, a gradual transformation to a culture of thorough communication on all types of issues, both good and bad, will pay handsomely in the long run.

L—Learn to listen. This skill is critical to develop to be successful in any area of life. But in reality, most conversations are counterproductive because they are not conversations at all. The dialogue is more like a collective monologue where each participant is thinking of what he or she is going to say when the current talker has finished his or her thought. Most perpetrators who commit violence have deeply held beliefs that they feel cannot be remedied except through an angry and, all too often, violent response. In this action of listening, we can often come to understand the issues at hand without necessarily agreeing with the position.

E—Evaluate and examine. If you currently have policies, procedures, and response tactics in place, it may be time to reevaluate your current strategies. Examining the records and reports from your security organization, reviewing artifacts of incidences, and looking at prior investigations to find the motives and excuses for violence may be enlightening. An objective evaluation of your organization's culture may be difficult, and an outside facilitator might be needed. But in reality, you need to ask the tough questions in order to determine whether or not, like the cartoon character Pogo discovered, "we have found the enemy and he is us."

A—Accountability needs to be established. Don't make the mistake of pushing your initiatives down to a lower level of the organization to complete a set of policies. This act is also a symptom of an unhealthy culture. If your upper management does not seem to see the risk, then having a risk analysis done against your business as it applies to a violence-prone culture might drive urgency. The age-old adage that "if everything is important then nothing is important" applies here. When profit and losses are the only real measurements of success within your business, then the indirect assumption is that the concerns and needs of the employees are a not-too-close second. Who within your business is accountable for your security and safety issues including violence prevention? Is it of high enough priority that it stands out among the cast of thousands in a fast moving corporate culture?

R—Response to issues. Whether it is a response to a concern or a response to an incident, there should be an established expectation known to all and communicated frequently. The execution of a plan will be the difference between success and failure. If you are a great planner but lack the skill to complete or implement a plan, then the hegemony of doing the same old thing and getting the same old result will harden. It is imperative that businesses develop cultures that place importance on speedy response times rather than ignoring problems and simply hoping they'll go away. If an issue is swept under the rug or addressed only on a superficial basis, chances are good that it will eventually manifest itself again. And, when it does, it will likely be even more serious as it's escalated with time.

So, be CLEAR in your corporate culture and your organization will be less likely to experience the frustration and disruption that accompanies violence in the workplace. A proactive approach would include the training of first-line supervisors on how to treat subordinates with respect even in a disciplinary situation or dismissal interview. We all want to be treated with civility and dignity even under adverse or stressful situations. Confrontation should not necessarily be avoided but rather done so in a professional manner.

Senior management should be the first to address this issue. How the boardroom deals with tough issues does matter to the rank and file. The word seems to get out somehow if the tone is disrespectful and harsh. Be aware that ambition drives behavior in many cases. The result may be an increase in harsh and eventually threatening or violent responses. Teach composure by example.

If you feel the issue needs teeth, there is always the policy route. If you have policies about how to treat each other and how to curtail unprofessional outbursts or harsh or aggressive behavior, certain individuals would feel that management wants a tight ship. Discuss this in your Crisis Management development process.

Employee pulse-type surveys oftentimes provide very insightful feedback, especially when they are conducted anonymously. Many large and small businesses use such surveys with customers and employees to get an accurate read on what is going on today. Over time, trends of improvement or the success of communication, training, or policy initiatives will emerge. If there is no improvement, keep trying. Make improvement in these areas an ongoing priority by setting short- and long-term goals. It is a commonly held belief that, like a customer service improvement process, employee morale and cultural change can be measured and scored. Index it alongside your production indexes. See if there are improvements in culture and productivity.

If you are in charge of the WPV prevention program, meet with your senior managers and solicit their support. Make these senior managers aware of how their ideas and attitudes impact and even dictate organizational culture. Recent incidents of organizations in similar businesses or locations can be used to demonstrate the realities of violence in the workplace. In this book, you will be given policy and procedural recommendations. However, winning the hearts and minds of your business's leadership will undoubtedly fall on you. So the key is to whittle your presentation down to a hard pitch and hit them squarely with the fact that violence in the workplace can happen anywhere and certainly in the business they manage today.

EAPs are key partners in dealing with cultural concerns within a business. The caseload at the EAP can be inversely linked to the health of the culture. If the EAP's work has increased, the health of the company's culture is probably under attack. Make sure the business has an EAP, and regularly communicate its role in the day-to-day operation.

As mentioned earlier, we are currently in the midst of an economic meltdown of tremendous proportions that is severely affecting hiring. Over the years, the economy's behavior has been quite cyclical in terms of its growth and decline. Create a plan around how your business will operate during a weak economy. Review your downsizing strategies. Believe it or not, emails have actually been used to notify an organization of the layoff selections. Ask yourself how you would like to be handled in the event of a downsizing or a dismissal, and then respond accordingly. Most large firms conduct exit interviews that serve two purposes: (1) they allow management to address employees' concerns and (2) they allow for the collection of valuable information from the employees' perspectives at their respective levels within the business. Issues around security and safety, as well as bullying, could be the root cause as to why an employee is choosing to move on. Be sure to interview those employees who are leaving for other employment opportunities. They may be more than willing to give candid feedback regarding your culture and WPV policies and programs. When an employee, with no personal agenda, leaves an organization, he or she can offer valuable insight into the real perceptions of your constituent groups. Nonconfrontational, conversational settings with a less formal agenda can net tremendous factoids relating to the health of your culture.

A Culture of Security Mindedness

As Case Study 2 indicated, often the change in the wind of corporate leadership can have either a negative or positive impact to the business. However, there are other factors that also help mold the organizational culture with regard to security and violence prevention. In Mary Lynn Garcia's book, *The Design and Evaluation of Physical Protection Systems*, she repeatedly talks about preventing, detecting, deterring, delaying, and responding to security incidents. Garcia's work is an excellent guide to determining the appropriate response to various threats and a methodology to determining the risks associated with various threats. This work is highly recommended when dealing with external and most internal risks of malevolent behavior.

The mere fact that employees are greeted with a well-thought-out, integrated security plan may, for some, be enough to demonstrate to both internal and external constituent groups that the organization takes security seriously. So physical security methodologies should be employed to deal with security concerns throughout your organization.

Further, it is imperative that similar security methodologies be developed to deal with technical risks of systems and intellectual properties of the business. Clear policies and procedures should be developed and maintained at all levels of an organization as the lifeblood of most businesses depends on the smooth and continuous running of systems and technical processes. The principle of evenly matching people, procedures, and equipment, including technological security strategies, is critical. Note that in this list people are first. All employees must be integrated and communicated to at every level of the organization because, at the end of the day, people need to feel that they are protected and cared for in the business. And, not only does the company care about the physical and technical assets of the organization but the human assets as well.

We all remember the tremendous surge in security emphasis after the tragic events of the Oklahoma City bombing and September 11. The need to understand an organization's security mindedness must be a daily part of an organization, and this can only be accomplished if it is a part of the culture.

It is the people who are at the heart of any successful organization. And, it is their attitudes toward the organization and each other that will ultimately prevent, deter, detect, and respond to violence in the workplace. The people within the organization need to be convinced that there are risks they can address. Business is not business. Business is people.

Food for Thought

1. What are the language clues telling you about the health of your business culture?
2. Are the changes in the economy/geopolitical landscape affecting or might they affect your organization?
3. How well does your company communicate positions, policies, and procedures?
4. Do the senior levels of your organization support and participate in the violence prevention efforts? If so, to what degree?
5. How is security viewed in your organization? Is it a priority only after an event?
6. Does your security organization have a place at the table with your senior leadership?

BUSINESS IMPACTS OF WORKPLACE VIOLENCE

INTRODUCTION

On August 4, 2009, a man walked into an LA Fitness Center in Collier, Pennsylvania, and opened fire. The shooting occurred just after eight o'clock in the evening, when the gunman walked into the fitness center with a duffel bag. The perpetrator entered an aerobic dance class, turned out the lights, and then opened fire on the room full of women. Three victims were left dead and at least nine victims were wounded before the gunman turned his weapon on himself (*Pittsburgh Post-Gazette*, 2009). The shooter, George Sodini, 48, left a detailed account of his actions and motives in an electronic log captured after the incident. This log will provide some important evidence as to why this type of thinking precedes a seemingly random act of violence. This incident further accentuates the premeditation of such acts of violence.

The way in which this story was handled by the media parallels the handling of similar events that have happened in places of business—the reporting was done after the fact and highlighted the short-term effects as they are often discussed in news reports. When these violent events happen, employees are evacuated, offices are shut down, employees are sent home with pay, and the entire senior staff refocuses its attention on the following questions:

1. How did this happen and who is responsible?
2. What do we need to do to calm the fears of employees, customers, stockholders, and investors?

3. How do we get this behind us quickly and return our attention to getting the organization back in the business of doing business?

4. What should we have done differently, and what should we do in the future?

While asking these questions is beneficial and provides a broad evaluation of the overall impact, some of the more subtle, and often more significant, effects are not addressed or even quantified. Unfortunately, the lasting effects caused by workplace violence may not be directly quantifiable. If this is the case, an indirect method of quantifying should be employed. For example, what is the overall effect to ongoing production after an incident? Is there a significant change in individual performance metrics in addition to attendance or disability claims? The time it takes to isolate the cause and effect may be significant and could be fraught with subjectivity.

In the LA Fitness example, the news teams took several ground-level and aerial views of the crime scene with the company name marquee prominently displayed in most, if not all, of the pictures of the event. The short-term damage this news coverage contributed to the organization's reputation is immeasurable. As a result of this incident, the need to vet customers in some way, and an evaluation of the general security of the facility, in addition to the concern for the welfare of employees and negative impact to sales at this and other locations, will certainly be impacted in the short term and possibly longer. Additionally, the question of what the corporation's response looks like as it relates to physical security, as a discipline, needs to be addressed. Will this response require a refocus or will the business try to resume business as it was prior to the incident? Will the organization begin to require bag searches, including magnetometers, in the short and long term? This reaction is, by no means, a recommendation, but all security solutions get thrown on the table as possible responses to the occurrence of a devastating incident.

The Problem as a Whole

Estimates on the actual monetary costs of violence in the workplace vary. The lowest estimate at the current time is $4.2 billion, which is provided by the Workplace Violence Workplace Institute (Kaufer & Mattman, 2001). However, this estimate does not include all of the business-related expenses. The FBI's National Center for the Analysis of Violent Crime (NCAVC), part of the Critical Incident Response Group (CIRG), located at the FBI Academy at Quantico, Virginia, published an extensive study that attempted to frame, address, and quantify the issues surrounding workplace violence. However, in addressing the size of the problem, the CIRG report stated, "Drawing on responses to the National Crime Victimization Survey, a Justice Department report estimated that an average of 1.7 million 'violent victimizations,' 95 percent of them simple or aggravated assaults, occurred in the workplace each year from 1993 through 1999. Estimates of the costs, from lost work time and wages, reduced productivity, medical costs, workers' compensation payments, and legal and security expenses, are even less exact, but clearly run into many billions of dollars" (2002). And so, the estimated cost of workplace violence and its multiple layers of impact throughout an organization is just that, an estimate, at best. The real cost is effectively viewed at the micro level to be fully understood. In other words, what is the effect of this incident to my company or organization?

Most large organizations and companies now have some sort of program to address violence in the workplace. According to this report, however, most small companies do not have violence in the workplace policies, let alone a program. If this is true, it is logical that a crisis management plan, which would include recovery, is also missing. So what are the costs of not having a program?

The types of costs can be divided in several ways. First are the immediate costs:

- *Downtime*—Depending on the severity of the incident, the operation at the affected site may be extensive. In the case of the Olympic Park bombing, the park was closed for four days. Research of the events demonstrates that this is an average amount of time for the organization to recover to the degree that it can reopen its doors. Some organizations may choose to close for business the day following an incident and sometimes even into the next day. However, many organizations try to reopen as quickly as possible in an attempt to move past the incident. If your organization is a physical product-producing shop or an integral piece to an organization's entire process, deciding when to reopen could be very impactful. As most technical businesses have backup systems, such systems could function as a behind-the-scenes method of spinning up a disaster recovery (DR) site or plan. But for a small business that does not have access to this kind of technology, a violent incident could be enterprise ending or, at a minimum, have a substantial negative impact on its customers. For manufacturing companies or service establishments, an instance of violence will cut into inventory, at a minimum, or disrupt any "just-in-time" manufacturing strategies. For a shooting or other violent acts like bombing, arson, or assault, a business may become a crime scene and could be taken over by crime scene investigators or fire investigators. To accurately calculate your business impact, take the daily production or productivity numbers of your site, multiply it by four and you will have an accurate average daily loss per incident. Other costs may appear in the following ways.

• *Loss of workforce*—This cost may come in the form of the victims of the actual event; however, it is just as likely that many of the members of an affected organization's workforce may just leave their employment with no obvious direct connection to the violence. Again, going back to the bombing at the Centennial Olympic Park, 10 percent of the workforce at the AT&T Global Olympic Park left the company, and this 10 percent represented employees who had not been directly affected. These employees were physically present during the event of the bombing but evacuated the area immediately after the detonation of the bomb. Some of these employees left their employment with AT&T immediately and yet others returned to work after the reopening of the park and then left after a day of work. Many of these associates left due to the emotional trauma of the event. When gauging the impact to the organization, the calculation of loss of staff means figuring the recruiting, training, and ramp-up or learning curve costs involved in replacing the 10 percent.

- *Customer/investor goodwill*—Goodwill is based on customer experience, attitude, and confidence in the company to deliver a product or service that deserves their loyalty. The same is true for the investor. Investors will look at the bottom line of the business in response to its ability to deliver consistent performance against the economy, industry, and month-over-month or year-over-year performance. A trend that is not explainable and the business' ability to recover quickly may have impact here. Macro trends have impact on investors. Industry-specific and competitive trends are also limiting. Abnormal bumps in results may send investors to higher ground—especially if there is negative press around the business' response to the specific event or if the reporting of a hostile or violence-prone area within the organization surfaces.

- *Falling productivity per employee*—Even if a violent incident is as simple as a threat, it will have an impact on a business. Every person within the organization will be off his or her game and watercooler conversations, instant messaging, and email chatter will increase. Keeping workers on task will be a challenge to overcome. Daily quotas or metrics will be affected. These areas are where impact is visible both in the short and long terms. Witnesses or victims to a violent incident may be the first to show changes but, over time, those employees who become increasingly concerned about their well-being at work may, intentionally or unintentionally, reduce their output. Customer complaints may increase during this time, thus creating additional stress for the now unfocused workforce.

- *Public relations and media impact*—These areas of concern can be intermingled in the customer/investor goodwill arena, at times; however, the repeated media coverage of an extreme event involving workplace violence may have impact. This is true especially if employees chose to speak to the media. Employees may paint a more negative picture of the work environment that is contrary to your PR department or senior management response. It is important to take this factor into account as a possible impact to business. This could also be measured as a monetary cost of violence.

- *Cost of increased security*—This initial cost may be as simple as adding some security officers to your site to control access or deal with the aftermath of the incident. It may also give a level of calm to the existing employees who are coming to work after a significant incident. Often, additional security is required when a disgruntled employee is dismissed and threats are made by the employee on the way out the door. The disgruntled former employee may even start sending veiled threats electronically to the key decision makers in his or her departure. The long-term cost may be missed in calculating the effects of violence. For example, if the affected business was not doing preemployment background checks prior to the violent incident, it may now add that ongoing cost of $35–150 per hire, depending on the organization's risk model. Or changes may need to be made to add electronic surveillance or electronic access systems in response to an incident. Organizations that strive to have proper plans in place should be proactive in conducting a risk analysis and security strategy *before* an incident occurs. Unfortunately, all too often, these measures are put into place after the event, sometimes in a less cost-effective, fast-track process that is more costly than a proactive approach. In several real-world instances, when a senior manager was threatened, the involved company or organization has done everything from paying for off-duty police officers to sit in the driveway of the home of the executive to hiring full executive protection teams. In one instance, the company paid for a home alarm system for an executive, which was, in this case, fast-track installed at a higher installation cost.
- *Cost of the investigation*—If a threat is made or an incident occurs, law enforcement may or may not be called. This choice depends solely on the policies of the business and the severity of the incident. In an ideal world, most violent incidents are reported to the local authorities for investigation. The cost in that scenario might be measured by the assistance that needs to be provided for the officers or detectives to do their jobs. This

process may require the company to provide employees to be interviewed, employee statements taken, and even requesting employees testify in court. If it is deemed to be an internal investigation that may or may not result in criminal action, the investigative resources may be an imbedded cost if your business has a corporate security department. There can be pay-as-you-go arrangements made with an investigative firm, and a cost, often as much as $300–600 an hour, may be involved. Also, the cost of taking employees off the job to assist in the investigation is a cost that is not often captured.

- *Legal costs*—In the previous chapter, you read about the legal issues and implications of violence in the workplace. Suffice it to say that there are many legal issues and implications and everything that happens after an incident drives up the cost. For example, there may be costs associated with civil suits that are filed citing negligence in the security that was provided by the organization or the hiring of an individual who had a violent history that was not discovered because no background check was done. Even if the allegations are groundless, the organization may be required to defend itself. The intangible costs occur when employees have to be pulled off the line for depositions or hearings at a time when their services are needed to perform their normal job functions.

- *Employee assistance*—If you are a pay-as-you-go customer for an outside service, the expenses involved in providing counseling to victims and witnesses may begin to spike. This is an important service to have in normal times, but its value will be obvious in the aftermath of any level of violence both from internal and external sources. Emotional trauma may manifest itself immediately or over time. So getting a real handle on the cost of an incident may depend on the time horizon you accept as comprehensive to an incident.

The message here is that your business will suffer both direct and indirect financial consequences that will ultimately affect your ability to operate your business smoothly. The key here is to have an effective violence prevention program that will not only mitigate the expense but also hopefully minimize the number of incidents your organization will experience.

Case Study

Chuck (not his real name) was a seemingly good employee. He had never really made any major waves, so it was surprising when a complaint by one of the security planners for a large international sporting event was made about Chuck. The planner, Steve, came back from a meeting red faced, visibly frustrated. Steve had just left a meeting with Chuck, who worked in venue planning, because he had gotten in Steve's face. The planner reported the incident to his director who then called the VP of Venue Development. After some discussion, management learned that the venue planner, Chuck, was described as "passionate" about his work and often seen as coming on a bit too strong. However, he meant well and was "harmless enough." So the Director of Security was assured that the incident was unfortunate but otherwise harmless.

We did not hear anything more about Chuck until a frantic call was made to the Director from the VP of Venue Development. During a discussion that escalated and became heated, Chuck had threatened to "flatten him." Apparently, his passion was interpreted differently when it was directed toward the VP. The appropriate security and HR response was made and Chuck was dismissed. However, the VP requested security be placed at his home for the remainder of his time in the city of the event (approximately six months from then). His request was more of a demand because he was a key planner and could not be replaced at such a late date in the process.

It was decided that off-duty sheriff's deputies would be placed in unmarked cars for the remainder of his time with the organization. The cost was negotiated to $35 per hour for 12-hour shifts. If you do the math, that is north of $76K. So, the actual damages, in terms of costs, the company incurred because of Chuck included lost talent, recruiting and training a new employee, $76K in added security measures, and a family that could have been put in harm's way.

Planning for Potential Incidents

1. First, violence prevention planners must scope the potential costs that the organization will incur if and when an incident occurs.
2. Proactive costs are cheaper than reactive costs because the expense goes through a process of thoughtful action and not reactive emotional thinking.
3. Take an outside-in approach as you develop a plan. Start at the fringe of your business and establish a plan that pushes the issues to the outer edges. The best way to tackle this is in layers. The outer edge of your building perimeter is not where you start. Focus first on the areas where your business predominantly takes place.
4. Include security and HR in your planning. Security is not an afterthought. It is a cost of doing business. Remember, the cost you pay in proactive spending will pale in comparison to reactive spending. For example, screening a potential hire or existing employee may be $150 if you do a background check and a drug screen. The cost of a negligent hiring may be in the millions. Pay me now or pay me later!
5. Create a business continuity plan that includes both a disaster recovery plan (DRP) and a crisis management plan. Know the differences and similarities.
6. Start by socializing the need by creating a policy that can be socialized throughout your business.
7. Train.
8. Communicate.
9. Train again.
10. Communicate again.

A more formal approach will be discussed in later chapters but having a plan is just good business. Violence can and will change your work environment and never for the better.

According to the CIRG FBI report mentioned earlier, 80 percent of all violent acts come from criminals outside your business and are unknown to you. So do not focus your efforts on workplace violence solely from individuals known to the business. The proactive approach focuses on conducting a risk analysis on potential threats of violence.

Calculated outside-to-inside thinking will break that cycle of solely focusing on violence from your employees, vendors, or contractors. It is recommended to use a holistic approach when approaching this process.

Small businesses or organizations have everything to lose. The fundamentals of this process should be taken to heart more readily in smaller organizations as proactive dollars and resources are smaller. When evaluating risk, understand that you can ensure against it, avoid it, or accept it. Accepting the violence risk can be the last thing your business does. It is rolling the dice each day you come to work. So what are the simple, cost-effective steps for even the smallest business?

1. Do a detailed risk analysis and be honest with yourself.
2. Follow a hiring plan that includes screening.
3. Negotiate as much security into your lease as you can.
4. Be a good neighbor to the business in your building, complex, or strip mall. See what expenses you can share.
5. Make sure you participate in associations that can assist you with threat analysis in your industry. Many associations provide you with volume discounts on security-related services like employment screening.
6. Make friends with your local law enforcement. They have many programs for the small business in their communities.
7. Consider the use of a security consultant if you have serious concerns. Most reputable security consultants can help to develop a right-sized program to fit your budget.

Prevention starts with awareness. If you have gotten this far in the book, hopefully you have a good understanding of the realities of failing to have some sort of prevention plan in place.

Food for Thought

1. If you have had an incident at your business, have you determined the real cost of that incident?
2. Does your company have an EAP contract currently? What is its capability if a violent incident occurs?
3. In your crisis management plan, who is going to talk to the press, stockholders, or customers? Are these

designated person trained to handle the difficult questions that will be asked?
4. When is it appropriate to use an internal investigative process or involve the police? Who makes that decision in your organization?
5. Does your business or organization belong to a trade or business association that may be able to provide some helpful information or services in your area?

References

Critical Incident Response Group. (2002). *Workplace violence: Issues in response*. Retrieved August 30, 2009, from http://www.fbi.gov/publications/violence.pdf/

Four dead in fitness center shooting. (2009). *Pittsburgh Post-Gazette*. Retrieved from http://www.post-gazette.com/pg/09217/98866955.stm/.

Kaufer, S., & Mattman, W. (2001). *The cost of workplace violence to American business*. Retrieved August 30, 2009, from http://www.workviolence.com/articles/cost_of_workplace_violence.htm/.

REACTION AND RECOVERY: TREATING THE WOUNDS OF VIOLENCE

INTRODUCTION

In 1986 when relief carrier, Patrick Sherrill, walked into the Edmond, Oklahoma Post Office, the Postal Service's need for a post-incident recovery plan was not on anyone's radar. This paradigm of a shooting incident at a work location was not a thought in anyone's conscious or subconscious, much less in anyone's planning queue. Prior to this incident, workplace disruption dealt with fires, earthquakes, and similar natural accidents or incidents that required an action plan. At the time, there was a paradigm for external sources of violence, so retail establishments, banks, and other robbery or burglary targets had scenarios in place that were part of certain industry types. Additionally, there were, in certain businesses, plans to deal with work stoppage due to labor disputes. Labor disputes require a coordinated plan to deal with management workforces, protection of temporary workers, and possible harassment from picketers. Certainly, there are elements of any crisis response plan that are universally applied to a disruptive incident. For example, if an evacuation occurs, there are certain safe distances defined when an organization would choose to evacuate its employees, visitors, and customers from its premises. However, evacuation may not be the appropriate strategy in all cases if a shooter has crossed into the interior of your business.

At a discussion of a post-incident recovery plan, it would be well advised to break the topic into two general categories:

1. *Preparation and prevention*—This refers to strategy and tactics to prepare, prevent, delay, or minimize the effects of violence in the workplace.
2. *Respond and recover*—If an incident does occur, this is the methodology by which an incident will be handled in the aftereffects of the incident regardless of whether the incident is large or small.

This chapter deals first with the latter—respond and recover.

Planning Strategy and Reporting Process

There needs to be a fundamental understanding of violence in workplace recovery measures or a "punch list" of elements that need to be in place in any and all organizations, regardless of size, to deal with an incident. If the entity is smaller, the model may be simple. Or there may be multiple roles placed on the plates of fewer responding resources. But a successful recovery will depend on the inclusion of certain key elements.

Each industry segment and business type has specific ongoing threats that are inherent to those particular entities. Security preventative and response strategies vary depending on the history of actual or potential threats or events. For example, the physical security for a nonpublic business that provides access solely by known individual and turns away or simplifies outside entry is a straightforward model. Normally, a business that deals with its customers, suppliers, or vendors in a business-to-business environment has a different physical security model and incident response strategy as opposed to entities such as a retail outlet, public banking facility, or event venue which is publicly open for business. The physical and security officer model that is effective in the "public welcome" environment is often very expensive and has routine incidents of all types happening daily. Therefore, there are very good models that exist in all environments that have elements which can be identified and discussed as a response to violence in the workplace.

It is equally true that no matter how much an organization proactively tries to prevent violence through the strategies and tactics that have and will be discussed, incidents will occur originating from both external and internal sources. This means that a good start point for dealing with violence is keeping the end game in mind.

The basic planning/response strategy embraces the following tactics.

Learn from your own history—create, maintain, and communicate incident information throughout your organization. Guard against information silos that reduce your ability to have a holistic model. Some of the information gathered and dispensed will be generic and used in your security awareness information and programs. Other information needs to be communicated specifically to leadership, decision makers, and planners. Trending by location, departments, or teams should be analyzed, so root cause analysis can be performed. Even if your overall culture is healthy, a subset of trouble within your business may exist.

Metrics in security have not always been in vogue. Throughout the recent past, more and more individuals and teams in business leadership and security leadership require metrics for funding and return on investment decision making. These metrics should also extend beyond incident numbers and trends. Bill Zalud in his article, "New Math: Security Means Business Performance" (August 2009), talks about the need for measuring performance, trends, and cost analysis against the security mission. He discusses how various companies including Honeywell International, Navistar, Inc, and a cast of other business luminaries are using metrics to define the mission of the security function and measure its activity. Metrics as they relate to violent incidents can also be measured not only in frequency and location, but against the rollout of policy against which understanding and effectiveness can be measured.

The incident reporting process should support the collection of:

a. Dates, times, and locations (be precise)
b. Victims and witnesses
c. A clear description of the event
d. Name (if known) and/or description of the perpetrator

e. All information should be electronically logged and assigned for follow-up and resolution. Establishment of a resolution will assist in future preventative planning.

Use the aforementioned information and possible incident scenarios to plan potential future events. The use of tabletop training is powerful in the assessment of an organization's preparedness. Tabletop exercises consist of the Incident Management Team (IMT) and key managers sitting around a conference table and receiving scenarios to verbalize the action plans. After action, reviews are effective in changing tactics or processes that didn't work as planned, were planned but not utilized, or were not planned or used. All of this evaluation activity should take place in a "no blame zone." Such a review is no time to find fault.

Organizations should have an established and documented process in place to assess threats that are reported from whatever source they derived. These threats should be reported through a process and team of trained responders. Some organizations call this incident management.

Incident management plans should include help for victims and witnesses to recover from the effects of violence in the workplace. Including this help in the plan may require planning and availability by EAP professionals or a network of mental health professionals.

Although employee training is certainly a proactive tactic, it is also helpful in the response scenario. Make all employees aware of the potential for violence, early warning signs, and how to report incidents, threats, and suspicions in a confidential manner, if necessary. In addition to this training, supervisors should also be given immediate response training. Supervisors should also be trained regarding disciplinary actions, including dismissals that have the propensity to take an ugly turn in the process. Supervisors should also be trained in methods to help them avoid disrespectful tone, language, or behavior that would incite a violent incident. The core IMT should receive an even deeper level of training. This more specific training will likely require an outside consultant, law enforcement, or internal and corporate security involvement if available.

The design of an organization's facilities and security systems needs to factor into incidence response planning to mitigate any violent incident. Questions such as "Is there ability for a retail clerk to alert an alarm company, mall security, or police that an incident is happening now and send assistance?", "Are employees trained how to use it and when?", and "Are there design barriers, such as man traps, or the ability to lock out or quickly escape to a safe room that can stop or delay the intruder or assailant giving the employees or customer time to exit to safety?"

Crime Prevention Through Environmental Design (CPTED) is an excellent tool to use in mitigating and preventing violent incidents, but it also has approaches that can be used in the development of response strategies to be implemented when an incident occurs and how there can be some mitigation of an event in progress. The National Crime Prevention Council (http://ncpc.org/) can provide you with specific information to assist you in the planning. The designs used in a structure that is built or an area that is built out in an existing building can reduce the overall effects or can even prevent tragedy. As mentioned earlier, Mary Lynn Garcia's book, *The Design and Evaluation of Physical Protective Systems* (Butterworth-Heinemann), is a great resource.

Downsizings and Terminations

In tempestuous economic times, downsizings, both large and small, are an everyday occurrence—or at least it may seem that way while watching news reports of unemployment challenges. However, it is the routine terminations that may pose the greater threat, especially if you have exhausted all other options and the potential candidate for expulsion from the organization has done the same. The ability of a company's HR department to lead or assist in this effort is imperative. However, there may still be some factors that lead to hostile, verbally threatening terminations that become exaggerated by controllable, contributing mistakes that could be minimized by just good management.

In the CIRG FBI report (2002) mentioned earlier (Chapter 6), the authors give a list of potential contributing factors to terminations that go bad. This list accentuates the areas of lost opportunities to create the appropriate culture.

- Understaffing that leads to job overload or compulsory overtime
- Frustrations arising from poorly defined job tasks and responsibilities
- Downsizing or reorganization
- Labor disputes and poor labor–management relations
- Poor management styles (e.g., arbitrary or unexplained orders, overmonitoring, corrections or reprimands in front of other employees, inconsistent discipline)
- Inadequate security or poorly trained, poorly motivated security force
- A lack of employee counseling
- A high injury rate or frequent grievances may be clues to the problem situation in the workplace.

The termination then becomes the last step in the mind of the soon-to-be ex-employee and frustrations can boil over.

One of the common mistakes not listed above happens with some larger organizations that are constantly reorganizing. The mistake occurs when the organization attempts to deal with a bad hire or troubled worker by passing the employee from one workgroup to another in the hopes that a new assignment, new supervisor, or new environment will somehow miraculously fix the unwanted behavior. This scenario can occur overtly through negotiation between workgroups and may, in fact, have a short-term positive effect. In other instances, however, the same scenario may be similar to rearranging deck chairs on the Titanic. Sooner or later, the employee will return to his or her past behavior as, in one sense, the organization has actually rewarded bad behavior. This same set of circumstances can also happen covertly by overblowing the employee's value or even inflating the performance review to make the move more palatable for the employee.

Now that we have discussed situations regarding downsizing or terminations, let's move to a discussion about the disciplinary process as a whole. Obviously, termination should be the last step in a list of actions that the organization can undertake.

The following are some recommended steps in disciplinary and termination discussions:

1. Involve the next level manager and HR in the process when it becomes apparent that dismissal is the last

option. If there have been incidents in the past involving the individual that have required the involvement of the security department, bring the security personnel into the discussion for perspective and assistance.

2. Choose the location of the conversation with the employee wisely. Ideally, a conference room that has two exits on opposite ends of the room would be the best option. If one of these exits leads to a street or lobby with no available entrance back into the employee areas of the business without a card key, that is even better.

3. If the termination can be conducted on a Friday afternoon, that is ideal. Make it the discussion near the end of the day, if possible. Such timing will allow the rest of the workforce to dwindle down and possibly be gone by the time the discussion with the employee is complete. On Fridays, most businesses have smaller staffing levels and most of the rank and file leave right on time to start the weekend.

4. Have all information and documentation together and prepare for the talk. Do not overwhelm the employee with a room full of people. If your business is a union shop, a union representative may need to be present—so arrange for that, if possible, before the meeting.

5. As soon as the individual goes into the meeting, have your IT staff wipe out all system and computer privileges to company systems to which the effected employee or contractor has access. If this person is an IT staffer who is the employee being terminated, use your best technology member to completely shut down the employee's systems taking care to look for backdoors or multiple user IDs and passwords. Acts of revenge on systems or processes could cost an organization millions.

6. If the location in which the employee works has electronic card key, retina scan, hand geometry, or key pad entry to any and all exits, make sure these codes are changed, and access denied while the discussion is in progress. If there are building security officers, make them available at a reasonable distance.

7. Experience has shown that it is not unusual to have an investigative interview and have law enforcement available, at some point, to arrest the employee should the need arise. This process is extremely tricky and outside the scope of this book. It is also possible that the now

former employee should be advised not to come to the work location for any reason and that to do so would be considered trespassing. A court order may be needed to follow through with this notification. A pre-meeting regarding these types of issues is normally led by the security department.

8. Have a table between the team communicating with the employee and the employer. Have the team sit nearest the door that leads outside the security perimeter. If the employee storms out of the meeting, leveling threats, leaving the building, heading for the parking lot, and then is seen returning, there may be genuine need for alarm. Make sure that if this occurs, there are tight controls on both ingress and egress. Contact law enforcement immediately and do not allow anyone to exit the business until the police arrive. Do not allow employees to exit into harm's way, if at all possible.

9. Documentation is the critical piece of any successful termination. Make sure all decision makers buy in on the move. A labor attorney might be the final sign-off.

10. If the reason for the employee's dismissal is violence or bullying related, then the need for all procedural and documentation processes is imperative. It would be distasteful to bring a bully or potentially violent individual back into the workforce after losing a wrongful termination suit or labor arbitration.

11. If the individual is calm and accepting of the decision, escort him or her to the workstation or office. By this time, all of your other employees should have left the premises and this fact will be appreciated by the individual who will feel that you treated him or her with respect.

12. Severance and job placement assistance are also helpful in reducing the sting of termination. Discuss these options and do not let your elevated sense of justice cloud a reasonable amount of consideration that will pay handsomely in how the employee ends up viewing his or her relationship with your company.

13. Avoid official references for your employees. It is recommended that you verify employment, dates of employment, title, and confirmation of salary. Often a background screening company will ask if you would

rehire the employee. That is a subtle inquiry to learn whether a termination was voluntary.

14. In the actual termination discussion, be courteous and structure the discussion toward the future and avoid looking to the past. Answer all questions but make the clear declaration the decision has been made and any discussion will remain about information and options. If prior meetings with the employee have included a strong performance discussion and included the use of intermediate steps of documentation, the final decision to terminate employment might not be a surprise. Hopefully the response will be one of relief and resignation might be considered.

15. In the case of dismissal for threatening, bullying, or other type of behavior that is not performance based, be clear about the fact that the behavior is unacceptable and will not be tolerated. There is some dispute as to a "zero-tolerance policy" of certain types of threats. (the discussion on policy will be discussed in a later chapter), but if the termination is for-cause, there is a golden opportunity to force the individual to look at his or her own behavior. Do not minimize this opportunity or call the dismissal a reorganization or downsizing decision. Play it straight up. This is an opportunity to, perhaps, change the unacceptable behavior going forward and even create a better employee for the person's next employer. If the decision is made to continue a person's employment, close monitoring, counseling, or some other action might be involved. Again, be specific about the reasons. This is not an opportunity for the employee to dispute facts. The investigation should already be complete and the facts should not be in dispute.

Threat Assessment and Incident Management

In the following chapters, proactive, preventative strategies and tactics will be discussed. However, let us concede that even with the best security plan in place designed to thwart external violence issues, policy, procedure, training, and early intervention via good management action or EAP, an incident that will need to be assessed still might occur. But, if an incident is reported and a violent act is not occurring now, a threat assessment may need to be completed. Efficient and effective communication is imperative in this case so that the threat does not move from a potential issue to an actual issue.

If the organization becomes aware of suspicious, disruptive, or threatening behavior that is either direct or veiled, the incident should be documented and a threat assessment should be initiated. This assessment may entail a core team being apprised and an immediate investigation conducted. Prior to this event, a threat assessment process, reporting procedure, and policy for appropriate behavior, including threats, should be published and communicated to all constituent groups including, but not limited to, employees, contractors, and vendors. Sometimes vendors may be notified regarding organizational policies in an official contract or orientation, or maybe something as simple as signage in common areas.

These policies should also include instances of threatening behavior involving customers or clients. If employees are alarmed by an email or correspondence, or verbal exchange, either in person or on the phone, the reporting process should apply.

Often in larger organizations, corporate or organizational security takes the lead in such cases. In campuses or organizations that have a law enforcement entity, the law enforcement entity should take the lead. However, if the threat involves an employee, HR should be consulted or, at a minimum, be included in the management of the incident. The importance is stepping up to the task.

Obviously the seriousness of the threat needs to be initially evaluated by collecting the following data:

1. What is the nature of the threat?
2. Is the origin of the threat internal or external?
3. How was the information of the threat received into the organization?
4. Collect all artifacts quickly—emails, extemporaneous notes, or memos.
5. Identify witnesses or suspect information.
6. Is there a weapon or delivery method involved?
   a. "I'm going to shoot the _____!"
   b. "I'm going to blow this place up!"
   c. "I'd like to cut her head off!"

7. Is there a history of violence involving the subject?
8. Other salient facts—Is the threat first hand or is it hearsay?, Is it directed at one individual or many?, etc.
9. If you have a background check waiver and consent on file that allows for an updated background check to be performed with your current provider, or, if law enforcement is involved, they may be willing to run the subject's name through the National Crime Computer (NCIC) to review any recent activity that might indicate an immediate issue.
10. Look in the individual's HR file or more importantly the "drop file" that a current or former supervisor uses for record retention.
11. Inquire about alcohol use, drug use, or recent negative changes in attendance or performance.
12. Interview witnesses and ask if this is the first time they have witnessed this type of behavior from this person.
13. If the unacceptable behavior comes from a customer, ask if there have been previous negative encounters with other employees.
14. Once this information is collected, choose a suitable location to interview the subject. If the report is vague or loosely documented, law enforcement may not be the appropriate interviewer. Corporate security professionals are some of the best trained individuals to approach this situation and are equipped to look for and identify deception in any denials. Use of the immediate supervisor or someone in the subject's immediate workgroup would be a mistake. Use an objective representative and a witness who can take notes.
15. Review the location strategy discussed above.

Do not forget that you can use outside resources in addition to law enforcement like trained threat analysts or psychologists.

Crisis Management

A simple assault occurs like a slap or a punch—a weapon is banished—a shove or other aggressive behavior has surfaced. Any of these examples require an immediate response. Law enforcement may need to be called to affect an arrest. Or an even more critical case—a shot has been heard. What is your response?

Emergency planning is common in today's businesses. This is especially true in heavy industry, manufacturing, or large facilities or businesses that have a long established history. Medical emergencies, fire, or flood protocols might be recognized. However the application and effectiveness of these plans might be uneven. Large organizations that are geographically distanced might have a "crackerjack" plan at the corporate headquarters that then fails to be translated out to the balance of the organization.

In a recent, special focus article in *Security Management Magazine* (June 2009), the author, William M. Lokey, points out the challenges of effective planning versus application to an actual event. In the article, Lokey praises the flexibility of companies that helped their employees relocate, or assisted in the overall recovery during the Katrina disaster of 2005, while yet other companies failed to think through the needs of employees who may be coming to help rebuild. Lokey cites an example of a contractor who requested housing for its employees who were there to help rebuild.

Katrina demonstrated that leaving the emergency response to a government entity, local, state, or federal government, is a short-sighted and flawed strategy. A well-planned, flexible, and funded plan at the business or organizational level is much more manageable and nimble.

Lokey points out there are "five major operational areas" that need to be addressed in any overall violent incidence plan.

1. Communication
2. Chain of command
3. Use of volunteer resources
4. Establishment of priorities
5. Media relationships.

In that article, he discusses in great detail the importance of focusing on these areas in the planning and execution of crisis management. Crisis may come in the form of violence which requires evacuation or some other form of immediate response and the activation of a crisis management plan that has been created, tested, adjusted, and kept current.

Case Study

Before the opening of the AT&T Global Olympic Village (GOV), almost two years of planning went into the security surrounding the sponsorship of the 1996 Atlanta Summer Olympic Games. Extensive emergency planning was coordinated with the Atlanta Olympic Committee (AOC), the various law enforcement committees, and infrastructure companies that had similar risks and security needs. Whenever possible there was joint security responsibility, security personnel had communication established via command centers, and emergency operation centers which were activated on a proactive basis.

Security contracts for electronic surveillance, contract and corporate security, dignitary protection, and performer and athlete security were awarded. Radio frequencies were coordinated, cell phones were issued, and landlines were strategically installed.

Public address (PA) systems were installed along with a sound system for the various performers who would entertain nightly on the GOV stage. Ray Charles, Kenny Rogers, and others were brought in for free concerts in the park.

Once the plans were put on paper in venue security plans (VSP), tabletop exercises were initiated and law enforcement, fire, and federal agencies like the Federal Emergency Management Agency (FEMA) participated in these exercises.

After the bombing in the Centennial Olympic Park just outside the GOV, the plans that had been put in place were activated, the park was evacuated, and the real work started. Interagency coordination became critical. The FBI became the lead investigative agency. The state of Georgia was the law enforcement entity that controlled the park's closed access and for four days recovery ensued. Without the communication and clear chain of command, the bombing event could have crippled the entire Olympic event. But, in four days, the park was reopened to record crowds.

Anyone will tell you that without volunteers there can be no Olympics. So there was concern that these volunteers would not return to their duties after the bombing. But they were kept informed, organized, and trained and *all* assisted in the recovery process and then returned to their assignments after the blast.

The first priority in this event was to find all the employees, volunteers, and contractors who were in the operation. It took over 12 hours to find everyone. Knowing that everyone was accounted for allowed the recovery process to proceed without interruption.

The media was an issue after the suspicion of Richard Jewell's involvement was leaked to the press. The 15,000 media representatives, hungry for information, made media relations a priority. Being a contractor for AT&T made the personnel, contractor, and key managers a target for interviews. Jewell was never charged and was later exonerated. However, during the actual games, the press wanted to interview everyone who knew him. PR managers shadowed the key managers to ensure they could continue their jobs without interruption.

Key traps to avoid in planning for emergencies including violence in the workplace.

1. Do not go into an event without a plan—make sure to take the time to prepare one.
2. Do not assume that violence is not one of the scenarios to entertain. Very often tabletop exercises use natural disasters as examples and violence is considered outside the realm of possibility.
3. If violence is included in this plan, be sure to consider it for both internal and external origination. Internal acts of violence have nuances like the perpetrator might know your emergency plans, evacuation rally points, etc.
4. Do not assume that senior managers should be the top of the chain of command in an emergency. It may be a trained security or safety leader.
5. If emergency response is under one roof and business continuation is under another, remember to communicate plans and strategies. It is better to resolve the interception points before, and not after, an event.
6. Do not forget to fund the project.

The line between preparation and response is often blurred. But the key message is contained in one simple phrase, *don't forget to plan.*

Food for Thought

1. Does your company, organization, or business have a crisis management plan?
2. Who in the organization "owns" it?
3. If an incident were to occur today, who is in charge?
4. Do you know the difference between disaster recovery and crisis management?
5. Where is your emergency operations center?

References

Critical Incident Response Group. (2002). *Workplace violence: Issues in response*. Retrieved August 30, 2009, from http://www.fbi.gov/publications/violence.pdf/.

Lokey, W. H. (2009, June). Don't let the plan be the disaster. *Security Management Magazine*. Retrieved from http://www.security management.com/article/dont-let-plan-be-disaster-005659/.

New Math: Security Means Business Performance. (2009, August).

EARLY WARNING SIGNS: CAN THE PROBLEM BE STOPPED BEFORE IT STARTS?

INTRODUCTION

Most practitioners agree that, in post-incident hindsight, all violent offenders have demonstrated early behavioral warning signs that could have been used to ward off or reduce the impact of violence in the workplace. The progressive nature of violence has symptoms, which if seen and recognized as such, can be precursors to violent acts in the future. Therefore effective interdiction tactics can be used in those cases. Unfortunately, statistics to how many are prevented through these interdictions are anecdotal at best. But it is believed that if minor threatening words or actions or veiled threats are addressed decisively and quickly, it is more likely that severe acts might be avoided. Further, as most violence originates outside the workplace and comes into the workplace uninvited, this debunks the notion that all violence can be eliminated. Even if all of an organization's associates are trained to spot warning signs that could lead to violence and even if the organization's reporting schema is robust, there is not a way to eliminate all violence. Here, the prevention mission meets good security processes including access control, sound physical security practices, and common sense.

This writing addresses the importance of creating a culture that acknowledges violence as a fact of modern business and creates a milieu of open and honest communication within the organizational construct. These actions should create an environment less prone to denial of the reality of possible violence happening anywhere in an organization. There are discussions in this work regarding the potential for devastation to the current and future success of the business if an organization decides to roll the dice with violence and not have a proactive strategy. So, now, the success or failure of prevention, containment, or controlling the escalation of violence becomes the responsibility of the individual members within an organization and these individuals' ability to prevent, report, and react to warning signs. Therefore, the earlier an individual recognizes the seed or a sign of potential violence becomes critical to the effective handling of an event.

Additionally, this work discusses the importance of quick, clear, and effective communication. Without good communication, both in prevention (policy, strategy, and training) and reactive (reporting, statistics, tactical and crisis management communication), there is scant chance to prevent a violent incident or mitigate its impact. Without good communication, escalation is probable and tragedy is more likely.

To augment these previous discussions, this chapter highlights the fact that violence can be prevented by interlacing good physical, logical, response strategies and tactics.

Gavin de Becker, in his ground-breaking book, *The Gift of Fear* (1998), discusses the importance of trusting and tapping into the basic instincts and intuitive thoughts about violence prevention in addition to the warning signs from within. It is recommended that organizations have employees; especially female employees read de Becker's book. These readers are encouraged to internalize the concept that, in the final analysis, it is the two steps of movement, in a defensive way before an act of violence is committed, that might save employees from harm. It is equally important that employees feel comfortable to communicate concerns giving notice and attention to actions of customers, contractors, vendors, and fellow employees to someone who has authority to take immediate action.

In review, there are three recognized types of violence that threaten any organization.

- Type I is violence perpetrated by someone unknown to an organization. As mentioned previously, estimates range from 75 to 95 percent that all violence in the workplace will fall into this category. Further to that, there are job types that can be identified as "high risk" to violence at work, for example, professions like bartenders, retail employees, taxi drivers, police, and security officers. These professions work on the firing line where violence is common and expected at some level. Physical security of the workplace can often help but also important are solid defensive and reactive training which are imperative to reduce the numbers and severity of violence. Often, robbery and assault is the motive for acts of violence in these cases and law enforcement are the first responders.

- Type II is violence that relates to individuals who are known to an employee(s) or known to the organization but not necessarily a part of the organization. Domestic violence is one of the more common examples. Additionally, health care workers like nurses and doctors are common targets with Type II violence. Customers, vendors, students, and contractors also fall into this category as well as church members or other such nonemployee connection.

- Type III is violence that occurs between employees. This third type is often the one that is seen as the most preventable if early warning signs are heeded. Type III violence often receives the most press. As was mentioned in earlier chapters, the employee who goes "postal" is in this Type III class.

The key point to this is that an organization's preventative and early warning systems need to address all three types of violence and not just one or two out of the three. Failure to address one of the three types of violence is likely in this modern world of limited resources but having an overarching violence prevention strategy led by a security organization and supported by senior management is critical. If no internal security organization exists, serious consideration should be given to forming one. If the organization still feels it does not warrant a defined and separate security organization, then some security function needs to be developed somewhere in the business. Some businesses combine other functions into one function. Safety and security is an example. This function will often fall under the umbrella of operations and is, too easily, pushed to the bottom of the pile of things to do. A lack of highly prioritizing safety and security should be strongly discouraged in light of the high stakes of not having a plan or response strategy in place.

Unfortunately and logically, smaller businesses do not have the size to support a full-time security function and should, therefore, consider engaging a consultant to develop a program that starts with physical and technical system and information security. Organizational information is a critical asset and should be treated as a core asset of your business. Ensure that cyber sabotage, cyber stalking, and threats that often come through your email or other web-based services are not left out of a safety and security program. If feasible, from a time-resource perspective, develop the program internally and do so by using resources like this book to ensure a solid understanding of the scope of such an undertaking. There are government web sites that provide some basic guidelines (see Department of Homeland Security (DHS) and FEMA web sites).

Type I—Early Warning Signs and Systems in the External World

Entire books, web sites, and training packets have been developed to deal with Type I violence. Good planning is the first step by which early warning systems and response plans are created that address how to handle intruders or criminals who target a particular type of organization in a particular location. In response to this area, there are some important recommended actions that should be considered.

1. Create or join associations that share intelligence. Often, suspected rings of perpetrators ranging anywhere from shoplifting rings to violent robbery rings or gangs who target a particular type of business or organization are known to others and normally those organizations are happy to share information. Often law enforcement assists here, but many organizations hold regular meetings to share information. Local American Society of

Industrial Security (ASIS) or Society of Human Resource Managers (SHRM) chapters are great places to become aware of current schemes and threats. Participation in these meetings by organizations should be a part of an early warning system.

2. Incident reporting systems are great tools by which trends and types of incidents can be noted or identified. There are many businesses in different areas. Attempt to determine if there is a way to generically or specifically share intelligence with business neighbors. Downtown business alliances and associations are another way to improve early warning systems. Although the Chamber of Commerce might be a good organization with which to be connected as a business, security might not be the focus and the security organization is probably not the appropriate representative at the Chamber of Commerce. However, if the organization has a membership in the Chamber of Commerce, make sure any attendees pass valuable security information along quickly to the security function's leadership. Again, communication is the key.

3. Establish a relationship with your local law enforcement entity or agency. If there are community watchdog groups or training for business owners, including CPTED, join and participate. Provide intelligence and risk assumptions and use these associations as an opportunity to network with other businesses, security professionals, or leaders in the business's immediate area.

4. "Good fences make good neighbors" is an old adage that applies to early warning systems. Alarm systems that provide early warning of intruders may fit into the risk model. Lighting, blended with other electronic measures, can react to security breaches by alerting quickly your security or duty staff. The concept here is to detect, delay, or respond earlier before the threat enters the building and comes in contact with any staff.

5. Use assets already purchased to their fullest. Cell phones, BlackBerries, and other common devices can be used as communication tools to send threat information or emerging facts about an incident to associates or key members of an IMT. The technology used every day in business

has features and functions that can help warn employees about threats, intruders, or other violence-related issues. Mass notification systems in the form of email and text message blasts, and broadcast phone messages are available for use in an emergency in these days where busy employees may let a call go to voice mail but who will not miss a text or an email. Study your associates' communication habits, then plan and test your technology leveraging these tools as part of an early warning system.

One of the biggest segments of business is the small business or organization with 100 employees or less, according to the FBI report on violence in the workplace. This represents almost 40 million workers. According to the Bureau of Labor Statistics, less than 45 percent of businesses with 49 employees or less have a violence in the workplace program (Figure 8-1). These businesses may

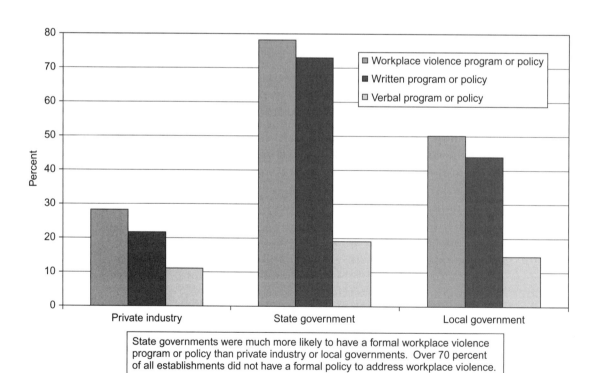

State governments were much more likely to have a formal workplace violence program or policy than private industry or local governments. Over 70 percent of all establishments did not have a formal policy to address workplace violence.

Figure 8-1. Percent of establishments having a workplace violence prevention program or policy, by size of establishment, United States, 2005. *Source*: Bureau of Labor Statistics, Survey of Workplace Violence Prevention, 2005.

not be able to afford full-time security organization and in many cases rely on shopping mall, office park, or law enforcement for their first and often last line of defense. This, according to the FBI report on workplace violence, is the greatest challenge to stemming the violence trends. This applies not only to Type I but Types II and III as well. Just staying in business on a daily basis is the primary focus and time and budget is often used up just staying competitive. The time spent in associations can also help network with other businesses that may be looking for the services your organization provides.

If the business has a security organization, it should make participation in these types of associations a priority. Attendance should be spread within the team to encourage participation. This will also help make key contacts within the local or regional security community. Most security organizations have access to newsletters, web broadcasts, and local meeting schedules.

Type II—Early Warning Systems for Individuals Known to, But Not Part of, an Organization

Although there are intersecting points between Type II and III violence, there are striking differences and risks. Contractors, vendors, and visitors in the form of friends and family of employees or ex-friends and ex-family are contained in this type. Although former employees are no longer part of an organization, they also ride the fence between Type II and III violence but will be covered in detail in the Type III discussions.

Contractors and vendors are often seen as quasi-employees in many cases. In some businesses, contract help comes in the form of temporary employees or consultants who have a one- to three-month relationship with an organization. The author has had multi-month contracts where he has been a part of senior-level meetings and often casual observers think or comment that they believe he works within the organization. The relationship between the contractors and employees should have a clear distinction which requires individuals to be background checked and include such individuals to sign privacy, confidentiality, trade secret, and proprietary agreements which cover the individuals' activities with the organization while under contract. Most good contractor agreements make it mandatory for the contractor, vendor, or consultant to adhere to the policies, procedures, and conduct that are required of employees. Violation of these compliance items then results in immediate denial of access and subsequent review of the entire contract relationship. This often means the contractor must replace an errant contractor to perform the duties required under the contract.

Some not so obvious constituent groups may include:

- Union leadership not employed by the company
- Cleaning contractor managers who are not assigned to the facility
- Plant watering contractors
- Contract/facility security officer's leadership not assigned to the facility
- Last-minute janitorial staff changes.

Often these groups become a constant in many organizations and become familiar with access procedures and can become known to on-site security forces. They are waved in quickly and allowed to move throughout a facility unescorted. If they have frequent needs to be there, then treat them as permanent contract employees and make sure they are certified to be a part of your organization.

Many of these groups fall into the visitor category and rightfully so. Unfortunately, they are not held to the same background or contractor credentialing requirements for the permanently assigned associates but can have frequent business on company property. So if a particular individual is routinely visiting company property, ask the person to be properly credentialed. Such visitors are often given free access, without escort, into restricted areas often by the contractors who are assigned to the facilities. Be diligent in not creating a hole that will allow a potentially violent individual into your facility.

Contractor credentialing is taking hold in many industries and is mandated in some like Hazmat Haulers and railroad contractors. Credentialing is much more than a background check. It gives wide flexibility and account-ability for the contractor. It can be extended to all nonem-ployees who have a frequent or ongoing relationship with a company. The DHS has helped in an attempt to roll out many of the recommendations of the 9/11 Commission. Contractor credentialing and background checking of indi-viduals connected to a business will be covered in detail in the Chapter 11 dedicated to background, drug screening, and credentialing.

The overarching function that needs to sync with an organization's violence prevention process is a good access control policy. An access control policy is normally multi-layered and segmented for both employees and contrac-tors to enter and move within the business. This applies to both physical and information/technical systems. System administrators should emulate the thinking found in safety and security policies in controlling access or, at a mini-mum, knowing usage patterns that are continually audited.

Some vendors will place their employees on the site of the customer for ease and focus of resources, which makes economic sense to one or both parties. This practice is often prevalent with shipping or trucking companies in the manufacturing area. Technical support personnel are often assigned to customers who choose to outsource these func-tions. These vendors may perform daily, weekly, or on-call tasks giving them access to people, property, and informa-tion ranging from limited to extremely open.

Temporary employees are in a similar situation and should be restricted in their access to the facility and infor-mation in a specific, focused manner. Levels of access should be constrained by times of day and days of the week in which they are allowed in a facility. There should also be specific discussion information system architecture that restricts temporaries in the systems they are allowed to access. If this is not feasible, for some reason, then the employment onboarding process should be followed strictly. This often creates conflict within an organization that is drowning in work and temporary employees who are caught in the HR onboarding process. Managing through such challenges is, indeed, an art and not a science. Getting the resources needed to run a business without shortcutting sound security process is sometimes difficult. Often, lower ranking managers will attempt to circumvent this process by taking the employee into the business "on their authority." This is a sign of a weak HR process that lacks senior management support and should be avoided. HR is often the gatekeeper of not allowing individuals to become a part of business. The disconnect is that many Type II violence comes from individuals who never are touched by HR. So in the case of temporary employees, follow the HR guidelines whenever possible.

Schools and college campuses have entered a particularly tough time when it comes to Type II violence. Students who are often the perpetrators of violence or staff who are part of the organization via their academic study are often under the radar of any HR or security organization when they enter the organization. The complexity and diversity of this issue is unique and growing. An entire chapter is dedicated to this growing issue of violence on campuses. But for the administrative staff, support personnel and teachers and professors of the various institutions, this is their workplace. In most cases, the students are there based on their academic qualifications and are focused on their academic achievements. Background checks of students are not in practice in most cases. Troubling histories might be unknown to the school. Therefore, the security process relies on reporting of issues to them through the normal incident reporting system which may result in an NCIC check by the campus police.

So the university or college warning systems rely heavily on the observation of fellow students, teachers, teaching assistants, professors, and other faculty and staff members, including security officers and campus police, to observe and report. In many cases, they can provide information to students and faculty of services available for students in crisis or fear. The "Jeanne Clery Disclosure of Campus Security Policy and Campus Crime Statistics Act of 1998" (20 U.S.C. § 1092(f)), commonly referred to as the "Clery Act," requires institutions of higher education receiving federal financial aid to report specified crime statistics on college campuses and to provide other safety and crime information to members of the campus community. Under the Clery Act, universities are required to notify students of issues in a timely way and most have plans to comply with this law. Most major institutions have instituted some form of mass communication to their students, staff, and faculty. The technology is improving but the upkeep of the information is indeed a challenge (Security on Campus, Inc., 2009).

The real challenge continues to be the overall cost and time to change culture, and decide on the appropriate solution and rollout. However, there are solutions out there and ingenuity is all that is required along with helpful partners.

Teresa Anderson, staff writer for Security Management, wrote a piece in the July 2007 issue of *Security Management Magazine*, which describes how the University of Pittsburgh worked with a supplier to integrate an existing ID system which is an access system for all the external doors of the 68 buildings on a 132-acre campus. With over 11,000 employees and 25,000 students, the task might have slid into the "too hard to do" box. But Joshua Cochran, the manager of integrated security, rose to the task. With a partner, RS2 Technologies, he was able to integrate an access system with an existing computer and network of electronic key locks. This was timelier and more cost-effective than trying to replace the existing system from scratch or having the individuals carry two cards according to the Anderson article.

Recently, in the case of a Yale graduate student, Annie Le, who was killed by a university lab employee, the access system helped to not only locate the victim but solve the case by determining the comings and goings of the suspect, Raymond Clark III. The entry system had recorded that both Le and Clark had entered the lab but only Clark had exited. So a robust, functioning access system is a valuable tool in both prevention and investigation (Kovacs, 2009).

However the preventative nature of a security system is, if a violence-prone individual is identified, the police or security can track the movements or even restrict access of a potentially violent individual. Although not entirely foolproof, it does help, at a minimum, delay ingress. Motivated individuals can gain entry and circumvent access systems by following an authorized user through an access controlled door. This maneuver is referred to as "tailgating."

So warning users to be suspicious of anyone tailgating them into a restricted area has risks, even if they recognize the individual. They might have had their entry privileged revoked for a reason, a violent reason.

Domestic violence is the fastest growing and most challenging piece of Type II violence. Prevention starts with an acknowledgment that it exists and creates counterproductive work results that make addressing the problem a challenge. The Centers for Disease Control reports that 96 percent of victims of domestic violence experience work-related problems. A more troubling result is 30 percent actually lose their jobs because of attendance or performance issues. Even if the violence is never acted out at work, the effects are costly. Estimates range between $3 and $5 billion annually measured in absenteeism, increased health care costs, and lost productivity. This ends up being about 175,000 days of work lost.

Jeanne Norday, who runs a Domestic Violence Community Council, was interviewed by Blake Jones of the Poststar.com who reported that one out of four women will experience domestic violence in their lifetime.

The confusing issues are that there is reluctance of women to report the abuse to their employer for fear of losing their position or reputation. The evidence may not be swollen eyes or bruises but a change in their reliability or apparent focus. Often the victim's abuser will hide car keys, take gas money, or even harass the victim electronically with text messages and emails. Unless the messages are through company servers, they might be unaware of the threats or harassment.

And the issue can spill not only onto work time but also onto work property. On September 9, 2009, in West Valley City, Utah, Charles Gordon followed his ex-wife to work, rammed her car chasing her into the building beating her severely at the Discover Card Service Center. Thanks to the quick response of the security force and fellow employees, the attacker was subdued until the police arrived. The perpetrator had previously assaulted the victim so badly that she had needed facial reconstruction. He was currently on a restraining order. It is undetermined whether Discover Card was aware of the restraining order. It is the policy of most companies to escort potential victims to and from their cars if requested. If the organization is unaware of the need for additional security surrounding a domestic violence issue, it will fall prey to the belief that the attendance, tardiness, or performance policy is the overriding process and take disciplinary action accordingly.

Some states, New York as an example, protect victims of domestic violence from discrimination if the company is aware of the cause. So the key here is to look for the changes in actions, not overt signs of violence. This is how an organization does the right thing, and this action may save a valuable employee resource.

Type III—The Perpetrator Is a Member of Your Employment Workforce

These are the employees who were hired through an often exhausting and thorough process, or not. It is the one that you background checked and used panel interviews to ensure capability and reliability, or not. It is the one who is a part of the work family and is seen every day, or not. This is true whether you believe it or not. They could have been with you for years. They do not necessarily fit an age group or demographic. They could be a young or old employee— highly skilled, highly placed, and highly valued. But at some point in time for reasons obscure, they began a process of internal change that created a deeply held belief that they have a right and a need to bring violence into the workplace. The changes may come quickly or over an extended period of time but there is a process. And like alcoholism, the disease of violence is progressive and unless recognized, reported, and addressed may end in extreme violence, even murder.

At the heart of all the cases that the author had personal investigative contact with, whether it was threats, acts of intimidation, sabotage in some cases, bullying and assaults, or even murder, they arose out of conflict. This manifests itself in conflict with a supervisor or coworker; conflict at home which spilled into work; conflict with a customer or contractor. Stress is often characterized as a cause, but the real factor of conflict that causes an increase in the level of stress is far more accurate.

Although the thought of a violent act as a solution might be laughable to most of us and certainly the person who is reading this book, we must try to understand to the perpetrator of the violent act the so-called need to affect revenge or act out to gain justice is deeply held and seen as the only path left. With perpetrators like Patrick Sherrill, their ultimate act is well thought out, planned for, and deadly. Others may move from an occasional veiled threat to a real threat to the eventual assault.

So what are the warning signs and what is the progression? In 1993, J. Anthony Barron wrote an easy to understand book addressing this phenomena. *Violence in the Workplace: A Prevention and Management Guide for Businesses* (1993) was a guidepost along the road of addressing the issue in the mid-1990s. Barron came up with his time-tested progression of levels of behavior that indicate which the author uses as the basis for the recommendations. These levels of escalation for intervention inspired the author's levels which are based on his experience.

- Level I—Change in demeanor inconsistent with past history
  1. The employee begins to exhibit an attitude of being a malcontent—complains about job assignments, polices, or safety rules.
  2. Argues with others openly and this may begin a series of complaints to first-line or immediate supervisors that may or may not be documented.
  3. Language becomes more street level and even profane. Displays fascination with firearms or violent events.
  4. May become involved in other unacceptable behavior like insubordination or unwelcome sexual advances.
- Level II—The attitude of us against them
  1. Paranoia and victimization regarding policies and changes in process. No change goes without comment or complaint.
  2. Suspected or even admits to acts of sabotage or theft; the motive is revenge for perceived injustices. Although on the surface the actions do not fit the crime the employee feels justified based on their situation.

3. Acts of intimidation, bullying, and real or veiled threats begin to be reported.
4. Cyber threats, volatile emails, or letters begin to arrive; sometimes they are anonymous and closely following disciplinary action toward the employee.
- Level III—The employee begins to act out
  1. Threats of homicide, suicide, or both.
  2. Angry outbursts with coworkers: fights or assaults.
  3. Sabotage of property, vehicles, or information including electronic files.
  4. Weapons may be brandished or used.

The action that can change the outcome is to intervene at Level I or, at a minimum, Level II. Once Level III is reached you are in the event. You will now have to manage the anger or actions of the employee. Dealing with anger in the workplace is covered in the next chapter.

Conclusion

The need to report these systems to an HR or security organization is paramount. The ability to do this anonymously or confidentially should be built into the process. Trust your instincts and be aware of changes in behavior that are more than having a bad day. Look for trends and patterns. Encourage open communication and train your key managers, HR professionals, and security professionals to root cause the issue. Record the information in a reporting process looking for departments or facilities that have large numbers of reports that would uncover devaluing management styles. If you are a small business, train your key managers even if it's just you.

Food for Thought

1. Does your organization have a security plan that blends and recognizes both external and internal threats?
2. What is your biggest concern with violence in your organization—internal or external violence or both?
3. Does your organization have a large reliance on contractors to provide day-to-day services to your business or facility?

4. What are your onboarding policies as they relate to contractors, temporary workers, and vendors?
5. Are visitor access and escorts strictly enforced?
6. What is your company's policy in regards to domestic violence?
7. If you had a concern about a fellow employee, who would you advise and how?

References

Barron, A. J. (1993). *Violence in the workplace: A prevention and management guide for businesses.* California: Pathfinder Publishing.

de Becker, G. (1998). *The gift of fear.* New York: Dell Publishing.

Kovacs, S. (2009). Yale female student strangled to death. Retrieved October 17, 2009, from http://searchwarp.com/swa547941-Yale-Female-Student-Strangled-To-Deathevidence-Will-Close-This-Case-Quickly.htm/.

Security on Campus, Inc. (2009). *Complying with the Jeanne Clery Act.* Retrieved October 17, 2009, from http://www.securityoncampus.org/index.php?option=com_content&view=article&id=271&Itemid=60/.

PROACTIVELY DEALING WITH ANGER IN THE WORKPLACE

Bonnie S. Michelman

INTRODUCTION

Workplace violence is a specific category of violent crime that calls for robust and clear responses from employers as well as from law enforcement. Although they may be the most publicized, homicides and violent attacks represent a small number of workplace violence incidents. It has been the experience of the writer that the majority of cases that occur in the workplace are lesser assaults or incidents like threats, stalking, intimidation, bullying, harassment, and emotional abuse. Many of these incidents are not even reported to corporate management, let alone police, and can be extremely dangerous or disruptive for the employee or workplace. Workplace violence is often perpetrated by angry employees, making it extremely important to identify and address anger in the workplace. This chapter discusses how to proactively diminish aggression, prevent violence, and empower employees and management to deal with anger.

Gaps between the realities of a job and the expectations of a job can turn into anger, which can sometimes escalate to violence. Because of this, some organizations acknowledge the risk and train their associates accordingly. The problem may even be cultural. In a recent CNN article (2007), male employees who were identified as "angry" were paid better than female employees who were viewed by interviewers as angry. In other words, male employees are rewarded for their propensity to be angry on the job. The lesson of this article is to make sure that your policies and procedures are consistent, and that you do not unintentionally reward bad behavior.

Strategy for Dealing with Anger in the Workplace

To defuse anger before it escalates into punishable offenses, employers should have a baseline program with multiple components to ensure the right foundation for a peaceful and safe environment. Steps that need to be taken include the following:

- A strong and clear workplace violence policy that includes the "lesser" forms of violence, which are usually more common and less understood.
- Consistent and customized training for all employees and management in aggression management, personal safety, and workplace violence.
- Adopting and practicing fair and consistent sanctions for behavior that is not considered appropriate within an aggression or anger context.
- Cultivating a culture of trust and respect among employees and managers toward each other and toward any visitors.
- Seeking guidance or help from internal or external departments or agencies when needed. This may include EAPs, the security department, outside psychiatric services, law enforcement, or corporate legal services.
- Procedures and protocols that help diminish the potential for violence or aggression. This could include a community policing methodology, a unified code system for a serious incident or problem person, and an incident response team.
- Environmental design is a critical component in violence prevention. This may involve landscaping, architectural considerations, design of integrated security technology, good lighting, location of strategic areas, etc.
- Administrative controls help increase safety in the workplace. Such controls may include redesign of staffing patterns to prevent people from working alone, to prevent customers from having long waiting times, to restrict movement by access control, or even to develop a system for alerting security personnel when violence is threatened.

The most effective strategy for dealing with anger or aggression in the workplace is behavior modification. In this chapter, we focus on three stages of anger that often lead to workplace violence: anxiety, verbal aggression, and physical aggression. We then offer some tips for proactively avoiding anger, a brief introduction to the idea of threat assessments, and, finally, advice on confronting an angry employee.

Managing Anxiety

People go through three stages when they are angry, the first of which is anxiety. *Anxiety* is a change in behavior and an involuntary reaction or response to something that happens. It is evidenced by a cluster of signals that can include the following:

- Sweating
- Minimal eye contact
- Face flushing
- Lip twitching
- Minimal or excessive talking
- Constant movement
- Shallow breathing
- Darker-than-normal facial color.

Anxiety may be caused by frustration, fear, disappointment, anger, jealousy, losing control, psychiatric issues, fear of injury, heat, and noise among many other things. It is important that anxious employees receive help to calm down, which will diminish the possibility that the anxiety will escalate into behaviors that are more aggressive or assaultive. Body language can be very revealing, as can facial expressions, space, eye contact, and verbal skills.

Giving anxious people the physical space they need in this stage is critical. Using supportive facial expressions and body language that is not aggressive will help people who are anxious to be less so. Where you sit or where you stand in relation to anxious people makes a difference. For example, when you move to within 2 feet of someone, you are moving into their private space. Most of us, depending on many different factors (gender, physical, cultural, and relational), use space to determine comfort. The closer a person is to us that we know and are comfortable with does not create anxiety. But if the relationship is work or some other more casual relationship, someone moving into our space can create discomfort. Try this exercise.

Line up four coworkers, two and two facing each other, and ask them to walk toward each other and ask one side of the four to say "Stop" when they begin to feel uncomfortable. You will see different distances based on height and even gender, but most will be well past the 2-feet mark.

Backing up or leaning back if you are sitting giving some space "back" to the person who is angry has the ability to release the pressure of the moment. Maintain a minimum of 2 plus feet and use supportive verbal skills as well, such as speaking in a calm and reassuring tone, not raising your tone of voice, and not speaking too quickly or too loudly. Listening carefully, not interrupting, and affirming their feelings are all crucial ways to help people gain control and improve their behavior. People need to feel understood, affirmed, and validated when they are upset. They need someone who is focused, and should not feel the person is distracted when dealing with them.

Ask open-ended questions in this stage, clarifying implied or concerning statements, redirecting anger to the past, and not using blame in any way. Other techniques that can help include walking with the person who is anxious, getting them to sit with you, rephrasing what they are saying, and kindly working with them in a confident but patient way. Often the person simply wants to vent and be heard. This act alone may deescalate persons concerns when they are anxious. Most of the time, people who are anxious do not escalate higher on the "conflict" scale; however, if they are not managed, they may.

Managing Verbal Aggression

If anxiety is not properly managed, it can escalate to verbal aggression, which is the second stage of distress. Many people can go from being anxious to being verbally aggressive in the workforce. They may show this by increasing the volume or rate of their speech, or changing their tone to one that is angry or threatening. There are many reasons people can become verbally aggressive. They may feel they or someone they love is being threatened, endangered, or insulted. They may feel a threat to their self-esteem. They may be frustrated with something not working in their favor in their progress toward a goal. Or they may be having some psychiatric or substance abuse issues that trigger verbal aggression. How someone in this stage is handled is critical to keeping others around the person safe. Telling people they are wrong, to "calm down," or that something is "for their own good," generally increases aggression.

People who are verbally aggressive often display the following characteristics:
- Darkening or reddening face
- Prolonged eye contact
- Protruding, stiff lips
- Quick and deep breathing
- Stiffened head and shoulders
- Violent gestures
- Belligerent behavior (yelling, cursing, kicking at the floor).

In this period, the aggressive person is testing the situation. Allowing the person to vent may be useful in deescalating the behavior. Being supportive with body language and facial expressions can deescalate the issue as well. However, some people may not be able to calm down or deescalate on their own. If this is the case, take an assertive strong stance by using clear eye communication and assertive verbal communication. Keep a calm voice, but be confident, setting limits that are reasonable and enforceable. Use the person's name, and, after he or she has been allowed to vent, respectfully but firmly intervene to express what behavior will no longer be tolerated.

Examples of aggression in the workplace may include an upset customer in a store, an angry visitor with a patient in an emergency department, or an employee who has just been given unwanted news by a manager or supervisor. In all cases, use good verbal and nonverbal skills to help an escalating person gain some composure. This is not always easy, as an aggressive person's behavior may be "hooking" the listener and getting him or her on the defense, or, worse, creating fear. Utilize deep breathing and positive self-talk about having confidence in handling the situation. Recognizing what needs to be done to diminish the person's escalation is very important, and the key is to not take it personally, which most people do. Staying objective, humane, and rational about this person's issue or problem, and the goal of keeping the behavior safe must be the priority. Setting limits with a quivering voice, not expressing confidence, using "tentative" language (such as "I *kind* of think you need to stop this behavior," or "We *sort of* need you to stop swearing and disrupting") is a recipe for disaster. Most people at this stage can be brought down to a more rational place with good verbal and nonverbal skills.

Managing Physical Aggression

After anxiety and verbal aggression, some people may escalate to physical aggression—no matter how well they have been managed in the earlier stages of anxiety and verbal aggression. In many cases, those who become assaultive do not have any intention of doing so; they have just lost control of themselves and somehow feel they have no other options. Anger builds on anger, and this can trigger rage and all the stress hormones that go along with it. Violence can occur in unpredictable ways.

In the workplace, employees must be frequently educated on the lack of tolerance for any physical violence, and the sanctions that will occur as a result of violence, such as termination or prosecution. This can be an effective deterrent to some violence. When it is not, and other actions have not been effective, people need to understand how to recognize when physical aggression will happen, and what to do to either stop it or get safe. Before someone is about to assault someone else, several physical characteristics are often present.

- The person's facial color gets white or much lighter than before (oxygen is going to other parts of the body prior to attacking a target).
- The person's eyebrows and head drop a bit, almost covering the eyes.
- The person's breathing is rapid and deep.
- The person changes his or her stance, rolls his or her shoulder, and moves into the fighters' stance, with one leg slightly behind the other.

- The person's verbalization often stops or is strained (most people cannot physically assault someone while they are engaged in conversation). If the person refuses to talk and begins looking away from the face, be aware of a possible strike.
- The person is rocking or moving back and forth, and then suddenly stops all movement.
- The person breaks eye contact with you and looks at the targeted area of the body they are going to attack.
- The person's body slightly drops or dips before an attack.

When a cluster of these signals is witnessed—and they often occur within seconds—it should be evident that someone may be in danger. The most critical thing at that moment is to get away from the person exhibiting these traits to an area of safety, and to get some help. Train employees not to be overly concerned that they are mis-reading someone. If their caution is misunderstood, it is better to be safe than to be concerned about embarrassment. Time is of the essence, and breaking the cycle of the act of the aggressor is critical. Even if they didn't plan to attack or get violent, the aggressor may have just lost control.

In this kind of situation, use defensive body language. Good defensive body language includes standing with one leg slightly ahead of the other so you can move quickly in any direction, maintaining eye contact, and keeping the head and shoulders straight and the hands in front. Using loud, shrill defensive verbal commands may help stun the attacker and stop the attack. Using hand motions to divert an attack-er's eyes away from the target will enable movement, which can be very helpful. Dropping something down in front of the attacker, or throwing something up in front of his or her face, can divert the attack and confuse the person enough to slow his or her actions or interrupt the violence. Even simple actions can be effective—for example, try getting up from your chair and using it as a buffer between yourself and the angry person. Additionally, diversions can be used to inter-rupt the aggressor's focus or intent. The best diversion is moving; head toward an exit or a barricade while continuing to face the individual, so you can block any blow that might be leveled. Again, this should only be used as a last resort; it is very rare that situations escalate to this level.

Being Proactive

The potential for violence is endemic to most workplaces, and the most effective tools for preventing violence are training, good judgment, and common sense. It is really important to teach people how to recognize when others are upset, angry, or volatile. It is necessary for people to trust their gut instinct about a situation and act on it in planned and prepared ways.

Often, workplace violence and conflict occur with an employee or a customer who has previously expressed dissatisfaction or anger. If employees and managers can be trained to take action early when something seems a bit wrong, it is far more proactive in diminishing violence. Often, other employees have a sense of their coworkers and can tell when something may be wrong, or observe that behavior has changed to become more antisocial, angry, blaming, or belligerent. Employees must be trained to talk to management if they see this occur, not to get their colleague in trouble, but simply to have the situation assessed properly for that person's safety and that of everyone else. Managers must learn to spot signs of employees who may be deteriorating in some way, or who may experience some psychiatric, anger, or substance abuse issues. Although not a simple task, confrontation is exactly the response that is needed when certain signs are seen. Managers should be able to collaborate with human resources, EAPs, the security department, risk managers, and legal experts to get consultative advice and to work as a team to see what might be really going on with an employee. With the epidemic of workplace violence and conflict that has occurred in our society, each situation should be approached carefully and comprehensively. Never make the assumption that everything is safe.

Threat Assessments

When there is an employee, a customer, etc., who may be acting in a strange manner, perhaps by making subtle threats or intimidating someone in some way, a threat assessment should be completed. If a company has a strong police department or security program, it can do a full background check to see if the person has exhibited signs of violence in the past. It is important to know what danger the company and its employees might face, and what outside resources (like law enforcement or psychiatric providers) can offer. Strong security operations can also be effective with investigative activities and by simply evaluating the risk and potentially dealing with the problematic visitor, customer, or employee on behalf of the company.

It should be a protocol that corporate security handles threat assessments in a clear and consistent, court defensible way that protects others in the corporation. Threat assessments can also serve as a deterrent, making people realize that certain behavior will not be tolerated and that they will not be able to manipulate coworkers or management. To prevent inappropriate behavior, inform new employees about how a company deals with any threats, conflict, or violence. Let them know that serious sanctions will be taken. This type of standard also gives all employees peace of mind; they will feel more confident that the workplace is safe, and that the company has high and unwavering standards.

A good threat assessment will analyze several things, in addition to the person's past behavior and record.
- The nature and context of the threat or unwanted behavior
- The identified target with as much specificity as possible
- The motivation of those making the threat
- The ability of those threatening to carry out the threat.

Even if the threat does not lead to a violent act, the threat itself damages workplace safety, instills fear, has financial and emotional impact, and needs to be comprehensively addressed and managed.

Confronting Angry Employees

Sometimes, managers need to have conversations or interactions with an employee or a customer they are concerned about. It may be a patient with some anger or psychiatric issues, it may be an employee who is very upset, or who is about to get bad news (such as a layoff or termination). In these cases, managers and others need tools (such as the ones discussed in this chapter) to help deflect and diminish potential violence.

In some cases, you may want to have security staff standing by just in case the situation escalates. Alternatively, you may just want to have someone else in the room (not necessarily a security person). Space and location are critical in interactions and meetings that might go awry; avoiding meeting potentially aggressive employees in closed spaces where help cannot be obtained quickly or where your associate does not have easy access to the door. In many cases, renovating an office with the door at each end of the office—so both the manager and the agitated employee can retreat from an escalating situation—can be helpful. It is also important to have doors that cannot be locked from the inside, so that potentially violent people cannot prevent anyone from leaving. Additionally, panic alarms may be very valuable in offices where people regularly deal with confrontations or tough situations (e.g., human resources, clinical employees, and customer service representatives).

Creating a duress code or a plan for people that work together can be a source of comfort and safety, should there be an incident. The floor plan and physical layout of a workplace should be reviewed and, if necessary, modified to improve workplace safety. Issues to consider include the following:
- Visibility
- Alarm capabilities
- Arrangement of work space
- Communication capabilities
- Adequate and clearly marked escape routes
- Well-designed, appropriate access control.

Conclusion

In this chapter, we discussed the three stages of anger that can ultimately lead to workplace violence: anxiety, verbal aggression, and physical aggression. We explained the warning signs that indicate these three stages, and discussed methods for deescalating situations that involve these warning signs. We also addressed the importance of being proactive in identifying anger, the benefit of threat assessments when dealing with angry employees, and some tips for confronting such angry employees. After reading this chapter, you should have a good sense of how to identify and diminish anger.

Though violence, conflict, and threats may never be completely abolished from the workplace, it is possible to minimize and deter a great deal of inappropriate behavior. In addition to avoiding uncomfortable incidents, this can lead to increasing employees' feelings of safety and confidence, and lead to higher productivity and loyalty. Due diligence should be comprehensive to keep this difficult issue in focus, and to ensure that all workplaces have the tools and power to manage issues that pose a risk to employees.

Food for Thought

1. Do you have an office or business environment that has a high risk of aggressive behavior from clients or customers?
2. Is part of your training of your associates on how to identify potential aggressive behavior?
3. Do you consider the configuration of your office in dealing with potentially aggressive or angry individuals?

Reference

CNN. (2007). *Workplace anger: Who wins?* http://www.CNN.com. Retrieved December 16, 2008, from http://www.cnn.com/2007/LIVING/worklife/08/02/angry.men.women.reut/index.html/.

VIOLENCE ON CAMPUS: A NEW AND EVOLVING THREAT

INTRODUCTION

Violence in schools and on campus has extended into the scope of violence in the workplace because of a couple of recently added, risk-changed categories of educational institution violence. Unfortunately, mass murder scenarios have worked up the ladder of education starting first at the high school level and moving to the collegiate level. Significant work was done after the paradigm-changing events that started with Columbine High School in April 1999, and later, within days of the eighth anniversary of that shooting, the events of April 2007 at Virginia Tech, followed closely by the shootings at Northern Illinois University.

The more recent tragedies at Virginia Tech and Northern Illinois University and, more recently, Yale University bring new attention to the problem of violence on college campuses across the nation. High school violence was brought to the forefront of the public's attention with the shootings at Columbine High School in Littleton, Colorado, and brought with it a wave of outcry and concern from parents about the safety and security of their children while the children are not under parental supervision.

The influence of the events, one upon the other, cannot be ignored as young, troubled, teens and young adults act out their personal frustrations or emotional and mental illness issues on the international stage. After these large-scale violent events, government entities have been tasked with creating reports to help explain, and hopefully chart a path to breaking, these escalations and the proliferation of violence in our nation's schools.

Safe School Initiative Report

In the wake of the Columbine killings, the Secret Service created a report entitled "The Final Report and Finding of the Safe School Initiative: Implications for the Prevention of School Attacks in the United States" in 2002. The Secret Service has an incredible history of protection and reaction to assassination scenarios and it is always blending its expertise against emerging scenarios in an attempt to create layers of safety around its charges—current and former Presidents of the United States (POTUS) and their families, Vice Presidents and their families, and certain other dignitaries. The author had the pleasure of working with the Secret Service during the Olympics—in the 1996 Summer Games in Atlanta, Georgia, and in the Winter Games in Salt Lake City. During that time, the Secret Service was considered the lead agency in planning the prevention of issues during major events. The Secret Service created a Major Event Division whose sole mission was to help prevent issues during National Security Events. National Security Events were then defined as any event where significant federal resources were staged in a planned event, like the Olympics, when held in the United States.

In this report, the size of the problem is discussed by drawing from several sources, including the U.S. Department of Education and the U.S. Department of Justice and Office of Juvenile Justice and Prevention. The report concluded that the odds of a child, in grades 9–12, being injured, or even threatened, was about 8 percent during the period of 1993–1997 (Vossekuil, Fein, Reddy, Borum, & Modzeleski, 2002). But now, "[t]he survey confirms that most of our society's children are exposed to violence in their daily lives. More than 60 percent of the children surveyed were exposed to violence within the past year, either directly or indirectly (i.e., as a witness to a violent act; by learning of a violent act against a family member, neighbor, or close friend; or from a threat against their home or school). Nearly one-half of the children and adolescents surveyed (46.3 percent) were assaulted at least once in the past year, and more than 1 in 10 (10.2 percent) were injured in an assault; 1 in 4 (24.6 percent) were victims of robbery, vandalism, or theft; 1 in 10 (10.2 percent) suffered from child maltreatment (including physical and emotional abuse, neglect, or a family abduction); and 1 in 16 (6.1 percent) were victimized sexually. More than 1 in 4 (25.3 percent) witnessed a violent act and nearly 1 in 10 (9.8 percent) saw one family member assault another. Multiple victimizations were common: more than one-third (38.7 percent) experienced 2 or more direct victimizations in the previous year, more than 1 in 10 (10.9 percent) experienced 5 or more direct victimizations in the previous year, and more than 1 in 75 (1.4 percent) experienced 10 or more direct victimizations in the previous year" (Finkelhor, Turner, Ormrod, Hamby, & Kracke, 2009). These statistics were obtained by screening children who were asked questions ranging from conventional crime, like robbery and sexual assault, to Internet threats. Figure 10-1 gives a picture of the categories of violence reported.

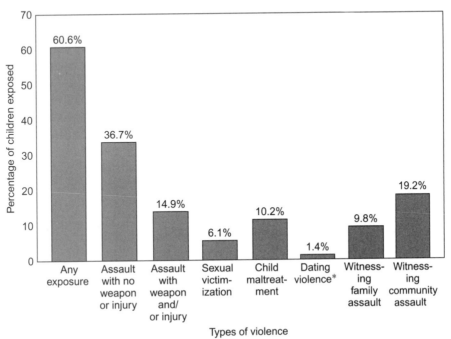

* Figures for dating violence are only for children and adolescents aged 12 years and older.

Figure 10-1. Past-year exposure to selected categories of violence for all children surveyed.

With 60 percent of surveyed children reporting that they had experienced violence in some form, it is understandable why parents are concerned. The figure concerning bullying tops 13 percent according to this report (Finkelhor et al., 2009).

Violence on College Campuses

Similar to the report statistics, current events demonstrate that violence on college campuses brings a unique blend of all types of violence because of the unique blend of groups found on any educational campus. For example, there is the staff of employees who work on campus in any capacity ranging from the cafeteria to administration. For these employees, who are responsible for maintenance of the day-to-day functions of campus life, violence is a real concern. This is the place where employees earn their livelihoods and, like any other school environment, have the challenges that come from the continuous change in attendees. Every year, a new group of students come to school or campus from around town, the state, or even from around the world, to a college campus with hopes of creating a foundation for the future. Additionally, there are faculty who constitute the academic component of any campus and, of course, the students—who's numerical size dwarfs each of the other groups. Added to these groups the visitors, parents, alumni, and event attendees, a college campus becomes a diverse group of constituents.

Institutions of higher learning are places where parents, very often, disengage from their children. This disengagement often happens for the first time and, in doing so, parents believe that they are handing the care and safekeeping of their children to the institution that can be many miles or states away. Parents often sacrifice their own peace of mind and meager savings with the desire that the son or daughter will earn an education that will secure the child's future. The incident at Columbine and the fairly recent tragedies at Virginia Tech, Northern Illinois University, and Yale University demonstrate a need to focus on the unique challenges of prevention, detection, and responding to violence on campuses without alarmism and without suggestions that campuses are not safe.

Epidemic style pronouncements of campus violence and broad proclamations of writers from the school of "Chicken Little" are common these days and there are no signs that this trend will be, in any way, truncated. So the strategies to address this type of violence should be planned, discussed openly, and addressed as a part of any school's overall security plan. These statements should, in no way, detract from the profound tragedy of the incidents at these institutions. However, a process built upon common sense, which is coordinated and communicated, should be followed. Hysterical thinking or advice should be avoided. Gratefully, a significant amount of excellent work has been done to provide generic recommendations, with respect to the prevention of violence, to educational institutions on all levels.

In June 2008, Applied Risk Management (ARM) produced a 114-page summary entitled "Campus Violence Prevention and Response: Best Practices for Massachusetts Higher Education Report to Massachusetts Department of Higher Education in June 2008." This well-written and well-documented review of the problem of violence on college campuses attempts to size the issue and give realistic recommendations that can be implemented and would not simply comply with legal requirements, like the Cleary Act, but also attempt to be reasonable in its size and scope. One of the points the ARM article makes is that the effect of campus violence is devastating but is, by no means, commonplace or at an epidemic level. And, like any workplace violence, the sensationalism that is fueled by the 24/7 news cycle seems to drive the issue to the forefront of both parental and would-be student concern that the life of the care-free student might be interrupted by gunfire.

James Alan Fox, PhD (2008) of the Lipman Family Professor of Criminal Justice and Professor of Law, Policy and Society, Northeastern University, is a major contributor to the work. He concludes that, "Epidemic thinking can tragically become a self-fulfilling prophesy by fueling a contagion of bloodshed. The overpublicized acts of two alienated students at Columbine High, in part, inspired the Virginia Tech shooter to outperform his younger heroes. As the death toll rose that fateful Monday morning last spring in Blacksburg, on-air news anchors tracked the unfolding drama as ignominious records began to tumble. Shortly after announcing that the shooting had become the largest campus massacre ever, eclipsing the 1966 Texas Tower sniping, television commentators declared, with nearly gleeful enthusiasm, that it had surpassed in carnage all other mass shootings in the United States at any venue. For the remainder of the day, viewers were told repeatedly that the Virginia Tech massacre had been the biggest, the bloodiest, the absolute worst, the most devastating, or whatever other superlatives came to the journalists, minds. Notwithstanding the cruel absurdity of treating human suffering as any sort of achievement worthy of measuring in such terms, little positive can be derived by highlighting such records. But there is one significant negative: Records exist but to be broken" (Fox, O'Neill, Depue, & Englander, 2008).

Therefore, practitioners who work on campuses everywhere know that the pressures are the same. The question all institutions ask is how valuable security dollars should be budgeted in concert with the health care component that focuses on the mental health and welfare of students while dealing with the overwhelming security demand for increased security. Priorities must be set and timelines established to meet the demand for effective strategies. This chapter is focused on the various dimensions of the problem and should not be viewed as comprehensive. However, as a dimension of discussing violence in the workplace, any book should at least raise the major elements of the problem that should be included in any proactive plan.

Campus Violence Prevention and Response: Best Practices for Massachusetts Higher Education

So let's evaluate the size of the threat based on 2001–2005 murders on campuses across the United States. The Campus Violence Prevention and Response: Best Practices for Massachusetts Higher Education Report to Massachusetts Department of Higher Education states, "Based upon information from the FBI's Uniform Crime Reporting program and the U.S. Department of Education's records mandated by the Clery Act, as well as information provided by news coverage, there were 76 homicides reported on college campuses nationwide between 2001 and 2005. Leaving aside cases involving faculty, staff or other non-students as victims, the count of undergraduates and graduate students murdered at school numbered 51, an average of about 10 per year. And of these homicides, as shown in Table 1, the majority involved acquaintance killings or drug deals gone bad, not rampaging shooters."

The report continues, "Of course, issues of violence and violence prevention extend well beyond the few widely-publicized crimes that form the tip of a larger iceberg. But even in the broader context of campus violence, the incidence of violence at college is rather low, as shown in Table 2, and the risk of serious victimization is typically far lower than the areas adjacent to most campuses. College law enforcement agencies reported an average of only seven serious violent crimes per school in 2004—two robberies, two forcible rapes, and three aggravated assaults. However, certain violent crimes— particularly rape—tend to be underreported. Therefore, we can assume that these statistics for violent crime on college campuses are an underestimate of reality" (Fox et al., 2008).

The actual deaths during that time period, which were directly related to crime, were low in comparison to violence in the workplace deaths as a whole. But The emotion and fear that is generated from these events may not have a solid basis but are still real in the minds and concerns of parents and students. Table 10-1 is a breakdown of the homicides committed in various ways for this period. This information was provided in the report referenced above and demonstrates that the overwhelming weapon of choice is a firearm but other methods are also used.

Virginia Tech Campus Shootings

Unfortunately, the event of April 16, 2007, was a game-changing one. Seung-Hui Cho, a senior at Virginia Tech, which is located in Blacksburg, Virginia, came to the 2,600-acre campus with two weapons, a 9-mm pistol and a .22 handgun that he used initially to kill two students in the West Ambler Johnston residence hall. According to the reports, the perpetrator's next incident happened 2½ hours later in a classroom half a mile across campus from Norris Hall, an engineering school classroom building.

Table 10-1. Characteristics of Campus Homicides in the United States, 2001–2005

Characteristics		Percent
Weapon	Gun	52.2
	Knife	11.6
	Personal	21.7
	Other	14.5
Sex of victim	Male	61.3
	Female	38.7
Victim role	Student	57.3
	Faculty	9.3
	Staff	9.3
	Child	5.3
	Other	18.7
Sex of offender	Male	90.8
	Female	9.2
Offender role	Student	35.5
	Former student	5.3
	Outsider	32.2
	Undetermined	27.0
Victim/offender relationship	Partner	12.5
	Friend	28.3
	Acquaintance	6.6
	Stranger	27.6
	Undetermined	25.0

Total number of homicides = 76

Source: Adapted from Table 1.1 in *Campus Violence Prevention and Response: Best Practices for Massachusetts Higher Education,* June 2008.

Cho, with planned precision, chained the doors closed to prevent exit from the building, and then proceeded to shoot 30 people—25 students and 5 faculty members—then eventually killing himself with a single shot to his own face. This single shot so disfigured Cho that it delayed law enforcement's ability to determine the identity of the shooter for some time as, in an initial search, his fingerprint came up "no match." Officers forced their way in to survey the carnage that included 13 who were mortally wounded and the 17 wounded survivors of the event. Several people were injured when they jumped from classroom windows to avoid being gunshot victims. The shooter still had over 200 rounds of ammunition and certainly would have killed more if the police had not forced their way in, as opposed to staying outside and taking a different tactical approach. With two different weapons firing, the police thought there might be multiple shooters, so their response was aggressive and courageous. Unfortunately, however, significant damage had already been done.

During the time of the first and last shooting, Cho returned to his dorm room where he changed his bloodied clothes, and mingled with other students, while making his way to the Blacksburg Post Office. From here, Cho mailed a package of his writings and videotapes to NBC that included his reasoning and ranting for the outrage. Cho, apparently, despised his fellow students as morally corrupt individuals, tainted by a materialistic U.S. culture.

Criticism abounds after an event like this. But the biggest on the ground complaint was the delay in the warning of a possible shooter on campus which took place 2 hours after the first casualties in the residence hall. Authorities believed, at the time, that the shooting was isolated to that location and that the shooter had left the Virginia Tech campus. This event was just four days before the eighth anniversary of the Columbine shootings in Colorado (msnbc .com, 2007).

Review of the event was undertaken by a panel that was quickly appointed by Virginia Governor Tim Kaine. A former superintendent of the Virginia State Police, Col. Gerald Massengill, headed up the effort. Hundreds of interviews were conducted ranging from the administration staff to hospital personnel. In a 2008 article written for *Change Magazine*, Gordon K. Davies, who also served on the panel, outlined areas of concerns and lessons learned. The concerns were divided into three categories: structural, managerial, and actions of the personnel on the ground. He concluded the following.

"The Structure of Mental Health Care in the Public health failed in this case. Further, since the structure of these services is similar across the country, it will continue to fail"

(Davies, 2008). Mr. Davies' basic conclusion is a lack of adequate resources. The services needed to address a mass casualty incident like the Virginia Tech shooting, at the time of the incident, were underfunded and outpatient services were needed. Davies also speaks to the issue of gun laws that made it easier, in this particular case, for the perpetrator to procure the weapons used to carry out the shootings. There continues to be ambiguities around the statutes, both Federal and State, concerning what prohibits "mentally defective" persons from legally obtaining a weapon. This is a reference to the enforcement of the Federal Gun Control Act of 1968 which attempts to prevent mentally troubled individuals, who have been diagnosed as being a threat to themselves or others, from obtaining weapons. Enforcement of this Act may have slowed the individual from obtaining a weapon but would not have prevented a motivated individual in all future cases.

Davies also states that confusion and inconsistent understanding and application of the Family Educational Rights and Privacy Act (FERPA) and the Health Insurance Portability and Accountability Act (HIPAA) also contributed here. Cho, in December 2005, was diagnosed as being a danger to himself or others. This information was not shared with the campus police department. This factor, if known, might have given police an opportunity to observe the current behaviors of this potentially violent individual in its jurisdiction (Davies, 2008).

Virginia Tech, apparently, had a system in place at the time of the killings along with procedures of actions to be taken if it became aware of a troubled student. The Care Team, which includes representatives from administration, faculty, student services, and legal, that works with students who have behavioral issues, is functional at this university. Mr. Cho had been reported for troubling behavior including stalking, violent writing, and refusal to participate in class activities. As described in the previous chapter, all of these issues could be precursors to future acts of violence. No action was taken by this group with respect to Cho.

There is a list of missed opportunities and lack of follow-up or follow-through by the campus counseling center. Calls were made by Cho but he was never diagnosed or treated.

A woman complained about Cho to campus police and he was given subsequent verbal admonishment to stay away from the woman at school and this led to a threat of suicide. The panel could not find proper documentation about this incident as it had either been destroyed or lost. The thread of incidents between the counseling system, behavioral problems, and complaints to the police was never effectively connected and this allowed Cho to follow a road to anger, outrage, and eventual violence.

Emergency response for these kinds of emergencies is handled by a committee. Not wanting to create a panic, a policy group of senior administrators, not including the police, was convened by Virginia Tech's president. The role of this committee was to oversee the communications response plan to the incident. The response came 2 hours after the first shooting at the residence hall and was vague in its communication of the magnitude of severity or that a suspect was not in custody. The police could ask for an emergency broadcast but did not have the independent authority to activate the system. Assumptions were made that the perpetrator had left the Virginia Tech campus when, in fact, he had gone to his own room on campus, picked up his manifesto, and proceeded to the post office. The reasoning behind the assumption was certainly well intentioned. The committee did not want to have a panicked campus or community. Similarly situated universities generally use a smaller group, which includes police, in the decision-making process.

An emergency operations center was not used in the response to this event even though the concept and capability to use one was part of the university's emergency response plan (ERP). A family assistance center was established but was seen, by Mr. Davies, as ineffective because it lacked leadership, training, and coordination of services. Volunteers were used in the family assistance center but they lacked the needed information to provide effective assistance. The overall response by the Virginia state government was seen as an exception, in the form of the Department of Public Safety, as "very good" according to the panel. The state police had the task to notify families of the death or injury of the victims. The other agencies, Department of Social Services, Department of Criminal Justice, etc., responded—some quicker than others—but in all the state's response was, generally, adequate. The Commonwealth Victim Services was the slowest agency to respond and did not arrive until two days after the incident occurred.

Mr. Davies concludes that the response by police and emergency personnel, including hospital response, was generally excellent. He describes the actions of emergency personnel as courageous, being the responders whose own lives were put in jeopardy. However, the aforementioned issues surrounding the failure to issue an all campus alert was probably a miscue. In all fairness, however, Mr. Davies points out that Cho had already committed two murders and was intending to commit suicide, so he probably would have acted out in some other venue even if all classes were canceled.

In the end, there were some lessons learned. Mr. Davies concluded that there were seven in this case. First, more outpatient mental health care services were needed at Virginia Tech. Second, enforcement of gun laws or statutes already on the books is needed. Third, privacy laws, as they relate to potentially violent individuals, are needed, and a thorough review and understanding of HIPAA and FERPA should be addressed as there appears to be a misinterpretation in this case. Fourth, communication may have contributed to the problem, especially regarding known violence or potentially violent individuals. Fifth, written plans should be individualized to each school—contrary to the concept of "one plan can be adopted to fit all." Sixth, response plans should be developed and practiced. Last, and maybe the most problematic, is how to create a system in which mental health records travel with the student.

Recommended Actions for Avoiding Campus Violence

The panel's work with respect to this incident was of great interest as it brings the focus onto a manageable set of action items. The Massachusetts report is quite detailed and lists a total of 27 recommended actions that it concluded need to be taken, after using several source documents, including the Davies article. This work is not meant to be an exhaustive study of this particular venue of violence. There is hope, by recognizing the issue in an emerging context, that if your area of responsibility is schools or campuses, this discussion will assist in your planning.

It is helpful to note, however, that there are some broad categories of issues that should be reviewed in the priorities recommended below:

1. Mental health services should be available for students and employees of schools and campuses in sufficient quantity to be effective.
2. Physical security is key. This is especially true with access control and camera surveillance.
3. Emergency communication processes should include both case of emergency reporting process at the classroom level and emergency in-bound communication to students that can give emergency instructions and directions.
4. Active shooter training should be given to the police, faculty, and even students and incorporated into the school ERP. These plans should be practiced in the form of "drills" on a regular basis. No one is looking for a training manual when the shooting starts.
5. Knowing how to report concerns about fellow employees and creating a culture that makes it a good thing is critical. A formal threat assessment and risk assessment process should be incorporated into the security plan.
6. Policies and procedures should be written and reviewed annually. As personnel changes, the process should continue to have an owner who is high in the organization. Human resources is a candidate for this job, security is its partner.
7. Victims and their families will need to be supported if an incident occurs.

Conclusion

Recognizing the need for planning and response is hard work. There is so much to do to run a school with change as part of the school's everyday existence with students coming and going, opting in and out, on a regular basis. But the work will pay off.

Food for Thought

1. Who is in charge of deciding when to alert students at your campus? Who creates the message?
2. If an incident occurred today, would your school have enough safety and security personnel to respond?
3. Who owns the process at your school?
4. Is there a good communications path between your mental health process and your security organization, whether it is campus police or security officers?
5. What is your training plan for your students surrounding active shooter?

References

Fox, J. A., O'Neill, D., Depue, R., & Englander, E. (2008, June). *Campus violence prevention and response: Best practices for Massachusetts higher education.* Boston: Applied Risk Management.

Davies, G. K. (2008). Connecting the dots: Lessons from the Virginia Tech shootings. *Change Magazine.* Retrieved from http://www .changemag.org/Archives/Back%20Issues/January-February%20 2008/full-connecting-the-dots.html/.

Finkelhor, D., Turner, H., Ormrod, R., Hamby, S., & Kracke, K. (2009, October). Children's exposure to violence: A comprehensive national survey. *Juvenile Justice Bulletin,* 1–11.

msnbc.com (2007, April 16). *Worst U.S. shooting ever kills 33 on VA campus.* Retrieved November 14, 2009, from http://www.msnbc .msn.com/id/18134671/.

United States Secret Service. (2002). The final report and finding of the safe school initiative. Retrieved from http://www.secretservice.gov/ ntac/ssi_final_report.pdf/.

Vossekuil, B., Fein, R., Reddy, M., Borum, R., & Modzeleski, W. (2002). *The final report and findings of the safe school initiative: Implications for the prevention of school attacks in the United States.* United States Secret Service and United States Department of Education. Retrieved from http://www.secretservice.gov/ntac/ssi_final_report.pdf/.

11

BACKGROUND SCREENING: IMPORTANT, BUT NOT THE SILVER BULLET

INTRODUCTION

The best way to prevent a problem from occurring in an organization is not to invite it through the door. Background screening is a process to determine suitability, integrity, and reliability of a candidate for a position as an employee, contractor, consultant, volunteer, or even a vendor. All of these constituent groups require background checks that have both similarities and differences. However, depending on the organization, prevention may focus on one or all of these categories of individuals as processes to be managed.

The first danger is to silo the background screening process by constituent group based on how each individual group interfaces with the organization. Very often, businesses may interact with these individual groups in very diverse ways. For example, the HR department may deal solely with different employee groups, which may include temporary workers. HR recruits, sources, and advertises for candidates at the request of constituent groups ranging from the highly technical to the semi-skilled; upper management to entry level. The HR department makes sure that employees receive the appropriate rate of pay, benefits, training, and orientation and may also even deal with behavioral and disciplinary issues, including violence in the workplace. Workplace violence, as has been discussed previously, may include issues like threats, intimidation, assaults, and bullying. Human resources is the group with which background screening is often associated.

Consultants and contractors may be brought into an organization by a particular work group, and also perform at the discretion of the particular group to whom they are assigned. These consultants and contractors are sometimes temporary in nature but may also stay connected with the organization for months or even years. Contractors and consultants may have access to every area and information system an employee has access to and, sometimes, even more. If the contractor or consultant is engaged to deal with or install an organization's software, it will often have the electronic keys to the organization's kingdom.

The first action of a planner who is charged with the setting or creation of policy or the administration, or management of the background screening process, is to set a minimum standard for anyone who is connected to the organization. This includes any person who has access to the organization's employees, facilities, or other assets regardless of whether he or she is an employee. Individual access should be the first consideration for inclusion into the background screening process. Each individual group may have a different approach or process for the background screening to be completed and by whom, but the approach or process needs to be identified and used consistently. To find out how complex such a process is, have a discussion with the facility's security personnel or building management group that manages access cards. During this discussion, a plethora of people can be identified who come into the organization, daily, who may or may not have been appropriately screened.

Once there is an understanding of the breadth of the constituent groups within the organization, the policies and procedures can be developed. Who, what, and when in the onboarding cycle do these groups need to be screened, how often, and by whom? For example, what about a security contractor? Should the background screening occur in-house or is there a process in place by which a background screening process has been verified? Imagine that an organization hired XYZ Security to provide unarmed security services and this contractor will have its employees deployed at each facility. Most states require the security contractor to license the company and its personnel. State Departments of Professional Licensing (DOPL) require security contractors to have a background check performed by the state providing the licensing. If the process is understood, specifically that this licensing requires fingerprinting, and a criminal background screen, it may be sufficient. The cost for these activities is borne by the security company which passes the costs to the organization in its contracted rate spread across all of its customers. A credential is issued by the state and is then required to be carried with the individual at all times. Are credentials verified as current with all security officers who work within the organization's points of entrance? Does the contract allow for periodic audit of the background screens to make sure they are at a level that is appropriate, depending on the organization's risk model?

A primary task is to understand the investment in these individuals by sector. How many different constituent groups does the organization have? Begin by creating a list of the various groups, by name, that also indicates the number of screens involved. Creating this list will provide the ability to identify potential costs. Take the time to understand all of the hidden fees and costs of doing a good, thorough background screen and determine whether the cost is direct or hidden in an administrative fee charged by the contractor. For example:

Employees—This group includes regular and part-time employees who are in the company' payroll. For instance, evaluate a business that employs 1,000 individuals. This business has a 15 percent turnover rate with a growth of 5 percent per year. This equates to approximately 1,200 hires per year at its current pace. Recognizing that there might be different background screening packages, depending on the job description for the individual being screened, the average cost per background check is $85. Therefore, the budget for the employee base in the next year is, roughly, $102,000.

Contractors, vendors, and consultants—These groups get the cost of background screening of security officers and cleaning staff pushed to their procurement group of approximately $50 per contractor. Contractors, vendors, and consultants typically have high turnover rates, so the cost of 300 contractors is billed to the company as an administrative cost. This equates to approximately $15,000. Vendors are screened by contract by the provider and that cost is hidden somewhere in the price. That cost could run to $3,000. HR has a full-time employee who administers this program. He costs the company $35,000. So this company's expense is $155,000 per year. Or is it?

A deeper look will determine if all costs are being considered. During this process, the HR department had a 10 percent failure rate. Most of this failure rate is due to potential candidates not disclosing critical information like prior criminal convictions or incomplete or inaccurate information regarding prior work history or education. As a result, the company went out to find additional candidates who could pass the background screening process. This represents an additional cost of screening 120 more employees, which results in an additional $10,200 in background screening expense. This, in addition to the cost of recruiting the additional candidates at $500 per candidate, results in a total of $60,000. The grand total for this "back of the envelope" estimate tops $225,000. This says that, in the next 10 years, this 1,000 employee company will spend well over $2.25 million.

Estimate this hypothetical company's revenue at $250 million, with an operating margin of 25 percent. If the company forgoes background screening, it could increase its margin by 0.09 percent driving the margin up to 25.09 percent or rounded way up to 0.1 percent. The question is what does it cost if background screening is not done?

Case Study in Background Screening

The classic case involving failure to conduct background screening that would have prevented a killing was the case of Jerrol Glenn Woods, a carpet cleaner. Woods fatally stabbed Kerry Spooner-Dean after cleaning carpets at the pediatrician's home in Oakland, California. Mr. Woods was a known felon who was released recently from serving a sentence. Woods was convicted of armed robbery and first-degree murder in May 1999.

The victim's husband, Daniel Dean, received a $9.38 million judgment against America's Best Carpet Care. The amount of this judgment was enterprise ending for the company. This amount would have comprised a little over five decades of background screening for the hypothetical company (Lublin, 2002). Beyond the moral sense, it makes good business sense, by any measure, to conduct some form of background screen to prevent inviting the problem through the door. In the example of the hypothetical company, this judgment would have paid for over 41 years of screening. Certainly, insurance may have picked up a portion of this cost … maybe. However, note how a basic due diligence check would have vetted this issue.

Relying on Resumes

Another business concern to be addressed is making a hiring decision based on using a resume the sole basis for information regarding a candidate. With national and international resources in use, it is imperative that background screens go beyond criminal history and extend beyond borders. In July 2007, *Security Management Magazine* reported that somewhere between 20 and 30 percent of all new hires in the Asia-Pacific international market have inflated or falsified their job experience, certifications, and education. This was reported to *Security Management* by Bart Valdez, President of First Advantage Employer Screening (Elliot, 2007). If these factors are a part of the decision matrix, a thorough review is needed of the information provided for the hiring decision. It is also recommended that employment applications are a requirement for all employees, including those in entry-level positions all the way up to those in the executive suites. An employment application is a legal document that should be signed by the candidate for employment. The employment application has individuals attest to the information provided as true, accurate, and correct. Be certain, when making hiring decisions, that each applicant and hire completes an application.

It is always interesting to see how job titles change from the transition from resume to application. Dates get a little tighter and areas of responsibility get a little less broad.

The application has a sobering effect to the provider of the information—the applicant. The application process is also the appropriate time to have candidates complete a separate document that is used to actually do the screening. This document should have specific language that allows the organization to check an applicant's background based on specific criteria that may include criminal history, work history, and education history, in addition to any appropriate watch lists kept by the Office of Foreign Asset Control (OFAC) and Office of Inspector General (OIG). The background screening authorization document is separate for several reasons but the best is very practical. Many sources, including former employers and educational institutions, require a waiver and consent to be mailed or faxed before any information is released to an organization or its screening partner. If this document is secured up front, it is available when a request is made for it from a provider when it is needed to complete a background screen.

Choosing a Background Screening Company

If there is a conviction that screening is needed in a specific business or organization and it is a good investment, there is a strategy to determine the best course to take in the establishment, adjustment, or even a fine-tuning of a current approach. The question may be—how much is an implementation of background screening going to cost and how long should it take? The screening industry is becoming more and more commoditized. The cost of data is dropping and screening companies, whether court data driven or those that administer drug testing, always attempt to keep associated costs in-line by further automating their processes. If there has not been a recent pricing discussion with your provider lately, with your current provider, this should be done as soon as possible. For example, if the cost for an identity check is $8 and for a court search $18.50 and 1,000 checks are conducted per year, that is far too costly. The author disagrees with an annual request for proposal (RFP) process for the background screening process and pricing that some organizations use just because it is an internal purchasing policy. This approach can be costly for both the organization and the provider and does not make good economic sense. If the right provider is selected, the ability to have a frank pricing conversation includes the current organizational strategy and the provider's pricing strategy. If there is a level of comfort with your current service, look for ways to decrease costs by using annual or monthly minimums. Most legitimate providers are happy to get an organization in a term and commitment relationship. If the organization is purely price driven, it is probably a customer that is looking at the process as merely a cost of doing business instead of a good business practice.

The creation of better analytics that determine identity and get more information back in real time is often the goal of both the organization and the provider. This is often a point of contention. Screening companies often claim speed and accuracy that is often questionable. So a conversation goes like this, "you say your current provider can get the screen done in three days, our company can do it in two." What is the truth here? Can a background screen be done in less than two days? Sure. It depends on the screening package and whether or not the search nets a "hit." A "hit" is a discrepancy or negative information that gets returned from a source. If the candidate has a clean record and has provided good, solid, and thorough information, and the screening request package is not too complex, the search could come back in two days or less. Most of the up-to-date criminal information is retained at the county level within the United States. There are over 3,200 counties in the United States. Many are now online or rolled up into a state repository. This speeds up the process dramatically. With some of the current screening packages, an individual with a clear record could come back in less than 24 hours. However, if the person lives, or has lived, in a county of the United States that is remote or not online, it could take 72 hours or more. The question to ask a current or prospective provider, then, is the *average* turnaround time. The average time should be under 48 hours. The key then lies not in what the provider promises but how they say it or, in this case, how the information is requested.

Next, and even more important, is that the background screening provider has a process that complies with the

FCRA. There are currently over 2,500 screening providers in the United States—most of them are quite small in size. A small screening provider is not necessarily a bad thing, by any means. The smaller companies often work hard to keep their business and provide some customized services and excellent customer service. The National Association of Professional Background Screeners (NAPBS) was formed in 2003 as an industry organization to further professionalize the industry. It is then recommended that, at a minimum, an organization's provider belong to that organization (National Association of Professional Background Screeners, 2006). Potential providers should also be questioned regarding the efforts that they make to comply with this law, in addition to any state and local laws (see Chapter 4).

The purpose of the FCRA is described under section 602 of the act which states:

§ 602. Congressional findings and statement of purpose
[15 U.S.C. § 1681]

a. *Accuracy and fairness of credit reporting.* The Congress makes the following findings:

   1. The banking system is dependent upon fair and accurate credit reporting. Inaccurate credit reports directly impair the efficiency of the banking system, and unfair credit reporting methods undermine the public confidence which is essential to the continued functioning of the banking system.

   2. An elaborate mechanism has been developed for investigating and evaluating the credit worthiness, credit standing, credit capacity, character, and general reputation of consumers.

   3. Consumer reporting agencies have assumed a vital role in assembling and evaluating consumer credit and other information on consumers.

   4. There is a need to insure that consumer reporting agencies exercise their grave responsibilities with fairness, impartiality, and a respect for the consumer's right to privacy.

b. *Reasonable procedures.* It is the purpose of this title to require that consumer reporting agencies adopt reasonable procedures for meeting the needs of commerce for consumer credit, personnel, insurance, and other information in a manner which is fair and equitable to the consumer, with regard to the confidentiality, accuracy, relevancy, and proper utilization of such information in accordance with the requirements of this title. (FCRA, 2004)

When reading this statement of purpose, the terms "accuracy and fairness" and "reasonable procedures" and in paragraph 4 (b) the word "personnel" are used. Employment falls under this act. Therefore, the sources used should be primary data sources, whenever possible, and accurate and reliable. The agencies that have this data are known as Credit Reporting Agencies or CRAs. So, when looking for a screening partner, make sure they comply, in fact and in spirit, with the FCRA.

Within this process is the consumer's right to appeal the accuracy of the report. Any screening process should allow the consumer, who is now a candidate for a job, a way to appeal the results of the screen. This process should point the candidate directly to the provider. Working with the consumer is the responsibility of the provider to assist the consumer at no additional cost to the organization. Make sure the provider has a solid process.

Another important provision that should be fully understood is the provider's process regarding Article 613 of the FCRA which states:

§ 613. Public record information for employment purposes [15 U.S.C. § 1681(k)]

a. *In general.* A consumer reporting agency which furnishes a consumer report for employment purposes and which for that purpose compiles and reports items of information on consumers which are matters of public record and are likely to have an adverse effect upon a consumer's ability to obtain employment shall (1) at the time such public record information is reported to the user of such consumer report, notify the consumer of the fact that public record information is being reported by the consumer reporting agency, together with the name and address of the person to whom such information is being reported; or (2) maintain strict procedures designed to insure that whenever public record information which is likely to have an adverse effect on a consumer's ability to obtain employment is reported it is complete and up to date. For purposes of this paragraph, items of public record relating to arrests, indictments, convictions, suits, tax liens, and outstanding judgments shall be considered up to date if the current public record status of the item at the time of the report is reported.

b. *Exemption for national security investigations.* Subsection (a) does not apply in the case of an agency or department of the United States Government that seeks to obtain and use a consumer report for employment purposes, if the head of the agency or department makes a written finding as prescribed under section 604(b)(4)(A) (FCRA, 2004).

What this means for the organization is that the provider should notify the consumer (the candidate) immediately if information is returned that could prevent him or her from being hired into the position. It is recommended that the provider use a belt and suspender here. If the candidate has an email address, notify him or her that they can download the Article 613 notice from a secure web site in addition to sending the person a letter in regular mail. Give the candidate every opportunity to resolve inaccuracies. Often the candidate will tell the potential employer that he or she will appeal the results but the employer never hears from the candidate again. In other words, the issue is really the candidate's, but he or she will say the report is inaccurate to save a little face. Either way, the inaccuracies should be resolved prior to making a hiring decision. Be reasonable in the time that is given to the candidate to resolve the issue. It is recommended at least five days be allowed for the resolution process. If the candidate does not appeal the report by contacting the provider, move on to the next choice (FCRA, 2004).

Ask the provider questions about overall coverage on any database product it has. This is especially true for identity tools and multistate court record databases. Make sure there is an understanding of the strengths and weaknesses of the so-called National Criminal Files. In reality that phrase is a misnomer. There is no holistic database in the US that covers the over 3200 counties in every state in an up to date manner. However, there are improvements in the data and new access to online FCRA sources, like county court records, and this is often very reliable and helpful.

Basics of a Background Screening

The question is then, what is a good basic check for a particular organization? The list below is a recommended place to start. Additionally, consult with the HR department, security and legal advisors, in addition to the background screening provider. Do the homework regarding the risk associated with the organization's business or industry. The ultimate background screen may require a more comprehensive check, but the following is a good baseline check to get you started.

The most important component to the background screen is *identity verification*; in other words, the interviewer must know who is sitting across the desk in an interview. This check should do several things. Do this any time that is needed in the process. This verification does not fall under the FCRA. It is not a background check. It is identity verification. According to the U.S. Department of Justice, over 9 million identities will be stolen this year alone (United States Department of Justice, 2009). Most reputable providers have robust tools to use data identifiers, validate, and verify them as issued, active, and belonging together. It is also a way to get past addresses that can be used to compare with an artifact like a resume or an application. Do not waste time on candidates who cannot make you feel warm and fuzzy about who they really are.

If a job offer is made, use E-Verify. E-Verify is a screening tool used to ensure that a candidate has a legal right to work in the United States. It is a good business practice and it is free to the employer. Having Immigration and Customs Enforcement (ICE) show up at the corporate headquarters or any site will definitely cut into the workday. Federal government contractors are required by law, since September 2009, to use E-Verify on all new hires. This process augments the onboarding I-9 process, which requires verification of applicant identity via artifacts including passports, driver license, and social security cards. "The E-Verify system is operated by the U.S. DHS in partnership with the Social Security Administration" (United States Citizenship and Immigration Services).

Background screenings should cascade from the establishment of identity. The author recommends that background screens occur at the post-offer/pre-hire stage. This saves money as there may be upwards of 10–50 candidates for a single position. If identity verification is conducted on each serious candidate, the bulk of the budget can be saved to conduct the important background screens. This process can be streamlined by putting job candidates into screening categories.

1. Temporaries and service employees—Screening package one—Identity, criminal, and prior employment. Watch lists including OFAC and E-Verify.

2. All regular full- and part-time employees—Screening package two—Identity, criminal, prior employment, and education (highest level). Watch lists including OFAC and E-Verify. Professional licensing might be appropriate in some industries and references.

3. Key functional areas like ALL Executive-level positions— ("C" levels like CEO and CFO), legal, Corporate Security, Human Resources, and Internal Auditors—Screening package three—Identity, criminal, prior employment, and education (highest level). Watch lists including OFAC and E-Verify, civil and credit, references, and verify all professional licenses.

Rescreens should be conducted when a person is promoted to a position of increased access or responsibility. Further, if a position moves from category two to three, the rescreen should be conducted using the larger scope of background screen. It should be noted that the higher a person's status is within the organization or when the person has critical access to customers, assets, signing authority, or information, the more robust the check becomes. When the issues of Sarbanes-Oxley or the scandals of the 2008–2009 economic meltdown driven by the acts of less-than-scrupulous individuals are considered, it pays to do the homework up front. A full check, guided by the legal department for key hires, makes a lot of sense as these individuals can hurt a business in a very public way.

Social web sites are an emerging area of screening value. These, in the author's nonlegal opinion, are really primary sources that can be viewed for information relating to a person's character. Racist or discriminatory statements on blogs or personal web site pages make for interesting reading. Such character defects come with a candidate into the workplace.

The employment application can serve another important purpose. If the application is falsified in any way and the screening process determines the candidate was intentionally deceptive, there is no concern regarding appealing false positives. For example, if the candidate says she has a degree from Texas A & M in Business Administration and she merely attended, but never graduated, she has falsified a company document. If the organization has a code of conduct and policy that requires employees and potential candidates to be truthful and accurate and it states this on the application, the hiring process can be stopped. Any offers made to the candidate should have the caveat that the offer is subject to a successful completion of a background screen.

Another question to consider is should persons with "a past" be hired? This is a risk/reward question that will be addressed in the policy chapter. In brief, the answer to that question is "maybe." The answer should be based on an accurate understanding of the details and timing of the offense. If there was a drug possession charge five years ago when the candidate was 19, should that be reason enough not to hire? These issues should be discussed in a policy committee.

In the first book that the author cowrote, *Background Screening and Investigations: Managing Risk from the HR and Security Perspective* (Nixon & Kerr, 2008), the anonymous story of a senior executive of a company hired a C-level executive based on his vast, and impressive, educational and military background. The only problem was that the newly hired executive never graduated from college and never served in the military. This hiring decision cost the hiring organization several hundred thousand dollars in relocation expense, lost time and direction, not to mention credibility in its particular industry.

In thinking through the process of background screening, it is important to note the current level of background checks for the majority of companies is a balance sheet approach. In other words, a person's history is evaluated as though looking in the rearview mirror, and past behavior is used as a predictor of future behavior. However, some practitioners feel more evaluation is needed. Looking at ongoing monitoring, especially with employees, contractors, consultants, or volunteers, is being tackled with a concept of credentialing workers.

Case Study: RAILSAFE

The rail industry developed E-RAILSAFE for its contractors for Class 1 carriers. E-RAILSAFE was designed to promote workplace safety and increase security awareness and for Class 1 Railroads in cooperation with the contractor organizations that supply workers. Combining background screening, security training, and compliance tenets, this program attempts to credential a group of workers who migrate between carriers. This model is interesting. It attempts to address the issue of unknown flexibility needs that can address the changing resource requirements for a particular industry. The credential has to be renewed and requires periodic screens to maintain it.

The author was discussing this program with a sales manager of a client who bemoaned the inability of the medical industry to police its members. When the trillions of dollars this nation spends in health care and the need to know who is qualified to be credentialed are considered, would a centralized process be viable? He says no. It is not a priority. Credentialing does exist, but it is as diverse as the number of providers and health plans. Further, providers can move between plans and facilities. In reality, this author believes that cost containment of screening is always attractive when costs can be removed from an organization, applied consistently, and standardized for a large group of "contractors" who move between organizations.

At the very least, this is a way to look at the problem a little differently. The differing focuses from various views of screening demand an overarching function that can help foster policy for all functional areas. It is recommended that if the organization has a security function that they participate in, or even lead the effort from a policy perspective as HR is focused on employment. Purchasing, or some other function, leads the contractor efforts, and vendors and consultants are led all over the map. All have access to some level. All need to be screened in a consistent and transparent manner.

Food for Thought

1. Does your organization have categories of risk that are addressed by different packages of screens or is yours a one-size-fits-all model?
2. Do you screen or credential? Do you understand the difference?
3. What is the cost of recruiting and training in your business? If you have a bad hire that you could have screened out and you have to replace them, are you counting this as a cost of doing inadequate or thin screens on new hires?
4. Is the security organization involved in policy and standards of doing background checks in the organization?

References

Elliot, R. (2007). Screening in Southeast Asia-Pacific. *Security Management.* Retrieved December 16, 2009, from http://www .securitymanagement.com/article/screening-southeast-asia-pacific.

E-RAILSAFE. (n.d.). *E-RAILSAFE.* Retrieved from http://www.e-railsafe .com/.

Fair Credit Reporting Act (FCRA) § 1681, 15 U.S.C. §§ 601–625. (2004). Retrieved from http://www.ftc.gov/os/statutes/031224fcra.pdf.

Lublin, J. S. (2002, March 11). Check, Please: Who are those people working alongside you? Too often, nobody has bothered to ask. *Wall Street Journal, 25.* Retrieved from http://www.firstcontacthr.com/ pdf/checkplease.pdf.

National Association of Professional Background Screeners. (2006). *NAPBS.* Retrieved from http://www.napbs.com/.

Nixon, W. B., & Kerr, K. M. (2008). *Background screening and investigations: Managing hiring risk from the HR and security perspectives.* Burlington, MA: Elsevier.

United States Citizenship and Immigration Services. (n.d.). *United States citizenship and immigration services.* Retrieved from http://www .uscis.gov/portal/site/uscis.

United States Department of Justice. (2009). *United States Department of Justice.* Retrieved from http://www.justice.gov/criminal/fraud/ websites/idtheft.html.

12

POLICIES AND PROCEDURES: CREATING A FRAMEWORK FOR PREVENTION AND REACTION

INTRODUCTION

Thus far, we've discussed various facets of violence in the workplace as well as specific policy and procedure to follow in the prevention and resolution and restoration processes. At this point, it's time to synthesize the information provided and create a Violence in the Workforce Program (WPV) that is initially outlined in interlocking *policies*, *procedures*, and *business rules* that address inevitable problems and create a flexible solutions with specific processes that address any ongoing and changing issues. It is important that these violence prevention and reaction policies, procedures, and rules interlock and support one another in conjunction with all known risks a particular organization faces, its culture and its communication processes, hiring practices, organizational structure, and training strategies for both new and current associates. These policies, procedures, and business rules should be trained on and socialized through all levels of management and reinforced periodically. An effective reaction to any potential or actual event is predicated on each and every associate having a clear understanding of the policies, procedures, and rules that provide direction in the prevention of and response to workplace violence.

To begin the policy process or to review the policies that are already in place, it is time for the security professional to look across the aisle and partner with the HR professional and jointly engage in policy discussions. This process will blend the program organization-wide and give the process authority and credibility throughout the business. Normally, the policy process is broken into distinct discussions. First, policies should create a general purpose and guidelines. Second, procedures produce the reactive steps and enforce rules that draw lines that should not be crossed, therefore, driving organizational behavior. For example, if the business never hires a convicted, violent felon, then the hiring process would never allow a known felon into the interview process under any circumstance. This becomes a business rule that cannot be violated.

Policies are the what, why, some who and when, but very little how. The policy setting process begins by determining who develops the charter of organization and who is responsible to drive or lead the process. The procedures determine who is responsible to the reactive component of whom, how, and when reactive or proactive measures are taken. The rules should be codified and known to the implementers and action teams who are responsible for the day-to-day enforcement. Prior to policy development, consideration needs to be given to the ethical, legal, and organizational culture. It is recommended that if the organization has a policy committee, the stakeholders of prevention and reaction to WPV be asked to provide input. Moving from theoretical to actual policy development is not an easy jump. For example, there may be reluctance by the workforce, union representatives in some cases, or front-line managers to deal with the issues making early intervention and reaction to symptoms, or even dealing with the actual events, difficult. This reluctance results in lost opportunities to mitigate or eliminate the problem when it is the most manageable. As mentioned earlier, violent individuals will only accelerate and increase their impact over time. Early intervention with a suspected violent situation or person means less disruption, and even avoidance of tragedy, within the organization. Therefore, policies and procedures must make the act of reporting incidents a requirement. The methodology must be clear and compliance encouraged. These issues need to be surfaced, discussed, and addressed in the policies and procedures that are codified and modified over time.

Guidelines for Effective Workplace Violence Policy Programs

In the cornerstone text for *Human Resources Management*, Twelfth Edition, by Mathis and Jackson (2008), the authors offer guidelines in effective policy programs. The author acknowledges this work and has used the general categories as inspiration to create categories tailored to the focus to WPV.

1. *Consistency of application*—The policies created must align with the goals of the organization and be consistently applied by all of the managers in the organization. When facing a challenging process or person, managers seek guidance from policy bodies. However, caution should be taken to ensure that policies are not written so tightly that they are routinely broken without consequence. When this happens, the policies become meaningless beyond filling a binder or shared server file.

2. *Required for risk mitigation and due diligence*—The policies, procedures, and rules in force must be needed to create the desired outcome and adjusted as the milieu changes or the risks morph. Policies need to be reviewed at least annually or if the risks change or the legal environment changes. Failure to review and update procedures could inadvertently create holes in the process or be outdated based on emerging risks to your business with regards to violence. In some cases it might mean that a legal liability was created. For example, if policies are so old that they do not address the misuse of email or text messaging to bully employees or threaten coworkers, then the appropriate process to deal with this emerging threat falls short.

3. *Relevance to your mission*—Does the policy, whether it is being created or is under review, fully apply to the risk model, the organization, and does it align with the business culture? Policies need to apply to all employees, contractors, and consultants, vendors and visitors. For example, if the background screening being done is asking for credit checks, evaluate if that really applies to the current employee base and associated job descriptions.

4. *Sensible based on cultural and legal requirements*—A legal professional should review all policies, procedures,

and organizational rules. The organization does not want, through the best intentions; inadvertently violate the FCRA, Equal Employment Opportunity Act (EEOC) or the OSHA Uniform Services Employment and Reemployment Rights Act (USERRA), or any other body of law. If policies are too complex to be understood by employees and managers who are charged with compliance, the risk of those policies being ignored or applied incorrectly increases. Using plain English and including examples of what a violation is and is not might prove to be beneficial. However, write broadly enough to allow the policy to be appropriate in scope with respect to the issues involved. Remember, your culture needs to be a factor in your planning. There are many approaches to process that are compliant but are consistent with company culture.

5. *Realistic*—In the case of WPV, it is certainly reasonable for employees to have an expectation of a workplace free of violence. It is also reasonable for an employer to expect its employees and other constituent groups not to engage in violence, acts of intimidation, threats or threatening behavior, bullying, or any other action that implies violence. Where the nuance may lie is in enforcement and action. It is reasonable that, if fighting occurs, all participants would be sent home until an investigation is conducted. Therefore, make sure that any procedures are realistic within the organization's environment for quick, fair, and accurate interpretation of the incidents. It is critical to advance the correct response to a threat or a perceived act of bullying as an example. But if procedures work well at the corporate office where plenty of security resources near the flagpole exist, does it work just as effectively out on the end of the string for the employees who are home based in Butte, Montana?

6. *Rolled out and reinforced*—The Internet and online processes, or the paper handbooks that are given to the employees during the onboarding process, can all be done in an organized fashion—documenting the program and process rollout so every employee is trained and informed. Chapter 13 discusses training and includes strategies that may help keep violence prevention in the front of the minds of all employees. Without a sound rollout, maintenance

and a refresher process of both policy and actions covered by policies, like screening, are disregarded or have a staggered start. Often the policies that need to be communicated are put into an employee handbook with the procedures often placed in an associated manager's handbook or guidelines that outline procedures for handling issues as they arise. The rules are found in both places but, certainly, there are some differences. For example, the employee handbook might indicate that the policy of the organization is to conduct pre-employment background screening and drug testing. It may also mention that the organization conducts annual, ongoing screens. However, rules concerning what specific kinds of checks are conducted and the rules surrounding the pass/fail criteria are contained in the managers' guidelines.

Unfortunately, according to a 2005 Bureau of Labor Statistics survey, most organizations do not have a policy that addresses all of the various forms of violence in the workplace. As you can see in Figure 12-1, the private sector has less than 30 percent of businesses that have violence-related policies and even fewer, 20 percent, have policies regarding clients and customers. Therefore, if an organization has a policy of any sort that acknowledges all flavors of the problem, it is ahead of the game. The policies should be broad enough from a violence source perspective to include customers, vendors, clients, domestic violence, and external violence. The procedures should be specific enough to address the violence or threats by type.

Background Screening Policies

In tackling this process, let us begin by discussing the first touch an organization may have with an individual who is entering its workforce. Again, this approach should extend to all contingent groups including nonemployees who have frequent access to employees or assets. Hopefully, at this point, the organization has an onboarding process that includes background, and possible drug screening, that, hopefully, weed out the obvious mismatches of individuals who would not fit into the organization's risk profile. Within the HR process, there should be a policy that

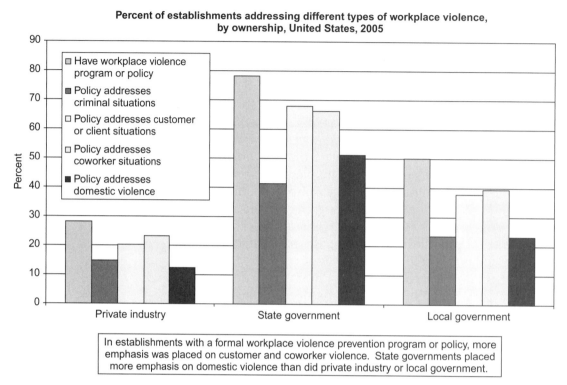

Figure 12-1. Sources of violence and policy coverage. *Source*: Bureau of Labor Statistics, Survey of Workplace Violence Prevention, 2005.

clearly states that *all* employees will be screened, and failure to pass the background check, based on specific criteria, means the offer of a job will be rescinded if the issue violates the organization's risk model. So assume that the candidate has been made an offer that lays out the responsibilities the individual will undertake as a part of your business and you have explained the benefits thereof. Contract discussions with contractors are made and consultants and vendors, who have gone through a vetting process, signed the appropriate agreements and are vetted through a screening process similar to that of the employees. These requirements should be included in a policy, generally, and specifically, in company procedures. Corporate security should be comfortable with types of checks being completed in addition to other constituent groups like HR, legal, and safety, and functional senior management should have full support of the process.

If the company already has a policy to screen all employees, it should generally state that exceptions to the guidelines of convictions that would deny a candidate employment. These policies and procedures should have a provision to specifically deal with exceptions. For example, if your HR and functional management are aware of a candidate who has a past incident that is normally a deal breaker in the hiring motion, the candidate has accurately disclosed the incident, like a criminal conviction or an employment termination for cause, but the organization still wants to make a hire, have a clearly stated and understood appeal process allowing the hiring manager to state his or her case. The case should be reviewed at a senior level by the chief security officer, director or vice president of HR, senior counsel, or senior manager who has profit and loss responsibility, or even the general manager of the business. Ultimately, these individuals have legal responsibility to the owners, stockholders, and board of directors as to why any policy guidelines are not strictly enforced. To say this doesn't happen is naive. There may be particular skill sets your business requires or the hiring decision makers feel the risks of impact are not great enough to pass on a talented candidate.

For example, having come from an Olympic background where "Ice makers" are not easily come by might require some flexibility. But these exceptions must be made with eyes wide open at a high enough level in the business to accept the risk. If company guidelines are, say, 7 years to be completely off of any court ordered sentence and it's been 6½ years, should that be close enough? These are the kinds of exceptions that the appeal process will face.

Access Polices

Organizations should have strong security strategies that prevent, deter, detect, and respond to external threats, including violence. Organizations should also have a tight facility and information system access policy that maintains a level of integrity around the perimeter (physical and cyber) and within the structure that keeps visitors from wandering through the facility or systems unescorted. Requiring escorts for certain constituent groups, like visiting family or friends, customers and vendors, nonemployee tours, and professional or civil meetings that you allow into your facilities on a regular or ad hoc basis, should be understood by all. Many companies design or retrofit facilities so that there is a layer of security requiring electronic card access between the meeting room area and general office areas. Food services can deliver lunches and snacks during breaks to the meeting rooms to prevent visitors from wandering off during downtime.

From the physical security perspective, these policies and procedures should prevent spouses or former spouses, friends and former friends, from gaining easy access to employees or individuals inside the business. Remember, domestic violence can enter a site without prior warning, so having an access process that addresses this is crucial. One of the most effective tools is to require some sort of early notification of upcoming visits. This practice should improve the efficiency of check-ins of large visitor groups and discourage surprise visits from potentially violent individuals. Therefore, procedures should require this process, presented in a clearly stated manner in post-orders of security officers, and routinely enforced. A little embarrassment of an employee who forgets to call down is a small price to pay to prevent an incident.

During a recent incident in which a former spouse was attacked while entering her workplace, the security director was quick to point out it is the policy of this particular organization to escort its employees who work late or request an escort to their cars or even meet an employee in the parking lot and walk with the employee when they are concerned about personal safety or has been threatened.

Access cards and ID cards are often viewed as one entity but they are really two or more. A visitor should be required to provide an artifact for identification (driver license, passport, or any other government-issued ID) when requesting access to the premises. Countersigning by the known employee is also recommended. In some cases, there are companies that only require a vendor to produce a business card or an ID from the vendor's company to be granted access. As many companies do not budget much for tam-perproof or easily reproduced IDs, it is recommended that government IDs be the standard. Visitors receive an ID card that is temporary and expires after one day. Contractors may be given a permanent ID and even an associated access card. In many cases, these cards have very similar or even exact access to most employees if the contractor has a long-term contract. So the ID should designate the individual as a contractor and be different from the ID an employee carries.

All of the permutations and combinations just discussed concerning how an organization functions in regard to the ingress and egress of people into a location need to be covered in the access procedure. Such policies and pro-cedures should also be synced with post-orders, updated regularly, and explained to all, so that if a visitor is seen in the server room without an escort, an authorized employee can approach the visitor and ask, "May I help you?" All too often employees see access control as a security responsi-bility, but in reality, the real security comes from the rank and file who notice what and who is out of place and take the initiative to find out why this person or thing does not fit. Writing a policy and procedure that requires challenging unknown individuals as to their purpose on-site is mean-ingless if the reality is that the policy is not practiced.

The procedure of access control should address the issue of former and suspended or terminated employees. Collection of the employee's access card without notifying security or key personnel is risky and could be a hole in the process that all employees know about, including the employee who was just terminated, for acts of intimidation or threats. If a former employee can access the premises through a loading dock, truck entrance, blocked exit used for smokers or employees who do not want to go "all the way around" to the employee entrance/exit, is always a concern. All of the policies and pro-cedures in the world cannot pretend to deal with actual prac-tices. So the question that needs to be addressed is, "Do the procedures match the practices?"

The policy(s) that is central to this process is the one that deals specifically with acts of intimidation, threats or implied threats, cyber stalking, bullying, weapons, assault, and all other forms of violence. It is important that the organization clearly states the prohibition for these activities in or to your associates. This is not the time to be subtle. Clearly stating what it is that constitutes a violation that puts constituents on notice that violations are grounds for action against the offender ranging from disciplinary action up to and including termination for even one offense *and* prosecution. It should also state that all reports will be investigated and the appropriate action will be taken. The policy should state what functional group within the organization is the lead here. If it is corporate security, then specifically state it will investigate these acts. If corporate security is the group designated to receive the reports, state the fact that reporting is a requirement. Provide employees with the ways information can be reported. Do not make reporting difficult. A call, an email, an anonymous tip line—all of these examples are viable and all should be considered depending upon the size, scope, and geographical challenges of the organization. However the reporting structure is set, it should allow for 24/7 reporting.

The procedure that dictates how to respond to these reports should not be for complete employee-wide dissemination. Response procedures should be revealed gradually and include discussions about the plan, how and who should investigate, what deliverables are required, including investigative summaries and reports, who should review, and who the decision makers are by title. The smaller the organization, the more compact this process may be, but documentation of what will be done, by whom and when, should be understood. There may be immediate actions that need to be taken to ensure the safety and security of both people and assets. A "punch list" that outlines how to deactivate access to systems, as well as physical entry, should be developed and available for immediate use. If an error is made in deactivation, access can always be reactivated. These are some key areas that should be addressed in any response policy and in the more detailed procedures.

- What is the policy regarding weapons?
- Does the organization fully understand the implications regarding "zero tolerance"?
- How often are policies reviewed for accuracy, and are they up-to-date? Is an annual review enough?

- How does the organization define violence? Does the definition include bullying or implied threats like "You'd better get this done, or I'll whip your butt!" If the location's culture is such that these or similar comments are "okay" if the employee has a smile on his or her face and senior managers make such threats, the policy regarding "zero tolerance" can be misconstrued. This is considered "crossing the line" from just a casual comment and not appropriate. A quick consulting session may be more appropriate in this case than termination of a contractor in an employment relationship. And how many employees have threatened to "blow up" their laptops when the screen freezes when working on a deadline?

There should be an investigative component to such comments that can objectively look at the action and surrounding facts before disciplinary action is taken. This approach does not refer to clear acts or actions such as those of 9/11, but it may be the more appropriate response when a weapon is brandished or a punch is thrown.

Zero-Tolerance Policies—Is It the Right Thing to Do?

Many businesses and organizations choose to use "zero-tolerance" language in their policies. This statement constitutes a rule built in to policies that basically states that the organization dismisses and potentially prosecutes offenders for even a first offense. What this means is that any proven incident of violence or threat of violence is grounds for immediate termination, revocation of access privileges, or cancelation of a contract for services. The logic here is to denote the level of seriousness the organization places on violence or potential violence. This approach dictates a firm commitment to deal with any issue in a swift and consistent manner.

From a practical standpoint, a zero-tolerance policy may not be as effective as one might believe. Anecdotally, in connection with investigations undertaken by the author, early reporting was discouraged inadvertently. There are cases in which witnesses related earlier incidents of lesser degrees of severity during the investigation of a serious incident. If known by HR or management, the ultimate incident may have been averted by early intervention. The witness knew the company was firing employees for threats under a zero-tolerance policy and decided not to report the lesser incidents with the belief that he was doing the perpetrator a favor by preventing him or her from receiving severe, adverse employment action. If, in this example, the company had a little more leeway to levy discipline that was progressive and fit the offense, then the witness advised that he would have reported the incident in the hopes that the perpetrator could get help or a warning.

This position is, in no way, a call to be "soft" on perpetrators of violence. It is a flexibility that not only treats violence or threats of violence seriously, but also encourages reporting. No doubt, this is a fine line. But if a witness hears of or sees actions that are of concern and the policy is zero tolerance, then the most casual of comments may be grounds for dismissal. Again, the threat to throw your laptop through the window needs to be investigated and an appropriate disciplinary tactic applied.

Another example of confusion with the zero-tolerance position is the disciplinary process itself. If the organization's policy language is "subject to disciplinary action up to and including dismissal," your process could flex to a less severe action when activities like inappropriate language or gestures occur that cause concern from coworkers. Where the manager's guidelines might give recommendations for kinds of disciplinary language, like in first-time offenses of a particular action, a three-day suspension is the correct action. The concept of progressive discipline has been used in businesses for many years. The concept here is to use a set of progressive steps leading to disciplinary action that eventually results in dismissal if the offending employee does not mend his or her ways. If the organization favors progressive discipline, zero tolerance may not be the appropriate approach. However, for extreme violations, progressive discipline should never apply. The option should always be available for dismissal and prosecution of the violence-prone individual who acts out in the workplace.

Weapons Policies—Are They Necessary?

The mention of guns or weapons in America, at a minimum, will generate a lively discussion in most social engagements. Almost everyone has an opinion regarding gun control or the need to eliminate, modify, or alter current weapons policies at the national, state, or local level. As a society, firearms have been regulated in some form or fashion in an attempt to keep them from criminals or criminal activity while allowing weapons to be in the hands of law-abiding citizens and those organizations, like the local, state, and federal law enforcement agencies that protect us all.

These laws and regulations are continually debated from the local town hall to the local bar. Congress wrestles with the constitutionality of any regulations and this has been a hot button since the first attempts to prevent firearms back in 1934. The advocates of gun control argue that gun control is about keeping guns away from individuals who are at risk of using the weapon for illegal purposes. The debate around gun control extends to the purchase, ownership, and even transfer of weapons or firearms. Even the use of the word "weapon" is debated.

The two major pieces of legislation at the federal level are the National Firearms Act of 1934 and the Gun Control Act of 1968. During the height of the prohibition era in America, machine guns and short barrel guns, like sawed-off shotguns, were viewed as a real threat. Consequently, strict regulation requirements were enacted. In 1968, interstate transfers of guns, limits on certain types of assault weapons, mail order, and interstate sale or transfers of guns began to be regulated. The debate also deals with issues around the licensing of manufacturers, importers, and gun dealers. Deschenaux, J. (December 2000).

The aforementioned laws refer to society as a whole and leave specific gun policies to the organization to decide based on the circumstance. Policy can, and should, be created to prevent weapons from being on the premises of a business. Beyond armed security forces, in some instances and depending on the organization, weapons should be left in the hands of law enforcement and out of the hands of employees, contractors, consultants, and vendors. Care should be taken to include visitors who may have interactions within the organization in these policies.

If the appropriate level of physical, logical, and operational security is in place, there is no need for weapons in the workplace. If stakeholders in the organization are sensitive to and have a finger on the pulse of the employee base, safety concerns that might drive or motivate an individual to want to bring a weapon into the workplace will be known. If someone is living in fear of violence, he or she might risk bringing a weapon onto the premises if he or she believes that adequate protection is not afforded by the businesses security measures. Or if the person feels threatened by a coworker or contractor, vendor, or customer, the person might run the risk of hiding a weapon in a vehicle or briefcase. So, again, a holistic approach to the issue of violence deters the need to bring a gun to work.

Any policy should be clear, avoiding any gray areas that can be interpreted in a way that creates loopholes in the minds of employees or other contingent groups. The policy should be broad and comprehensive enough to include everyone. No guns, firearms, or weapons should be allowed on company premises. In Arizona, you need to be careful on the "premises" issue as there is a law that allows weapons in vehicles, but, in every other instance, make sure you are clear that weapons are expressly forbidden (Pangburn, 2009). Watch out for the word "authorized." This word may suggest to the employee or consultant who has a concealed carry permit who might view that permit as a license to bring a gun to work. Post notices about this policy at entrances, cover it in orientation training, have it in signed employee handbooks. Notify all constituents of the employer's right to search company property like lockers, desks, and any personal baggage that a person might bring to work like purses, briefcases, shopping bags, and rollers that often accompany traveling employees. If a company web site is used as a part of your policy dissemination process, be sure to highlight policies that address weapons. If there is not an electronic process, an acknowledgment can accompany the training (see the next chapter).

An important policy to have associated with weapons policies is the search policy. Be sure that such policies communicate that the organization has the right to look through boxes, purses, and any other thing that is brought in to the workplace. This policy can be written as tight as the risk is and include the right to conduct X-raying of mail and deliveries to searching purses when employees come to work.

Vehicles on-site will be the biggest issue to address. This topic should be fully discussed by the policy team. Many organizations exclude vehicles from policies due to the enforceability standpoint, and the organization's ability to draw the secure line at the door to the building.

CMT's Role in the Policy Process

The CMT is the core body that will eventually be on the leading edge of any incident, whether large or small. The CMT should represent all major stakeholders and oversee the response and recovery portion of any incident of violence. Many times this team is the leading resource in the design and training of the response team and then acts as the clearing house via the Crisis Management Center (CMC) when an incident occurs. Therefore, the CMT should participate in, if not write or help write, the many critical policies, procedures, and rules in the area of violence prevention and response.

The CMT will often receive additional training themselves as the ombudsmen of the company who will step forward to manage an incident over the direction of senior managers who are normally focused on the day-to-day business and not looking at these issues at the granular level. By doing so, the CMT is an asset and is often called out in responses to requests for information (RFI) or requests for proposal (RFP) as a business advantage. Business continuity and DR strategies that are real and not just on paper are differentiators in the marketplace.

Each member of the CMT will be able to give valuable insight to the risks and response impacts to his or her particular constituent group. This person can often respond to how a particular policy will be viewed or determine how and if the policy will be enforced on the line.

The CMT can also provide insight as to how training should be done in the communication phase of the policy process. Is an electronic or web-based training effective across the entire organization or will there have to be combinations of live and online-based approaches? The CMT can also provide effective input into reporting strategies that will be written into procedures that make sense across the enterprise. The CMT will know when a particular message may be diluted by certain senior managers. The CMT will identify the "sacred cows" that are not seen or understood by senior managers at the associate level with respect to policy.

It is mission critical to have the CMT stack hands on the process and agree that they can make the plan work if an act of violence occurs. The senior management representative on the CMT should assure the team that the executive leadership will stand behind the initiatives and support the dismissal of a high-producing sales executive who is a habitual bully.

Communication is a key component of any effective policy process. In the world of violence prevention and detection response, it may be life saving. Communication starts with the newly hired employee who is just entering the doors of the business for the first time. This might be a new consultant or contractor who is now going to be on-site for an extended period of time. One of the most effective processes used during the Salt Lake City Winter Olympic Games was the orientation. If a person was going to be on staff for the Salt Lake Olympic committee, he or she was required to go through orientation to be granted access to any venue during the planning phase. During the event phase, all volunteers, sponsor employees, consultants, police officers, and vendors were required to go through an orientation that was at the front end of all specific assignment training for the games. At first, the classes consisted of four to five individuals but, as the event drew closer, the classes swelled in size.

It was in these first days that the policies, procedures, and rules concerning security, safety, and violence in the workplace were addressed. It started the process of creating a culture of boundaries that affected words and actions.

The boundaries addressed words and actions that were unacceptable and enforced via the policies, procedures, and rules. It is a critical notification to all constituent groups that the organization is serious about deterring and avoiding WPV. Policies should be rolled out using electronic means, as well as having stand-up meetings that address this issue periodically in work teams. Annual reviews of policies that address workplace violence may happen during code of conduct or employee handbook reviews that call attention to violence as one of the key topics. In the following chapter, training will be covered which is the cornerstone to the WPV process.

Food for Thought

1. Does the organization have a full specter of policies that address violence prohibition and prevention?
2. Does the company have a weapons policy?
3. If the organization's employees were surveyed today, would they know all available methods of reporting an incident or suspected threat?
4. Who in the business is responsible to investigate acts of violence, threats, or acts of intimidation?

References

Deschenaux, J. (2000, December). Court strikes law banning workplace gun policies. *HR Magazine*, Retrieved from http://www.accessmylibrary.com/article-1G1-172516736/court-strikes-law-banning.html/.

Mathis, R. L., & Jackson, J. H. (2008). *Human resources management* (12th ed.). Mason, OH: Thomson South-Western.

Pangburn, J. (2009). http://www.AZBiz.com. Territorial Newspapers. *The Daily Territorial*. Retrieved from http://www.azbiz.com/articles/2009/10/17/news/doc4ad8a8d8022bc359419376.txt/.

Sources of violence and policy coverage. (*Source*: Bureau of Labor Statistics, Survey of Workplace Violence Prevention, 2005.)

TRAINING

INTRODUCTION

Anyone who has ever spent time in the military, mastered a musical instrument, learned a new language, or participated in any organized sports will recall the importance of training and practice. In the case of WPV training, people should be trained to develop skills that hopefully never have to be used in a real-life situation.

Law enforcement, first responders, and firefighters are constantly training to combat the negatives of life, whether the activity includes climbing ladders to fight a fire or facing an active shooter. This is not a skill a person is drawn to in most businesses and organizations. In fact, someone might choose such a profession with some idea that the risk for violence is decreased. In other words, no one goes to work wanting or expecting to be bullied, threatened, and certainly not shot! This paradigm is so foreign that many who have been trained to be aware of the potential for violence or those of us who have trained teams who deal with the realities of violence find a certain amount of resistance to fully engage in discussions or practical exercises without some degree of seriousness.

Depending on the industry or work environment, there might be some disbelief that anything involving serious violence, like we see on the news, could ever happen. Similar to addiction, denial is a systemic factor in overcoming the problem of violence and the prevention of it.

Imagine a person who was recently awarded a promotion to supervisor. This person may not recognize the fact that the job is one in which a subordinate or coworker could report an implied threat or any form of questionable behavior in the workplace. Perhaps even more likely, the job might put newly promoted supervisor in a position to be a target of a threat or act of violence. Part of filling the role of this job is dealing with unpleasant situations. The passion required of a person in such a position to learn the skills necessary to manage and even prevent threats of violence and actual violent behavior in the workplace is not like learning Spanish or Portuguese.

Even though an organization may have dynamic, well-thought-out, and well-written policies, procedures, and business rules, if the constituent groups within the organization are not aware of what to do and when to do it, the preparation activities become meaningless when a real need for action arises. The work that has been done, up until now, means that the hard work, coordination, and expense of the program are about to start. This hard work begins with organizing an effective training strategy that should include the following:

- Orientation training that includes initial WPV awareness training
- Initial program rollout
  - To rank and file employees, contractors, and consultants
  - To managers and functional leadership
- Annual employee WPV awareness training
- CMT training that is specific to WPV, first responders, and key constituent groups
- Tabletop exercises
- WPV drills or exercises.

Orientation Training

All employees and contractors in their course of connection to an organization need information that provides knowledge and direction with respect to how someone can get things done within the course of business. Who are the contacts and what is the purpose of an employee or contractor on-site? This general information is often overwhelming to new personnel and may be downloaded with a cadre of useful, and some not-so-useful, information that may complete a due diligence responsibility. Very often it is during this "new hire download" where most employers include information regarding violence in the workplace. This may or may not be effective, even though it is certainly viewed as efficient. Employees or consultants who are new to the organization are probably somewhat wide eyed as they're excited about the possibilities the new position holds. The creative trainer may be able to impress some valuable information upon these newbies.

1. Violence prevention is important and not taken lightly. Even casual remarks have consequences that should and will be addressed.
2. There are policies. Do not engage in simply reading the policy word for word. If the business has a well-written policy, the first few paragraphs should be tattooed in the minds of the orientation attendees.
3. Policies may be stored on an intranet that can be accessed by employees and contractors to allow for a more in-depth study. Certain points of the policy should be made crystal clear: acts of intimidation, bullying in the workplace, threats, assaults, and any other form of violence are to be reported immediately. Allow reports to be made anonymously if necessary.
4. Be sure to clearly state to whom the reports should be addressed and how to contact that person. Limit the contact information to one number and one email address if possible. Also, provide the encouragement of both the carrot and the stick. It is a part of each person's job responsibility to report acts of intimidation, bullying, threats, assaults, and any other form of violence in the workplace. Not reporting is a violation of policy.

Keep this training on point and to the point. Information contained in training should be reinforced in the employee handbook, whether disseminated electronically or in written form. The purpose of the aforementioned training conducted with new hires or contractors should cover any gap that exists until the employee is provided the level of training described below. This training may occur through either an organization-wide rollout of a new program or an annual review with current employees.

Initial Program Rollout

Planning is required if the business does not already have a program in place. A part of this planning may mean that training material needs to be purchased. This material should be of a caliber that creates awareness and includes information that addresses the question of why a new process is being rolled out. Consideration should be given to bringing an outside expert or two to guide the process. Companies will often roll out a program to its key managers for the purpose of getting candid feedback on the material provided and the effectiveness of the approach. By this time, the procedural process should already be created and the information is now being disseminated. The first task is to convince the audience that violence can happen at work. This discussion should include the possible sources of violence—both internal and external.

Domestic violence and bullying in the workplace should also be included. Although the number of homicides in the workplace is decreasing year over year, there are some indications that threats and acts of intimidation are increasing. Based on this data, the scope of training should be established accordingly. If the business functions as a retail, gaming, or entertainment environment, be sure to make the constituents aware of the potential for dealing with angry or violent customers or guests. Refer to Chapter 9 of this book for information pertaining to anger in the workplace. Define the organization's potential for violence ensuring constituents are always informed of the possible risks ranging from external sources to risks involving employees within the organization.

There are several media sources from which to draw to reinforce awareness in this training that extends beyond a regurgitation of FBI or other statistics. Use just enough of this data to size the problem for trainees. An extensive discussion into the facts and figures is not necessary to make the point that violence in the workplace is a reality and needs to be taken seriously by the entire staff. Employees involved in this training should be able to discuss what they see as the risks in their particular functional area. The trainer may be surprised to learn of new or emerging threats and even perceived threats within the organization. This learning can provide some time to develop countering tactics.

Have a discussion about recent acts of violence in the news, if possible, and research incidents in similar industries or geographical areas. If the company has experienced a recent incident, it could be discussed in a general way, being careful to maintain confidentiality for any witnesses or victims. Discussing examples demonstrates the continued need for vigilance. Talk about the progressive nature of violence, levels of violence, and the need to react quickly to the problem with decisive action. This is not a time for debate. Organizational policies should be discussed including those that apply to weapons, access policies, and the reporting process in place designed to facilitate getting all appropriate parties involved.

Interlock ongoing security processes and preventive procedures that counter known threats as part of the overall strategy. This should stress the importance of supporting and following security procedures. These procedures are set to aid in deterring and preventing violence in the workplace so that employees are kept safe while allowing them to focus on the organizational tasks at hand. The protection of physical and intellectual property is important too; however, protecting the people who are part of the business should be the most important mission.

Changes in coworkers behavior should also be a part of this discussion. Depression, mood swings, and inappropriate behavior like sexual advances should be viewed as areas of concern that may need to be called out in accordance with policy. Although sexual harassment is not a focus of the training, it should be discussed as a possible symptom of a deeper, emerging issue that very well may signal that a violent event is developing. These changes should not be ignored just as the escalation of angry, bullying, or threatening behavior—it all needs to be reported. The ability to reverse and even save the career of a colleague by reporting questionable behavior before a serious event occurs should be mentioned.

All employees need to attend this training. If the organization is serious about prevention of violence, all of the senior leadership should attend the training and be seen in the classes if the training is presented live. If the training methodology is virtually delivered via an intranet or web-based solution, a brief introduction in the training by the CEO or another senior manager demonstrates organizational commitment. There should be plenty of flexibility and an adequate window of time built into the rollout plan to allow vacationing, traveling, or absent employees the chance to be trained. Makeup sessions should also be offered. Keeping good training records is critical. If the organization has a training department, they are a great resource to help with a session strategy that ensures 100 percent of employees get trained.

As briefly mentioned, electronic or virtual rollouts are becoming popular and can be extremely beneficial in ensuring that all employees and associates are trained. The electronic approach provides a 24/7 rollout capability to the organization. For those who work on the weekends or late into the night, this approach can accommodate flexibility that allows focus on the core business during normal working hours. Web-based seminars have become the gold standard with the rise of home-based workforces and computer workstations being standard issue throughout an enterprise. Emails can be used to remind and notify managers of attendance. If an employee does not complete the training after being provided with repeated electronic reminders, the supervisor and eventually the managers can be notified to ensure compliance. Tests can be embedded into the web-based seminars and video can be streamed to give the presentation life.

Training for Supervisors and Managers

If training is created in modules, a supplemental module can be provided specifically for supervisors and managers who may receive complaints or reports of threats or implied threats. Supervisors and managers should be given an additional level of training that addresses tactics for intervention or additional resources to assist in the intervention. These resources might include things like EAPs, investigative resources like corporate security or HR, and intervention and coaching strategies that allow for intervention in the early stages of a potentially violent situation. These front-line and second-line managers have the most interaction with employees and are the ones who are most likely to be a witness to or hear about changes in attitudes and actions.

Union stewards and union leadership should also be approached about participation here. Policies and procedures concerning violence should never be a part of any labor negotiation or contract as the safety of employees within the organization is paramount to a business's vitality. But the reality is that some workers will report to their union representatives issues that may involve troubling changes in a coworker's behavior rather than talking to a supervisor. This is not the case in all union shops, but this issue does exist and should be considered when creating and evaluating your reporting processes. Do not assume because of this reluctance to follow a strict process of reporting an issue to management that a reporting employee disagrees with the policy. Each employee, regardless of his or her role within the company, has a stake here, and employees should be seen as a constituent group. The unfortunate dynamic that has to be navigated through in the labor relations area is not safety but concern that a direct report to the company management might be misinterpreted by fellow union members. It also is a concern that reporting may result in the loss of a fellow union employee's job. Needless to say, all constituent groups have a lot to lose if a symptom that might lead to potential violence gets rationalized away. Further, the supervisor may be the person whose behavior is troubling the associate.

A tactic that could be used to mitigate these issues is to have an anonymous reporting line as mentioned in earlier chapters that will allow any associate to report suspicions or concerns. Although it is better to have a cooperative witness, at least you would have some information to begin an investigation.

Annual Training

The threat of violence is constant but changes in its form. Annual reviews of the policies and reporting procedures for the workforce are a critical piece of the puzzle. This training provides a platform in which the effectiveness of the program can be discussed. It also exposes newer employees to a more focused view of the program. Some organizations break the review into a more detailed discussion for newer employees and a more truncated version for the seasoned employees. If the training is made compelling and is up-to-date, these two can be blended together nicely. Again, this is an opportunity to gauge the effectiveness of the program. Watch the body language of training attendees. The use of an outside resource can uncover issues that may, for whatever reason, not get reported via the established channels. The author has gotten good intelligence from attendees in seminars that he was able to provide, in an objective manner, to the principles of an organization. This approach removes personalities from the process and helps determine potential roadblocks to reporting and implementation of the program.

Another example of objective input can come through the use of an outside resource that can identify cultural issues that are troubling to the overall health of an organization. For example, there is a growing problem of bullying in the workplace. Bullying is alive and well on the national and international stage. A recent study in the *International Journal of Public Health* reports a decline in bullying among school-age children across all countries, including the United States. However, there is no clear evidence to explain the reasons for the decline. Conversely, in the workplace, the opposite is reported to be true according to a recent article published on NewStar.com indicating that bullying is at epidemic levels posing as aggression among workers (Bonner, 2009). According to Mkay Bonner, Industrial Psychologist, 37 percent of respondents, that is 57 million workers, report to have been the victim of some form of bullying in the workplace (2009). A recent twist in this increase was noted in a Personneltoday.com article that indicates one out of three women in the workplace is a victim of bullying (Gilbert, 2009). Based on this information, it is vital to teach that the culture in the organization does not support these behaviors and such behaviors are forbidden by policy.

The same approach is applicable in the area of domestic violence reports. There is concern that domestic violence may have a negative impact on a person's career. Any reluctance to report the threat of domestic violence needs to be overcome. As discussed in earlier chapters, the workplace can become a battleground for handling domestic disputes. Domestic disputes, unless reported, are unknown to the organization. Employees need to understand that domestic disputes may spill into the workplace, and that it is critical to report these potential issues. The training should focus significant time in discussion of the nature of this type of threat. Coworkers who are aware of domestic issues with the potential victim should be encouraged to risk a friendship to avert a larger tragedy.

Information and training relating to active shooters should be included in all levels of WPV training. There are significant risks to gatekeepers, security personnel, and customer-facing employees. Each of these risks should be addressed and response plans provided. The topic of active shooter is covered, in detail, in the next chapter. Do not avoid this discussion in training out of fear of scaring employees. The risk that an active event will happen is small but it is a possibility. Reinforce that active shooter training is provided as a precaution, just like safety training for passengers on an airplane, where the information is needed but, hopefully, never used.

If you have an inter-organization newsletter or blog that is updated with current information or events, consider putting WPV in the rotation of information that you provide to your constituents to keep the issue fresh in their minds. The message "it could happen here—so be vigilant" should be conveyed.

CMT Training Specific to WPV, First Responders, and Key Constituent Groups

Training of your CMT needs to be crisp, frank, and evergreen. The CMT consists of the individuals who will make the tough decisions like evacuating, calling authorities, initiating investigations, and weighing in on disciplinary actions. These are the individuals who will brief senior managers, address the press, law enforcement, firefighters, emergency responders, and family members. The CMT will mitigate the impact to the business, and make the on-the-ground decisions on the organization's behalf. The first step in assembling the

CMT is to define the positions needed to comprise an effective team.

- Incident manager—This individual will make key decisions and manage the critical response, depending on the event.
- Communications manager—This person will ensure that all who need to know are kept in the loop. He or she summarizes key facts and creates press releases and briefing communiqués.
- Logistics manager—This individual gets everything that is needed, when it is needed, and where it is needed.
- Technical support, EAP, legal, and security are other key areas. And the list goes on.

The aforementioned roles are discussed further in Chapter 14, but, suffice it to say, normally, the primary role of these individuals is not crisis management, in most cases. These individuals have day jobs. So this job is one that may be given as something to participate in on an as-needed basis. Safety, security, and HR are often great sources for key personnel. However, be sure that this team has senior management sponsorship so that it can act with decisiveness and authority. The team's ability to function should not be usurped when an incident occurs.

The absolute best training for this team will be general discussion of the organization and assignments of personnel to the team's various functions. In conjunction with this training, time should be taken for the team to engage in tabletop exercises. These exercises are extremely effective. An outside facilitator or a facilitator from the DR team or corporate security with a background in crisis management is desirable. Asking law enforcement for input is also suggested. Very often, law enforcement will participate in these exercises or, at the very least, are able to provide valuable suggestions to align the response with how things work in jurisdictions where the organization's facilities are located.

Some occupations that are at high risk of encountering violence on a routine basis require specific training. Hospital workers are a prime example. This is especially true in emergency rooms, psychiatric wards, and patient services in general. Hospital security is often required to respond to a situation and intervene without immediate police assistance. Security personnel may or may not be armed. The decision to employ armed or unarmed security is a risk decision made by the individual facility. In this case, training is detailed scenario based and routine practice is required. Such training is outside the scope of this book but is necessary.

Retail associates, convenience store personnel, bar tenders, and gaming employees all need job-specific training to deal with the inherent risks associated with these occupations. My own experience as a bartender in college leads me to believe that this training is often too vague and even nonexistent in smaller businesses. This fact is consistent with the overall lack of policies and programs existing in small businesses due to the monetary costs and time commitment these programs require.

Field Exercises

Field exercises are effective and can be expensive or impactful to your day-to-day business, so conduct these only after plenty of discussion and evaluation. The decision whether or not to evacuate is often a question. These are the kinds of scenarios that need to be evaluated and examined by the CMT during tabletop training. Definitely involve local law enforcement and fire personnel in this process. Let neighbors know that drills are being conducted to avoid any misunderstanding that would embarrass the organization or disrupt another organization or business. It is not a good practice to panic business neighbors, create traffic issues, or invite the press to present a not-so-flattering exposé that would suggest "poor" crisis planning. Be very cautious here.

Summary

Key elements should stream through your training. These key elements include:
- Policies
- Procedures
- Business rules.

Key participants will receive more in-depth training by constituent groups. Key groups include:

- All employees via orientation and annual reviews
- Supervisors and managers
- CMT and first responders
- High-risk group training.

Key methodologies for training include:

- Classroom and electronic delivery
- Specific classroom for CMT and first responders
- Specific classroom tabletop training
- Field exercises.

Key considerations include:

- The use of outside resources like law enforcement or security consultants will keep the discussion interesting and contemporary.
- In times of crisis, people fall back on the level of training that has been provided. Therefore, consistent reinforcement is necessary to keep the process evergreen in the minds of all associates and key team members.

Food for Thought

1. Does the organization do any formal training in regards to WPV?
2. If so, does the training provided seem dated or irrelevant to the issue of WPV?
3. Has the use of tabletop exercises ever been considered in the organization?
4. Is an internal resource available to conduct training or are outside resources more effective?
5. Does the organization have a CMT?

References

Bonner, M. (2009). Working solution: Workplace bullying is increasing. *The News Star*. Retrieved from http://www.thenewsstar.com/apps/pbcs.dll/article?AID=/200910270115/BUSINESS/91026027/.

Gilbert, H. (2009). Personneltoday.com. Reed Business Information. Retrieved from http://www.personneltoday.com/articles/2009/10/15/52566/workplace-bullying-experienced-by-one-in-three-young.html/.

INVESTIGATING INCIDENTS: RESPONDING TO AN ACTIVE SHOOTER

INTRODUCTION

With all of the work an organization has done up to this point, it is hoped that it has created a culture of understanding and communication that will systemically prevent a violent situation from ever forming on its premises. This extends into the external threats as well. The previous chapters established a roadmap for the organization to follow to create a series of layers of security that can prevent, deter, and detect an attack early enough to mitigate its escalation to severe violence. In addition to work done in the establishment of policy, along with a robust training protocol, it is further hoped that the organization is working proactively to root out any issues of violence that are in the early stages. Early identification will serve to nip the whole issue, which may be in the very early stages of potential for violence, in the bud. Unfortunately, no matter how much work is invested in a program with significant time and resources focused on the prevention of workplace violence, an incident still may occur. With the proper planning and strategies in place, the majority of these issues should be in the nature of an implied threat or as a minor act of aggression that is dealt with decisively.

The preceding chapters are host to an in-depth discussion of the types of violence that may originate from both internal and external sources. These discussions include guidance regarding the need to change awareness and culture to attack the issue of denial of the problem of violence happening where you work, volunteer, or attend school. In addition, discussion regarding legal issues, the need to communicate, policies and procedures, and proactive strategies to prevent, deter, delay, or prepare to react to an incident of violence in the workplace is addressed. There is also a discussion that covers dealing with anger in the workplace and associated strategies to address the issue and deal with it in the earliest stage possible along with the need for training and awareness, and creating teams with specialized roles and skills. Preparation is complete and, hopefully, none of these plans will ever have to be initiated.

Unfortunately, it is realistic to suspect that even with the best of plans and designs, violence might occur. And if violence does present itself within the organization, everyone will need to know how to react to the incident by dealing with the threat, implied threat, assault, act of revenge, or even an active shooting. If an act of violence occurs, it will then be the opportunity to react and minimize and mitigate the effects of the incident. Timely actions will help deter similar activities in the future and help employees and the organization prepare to recover. It is at this juncture when all involved will need to act with confidence and decisiveness.

In discussing the recommended actions, the following divides potential incidents into categories that have similar methodologies of response.

1. Threats, implied threats, and acts of intimidation—This includes verbal and written, including electronically transmitted messages.
2. Assaults, battery, or fighting; physical violence that is normally nonlethal—This includes domestic violence in the workplace.
3. Violence involving weapons—Guns and knives are the primary threat here, but bombs or intentional sabotage, vandalism, or cyber attacks are possible.

In this chapter, we briefly cover the first two types of incidents for the sake of a comprehensive review, but the real focus is on the third type of incident, violence involving weapons, which we explain by focusing on active shooters.

Threats, Implied Threats, and Acts of Intimidation

In the case of a threat, a violation of established policies has occurred within the mind of the person reporting the threat. The reporter has hopefully received training in what to report and to whom to avoid losses of valuable time to formulate a response. The allegation should be documented immediately and the threat assessment process should ensue. This activity usually means that the facts of the incident need to be established. So the appropriate investigative organization should initiate an investigation which should gather all the artifacts available, like spontaneous notes from witnesses or supervisors, emails, witness statements, and other salient facts concerning the incident.

If the incident was severe enough, some mitigating actions may have already occurred. The parties involved have been separated or even sent home. If the individuals are still available when the investigative component is on scene, statements should be taken to establish both the facts of the incident and information that might explain the history and define the relationships involved. If the threats are more general in nature, vented toward the entire company or leadership, the interview can be used to decelerate the emotion. The investigators in the author's experience came from the corporate security group. However, HR is often the lead in smaller companies. Often a middle manager or a level of manager removed from the subject might be the appropriate interviewer.

Other evidence should be isolated quickly in case it becomes important later. For example, witnesses might send an account of the incident to a friend via email. That email becomes a spontaneous piece of evidence that may clear up discrepancies or document states of mind of witnesses or the suspect of the incident. Data capture of not only emails but also web activities should be obtained. Any security video should be obtained and a copy made and certified. A witness to accompany the designated investigator should be used if he or she is not a trained investigator. Remember, there may be geographic constraints that might cause getting the evidence from point to point, making chain of evidence a challenge.

A determination needs to be made as to whether or not this is an isolated event or a part of a series of events that have gone unreported. For example, the witnesses will advise, if asked the question, if there have been other incidents that the witness noticed that went unreported or did not seem significant at the time. Now in light of the current situation, the witness may recall a past incident that may indicate an acceleration of frequency or intensity. Look for patterns of behavior. Clustering of patterns and incidents are key indicators of a potential queuing of emotion or frustration which may create a more severe outcome in the future.

In the experience of the author, violent individuals have an exaggerated sense of justice and fairness. In their minds they know right and they know wrong. It almost appears that when the right is maintained then the potentially violent person is in control. The threat may be an attempt by this person to right a wrong that cannot be controlled by conversation or complaints. This person feels powerless.

It is important to look outside the organization for information or prior acts of violence. Check in public records, if possible. Most offenses occur where the person lives, works, or has studied. Check with local court systems for records of violent acts, both civilly and criminally. Former employers may be reluctant to assist but contact the security organization of the former company, explain the situation, and maybe that group will share whatever information they can provide legally.

You may also call the main line of the former employer and ask for the individual being checked. If the response is that the person no longer works there, ask for whoever is taking their calls or ask to speak with the former supervisor. It is possible that the person investigating may be able to speak with a coworker or person who knows the subject and who may be able to provide some helpful information.

Overarching Security Posture

Risk analysis with regard to potentially violent risks should be done prior to any potential events happening within the organization. Potential adversaries should be identified in addition to any persons who are of like mind and disagree with the overall activities or business in which the organization is engaged. For example, if the organization is or has an animal testing laboratory as part of its business, including those found on university campuses, organized adversaries exist that cannot be identified specifically who disagree with related daily activities. These risks should be factored into day-to-day business operations and built into a baseline security plan. If a specific threat is received, the overall security levels can be ratcheted up to accommodate the particular threat. Protocols can be built in that protect a specific employee or location. This activity may require a more rigorous access process during a threat situation.

For example, if awareness of a domestic abuse situation involving an employee comes to light, there is an understanding that this nasty breakup may give rise to an incident. This understanding and awareness should prompt the initiation or improvement to parking lot security or, if the location is in a lease situation, prompt notification to the building owner to increase parking lot patrols. Vehicle and person descriptions should be provided to building security forces. If the organization does not have these types of resources, in most jurisdictions the organization can engage off-duty police details until the situation is resolved. This proactive cost is a small price to pay to deter a tragedy.

If the organization's WPV plan has a CMT, be sure the team is trained to assess threats. If not, consider seeking assistance from law enforcement or an outside consultant who can review objectively the potential risk and provide recommended actions. Certainly a part of the process is to determine the seriousness of the threat and determine whether there is immediate or imminent danger. If the incident is minor and isolated, the decision may be made that dismissal is not the appropriate action and then requires some other form of discipline and action plan to prevent reoccurrence of an internal threat. Or the decision may be made that, based on the type of threat and the circumstances thereof, a discussion with HR and legal may be needed to establish whether a violation of policy has occurred and what appropriate action should be taken regarding the employee.

Another issue to determine is what effect the incident has had on the witnesses, victims, and morale. Do not forget to offer counseling to employees who are affected, either directly or indirectly. EAP counselors can be used as a resource in such cases. Keep the process focused in a 360 degree circle around the subject. These counselors can affect those who come forward with information and those who sit in the shadows and stay silent. This is especially true with business bullies who have abused their positions or even used physical stature to intimidate or humiliate fellow workers. Again, look for patterns of behavior.

Do not assume that a current mental health care professional who may be a part of the EAP process, or even on staff, has the specific training to deal with potentially violent individuals just because he or she is a licensed psychologist. Do the homework here and ask questions about the person's clinical experience in dealing with potentially violent individuals. If this resource does not have that particular skill or background, take the time, effort, and expense to get a professional who can help provide a level of comfort in the creation of the action plan.

The way to mitigate truly or eliminate the threat is to deal with the individual hoping to change his or her decision to ultimately act out on the threat. If the threat was made to scare or control others, then an ultimate violent act is not the motivation. But if the threat is a precursor to an event, then the question is what needs to be done to convince the individual not to commit the violent act. An analogy to this is the bank robbers who decided not to rob the convenience store this particular night because a police car was in the parking lot. They will wait until the police car leaves. The decision to rob the store is already made—it simply becomes an issue of "when."

Continue to look internally for prior evidence of violent tendencies if the subject is known and is an associate with access to your people or systems. Determine whether a prior incident was not reported and why. This relates to your current culture and how it sees outbursts or threats. If there is a high tolerance for threats or threatening behavior, then the likelihood of an actual incident may be closer to happening if earlier threats were not known. Remember that violence and its intensity is often progressive.

Cyber threats and cyber stalking should be taken seriously and the appropriate precautions taken. Refer to Chapter 15 for more insight on this emerging concern. Virtual threats should be considered just as serious as face-to-face verbal threats as many employees now work in virtual settings, like home offices, and report remotely to managers and supervisors.

Assaults, Battery, or Fighting

No one wants to hear that a coworker or friend has been assaulted at work. All of the steps to investigate the incident need to occur *after* the immediate action is taken, separating the parties if possible and the police have been called. In this situation, the main objective is to protect bystanders, gather preliminary information, and assist law enforcement. Minor assaults that seem harmless may turn into a major liability once the victim speaks to a spouse or family member and he or she reports that the employers seemed unsympathetic or encouraged the victim not to report the incident. Be very cautious here. What may be "no big deal" has the potential to turn into a real headache later, so conduct the due diligence and investigate thoroughly the situation and take care of aftermath.

For example, pushing, shoving, and other more minor violent acts should not be tolerated and a full investigation should be conducted. Once the basic facts are known, a decision to call the police should be made quickly. If police review the incident and decide not to file a charge, there may still be a violation of policy that needs to be addressed. The victims or participants in the aggression need to be dealt with and this may require disciplinary action. A key point here is to make the most of the post-event by having stand-up meetings and, where appropriate, email blasts that reinforce the organization's violence prevention policies. The recent incident should be discussed in a sensitive and anonymous manner that lets the rest of the staff see and understand that certain types of behavior will not go unnoticed and will not be tolerated. When this communication is handled in a sensitive way in which it does not embarrass victims, the rest of the associates can be clear that the organization is serious about having an environment that is free from violence. This communication will pay immeasurable dividends by sending notice that aggressive behavior is not a part of the organization's culture.

Violence with Weapons: An Active Shooter

An active shooter is an incident that receives a tremendous amount of review, press, and has, unfortunately, become common in today's society. As mentioned several times in earlier chapters, the good news is that the number of shootings or homicides is declining since the peak in 1994 of over a thousand to less than 500 in 2006 (U.S. Department of Labor, 2009) (Figure 14-1).

For the individual who goes to work expecting to be safe inside the walls of the organization, one incident of an active shooter can not only be life-ending or life-changing for the victims but for their families, witnesses, and company officials as well. The risk is still there and the need

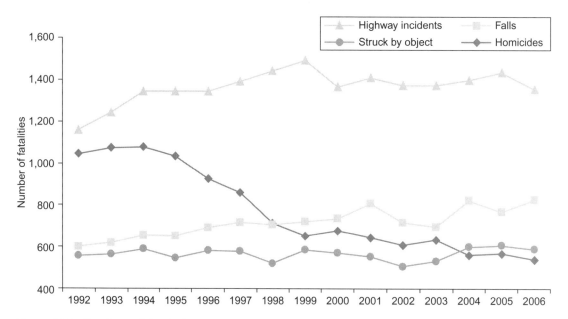

Figure 14-1. Numbers of deaths in the workplace from 1992 until 2006. *Note*: Data from 2001 exclude fatalities resulting from the September 11 terrorist attacks. *Source*: U.S. Bureau of Labor Statistics, U.S. Department of Labor, 2009.

to be prepared still needs to be addressed. Therefore, the organization should train its employees how to respond to an active shooter.

The DHS created a very useful document that can be downloaded from the web that provides a very useful outline of addressing the issue: http://www.dps.mo.gov/ HomelandSecurity/documents/Active%20Shooter/DHS%20 ActiveShooter_Response%20Booklet.pdf. The process outlined in this document, which is available to the public, recognizes that most shooting incidents last anywhere from 10 to 15 minutes and that employees must be ready to deal with this issue if it occurs. Remember that people fall to their level of training in times of crisis, so make this information available and reinforce it in the training process. If employed by a large organization or company, consider training a core of individuals who can act as leadership in an incident.

The information provided by DHS was used as inspiration for the following overarching suggestive actions for all employees.

- Everyone should be aware of their environment—dangers may erupt and seconds, not minutes, are the metric for survival.
- All should know where the exits are—part of orientation training should include evacuation training. If employees become aware of gunfire, they should move away from the event and exit the immediate area, if possible. A recognized concern is members of staff who may become the shooter who will also know the facility. An internal shooter will know that exits will be used when the event unfolds, so exiting the building may not always be possible. That is why the next point is often a more effective tactic.
- If employees have an office or are close to an office, they should move to or stay in that office and secure the door. Conference rooms or other office-type spaces may not have lockable doors, so the door should be barricaded in any way possible. This may require moving heavy furniture or wedging objects against the door to prevent the door from being forced open by the shooter.

- Unfortunately, if the shooter is currently in the employee's immediate area, the only option will be to try to take the shooter down by tackling him or her. This may not seem reasonable but if employees cannot find immediate safety, there may be no alternative but to move quickly toward the shooter.

Remember that if an employee is in a public setting or this associate is a manager or supervisor, his or her moves and directions will likely be followed by subordinates, visitors, and customers. So be aware that employees may be in leadership positions whether they like it or not. As a result, they should be prepared to give direction. If the employee makes a decision to evacuate, chances are many will follow. This person should not spend time trying to convince anyone that this plan of action is the right decision. The move should be made, leaving all personal belongings behind. If possible, this person should help others escape and follow the direction of police who may be coming into the building when employees are exiting. A key point is to remind those exiting the building to make sure their hands are visible at all times. Police tactical teams will be entering the building, weapons drawn, and they will be looking for the active shooter who may decide to leave with the crowd to avoid detection or continue the shooting spree against the police. So having their hands in clear sight is an important topic on which to train.

It is possible that others may be wounded. If the decision is made to assist the wounded, try not to move them, if possible. Remember, the incident is fluid and if employees are to survive, they must be decisive and move quickly. Once employees are at a safe distance, they should call authorities if police are not on the scene.

Hiding out, however, may be the only option. Employees should try to stay clear of the shooter's view. Often, the shooter is looking for targets of opportunity and if the employee is not in the shooter's view, the employee may be spared. Barriers between employees and the shooter delay the shooter's movement and the shooter is more likely to move on. Employees should remain silent, turning off cell phones, and remaining quiet until convinced the incident is over. Police will clear the area methodically and as quickly as safety allows.

As mentioned earlier, if hiding or evacuation is not an option, the only option available is to take aggressive action against the shooter. This may include yelling, throwing any object within reach at the shooter to confuse and delay the shooter. Remember, there is a very good chance that law enforcement is approaching the shooter's position and by delaying or disorienting him or her, these aggressive acts may save a life.

When law enforcement arrives, they will be in teams wearing regular uniforms or tactical gear like helmets and external vests. They may be carrying rifles, automatic weapons, or shotguns. They may even be seen pushing potential victims to the floor to protect them from harm. Law enforcement will be giving commands that employees need to follow immediately and explicitly. As mentioned earlier, employees keeping their hands visible is critical and, when they see law enforcement, they should raise their hands. If an employee is carrying something for some reason, he or she should drop it. Employees do not want to be seen as a threat or be confused as being the shooter. If evacuees cross paths with a law enforcement team entering the facility, they should continue in the direction from which the law enforcement is coming—not stopping or asking for directions.

When a call is placed to law enforcement or 911, the caller should provide the location of the building or facility, the location of the shooter(s), and any description of the shooter(s) describing weapons and numbers of weapons. Callers should let the contacted party know of any potential victims of whom they are aware, including the location of those victims, if possible. Victims will probably not be attended to by the first responders, but once the area is secure, medical responders will assist them.

More than likely, once employees are in a safe location, they will be asked to stay put until they have been questioned regarding the incident. These are "safe zones" which act as assembly points, so an assessment of the situation is made and the investigative phase of the incident commences. Remember, the one thing that is consistent in the active shooter scenario is that it is fluid. So getting to and staying in a safe area designated by law enforcement is critical. Very often, these locations are part of the evacuation plan the organization has created and reviewed with law enforcement or the fire authorities, but circumstances may dictate a change to that plan in which law enforcement may have to designate a new location due to the circumstances associated with the event. If the location of your assembly point is not in the line of sight and is 300–500 feet away, it may be acceptable.

Aftermath and Recovery

As has been mentioned in previous chapters, a business continuity plan (BCP) should contain a DRP and an emergency plan (EP). Each of these outlines the response aspects of the violence in the workplace response plan. Along with the natural disaster response to fires, earthquakes, and floods, man-made disasters like shooters and intruders should be codified for the CMT to administer. Again, in that plan, work with local police to establish an assembly area that is known to employees and conduct fire drills in cooperation with the local fire department.

One important factor is to recognize that if the news media show up, there may be news bulletins on the radio and TV that may be viewed by family members. The ability to remote route inbound calls to a secondary location should be done whenever possible so that calls will not go unanswered. Unanswered calls create panic in the minds of family members who need to have information. If a number is established for family members to call, this number can be provided to the news media that will assist by broadcasting the contact information. Local hospitals will also receive calls regarding a mass casualty situation and will need to deal with panicked family members who attempt to ascertain the condition of a loved one.

Train employees by using tabletop and training exercises that focus on aftermath and recovery. Local law enforcement is a valuable resource in this process. Most police departments have community relations functions or details that are more than happy to get citizens to participate in protecting themselves through proactive planning. It is important to make the training meaningful. Tabletops are the first step to talk out how an actual event would unfold. The tabletop training can help identify holes in EP planning. It will also create an atmosphere of empowerment. The tabletop process creates the underpinnings for a field exercise that will address the active shooter scenario. The DHS (2008) made some valuable suggestions for this training.

The DHS Active Shooter Guide lists the following field training exercise areas to be covered:
- Recognizing the sound of gunshots
- Reacting quickly when gunshots are heard and/or when a shooting is witnessed
  - Evacuating the area
  - Hiding out
  - Acting against the shooter as a last resort
- Calling 911
- Reacting when law enforcement arrives
- Adapting to the survival mind-set during times of crisis.

As mentioned earlier, be a good neighbor to businesses by letting them know that exercises are being conducted. Make sure law enforcement and fire services are engaged and informed. These public servants are an integral component to a successful exercise. Police and fire personnel can fill in holes in the mapping of expectations within the CMT and employees.

Remember to plan for assisting employees with special needs. Have assigned resources who will make sure these individuals are evacuated safely. Examine the various evacuation routes from all areas of the building that the special needs individuals in your organization frequent, including restrooms and break areas. Comply with all Americans with Disabilities Act (ADA) requirements in all cases.

Consider a floor warden system that assigns individuals who have demonstrated leadership capability to act as evacuation coordinators. These wardens may be managers or members of a safety committee who have the willingness to assist and direct associates to safety. These employees are the calm ones. Former military personnel might be considered for these roles if they are a part of the workforce. Former military personnel are often used to deal with evolving and fluid situations that require disciplined movements.

Once the immediate situation is resolved, there is a need to fully recover and deal with the immediate aftermath. One of the most critical needs will be to account for employees, visitors, vendors, and contractors who were in the building at the time of the incident. Remote access to electronic entry logs from the card key system would be helpful to knowing who was in the building. Paper visitor sign-in logs may not be available immediately. Therefore, a discussion of this scenario will need to be had and a work around created if the work location is a crime scene and not accessible for some time. Do not assume that because a person was not scheduled to be at work on that particular day means that he or she was not there. Start at the macro view of the entire workforce, including contractors and vendors, and work to the micro view making sure everyone is accounted for who *may* have been in the building. Ask employees who are there if there were any employees or visitors present at the time of the incident who may have come in to pick up a forgotten item before taking a day off. In other words, think widely.

Notification of family members is critical for victims and witnesses who may be delayed in calling their families because of the commencement of the investigation. Employees may have left cell phones sitting at work stations when the incident unfolded. If the organization has a PR manager or team, have them craft a communication to the press, being careful not to step on toes of the public information officers from the police department.

The psychological damage may not be apparent immediately. Have EAP and health care professionals whose job is to see below the surface conduct an assessment. There may be delays in reactions by victims. Make sure all parties are debriefed to ensure that all involved can express how they feel, in addition to what they experienced.

Execute the BCP by determining any gaps in the organization due to the incident. Key managers may have been part of the casualty roster, and adjustments need to be made to the business process to ensure gaps are minimized in the disruption.

Communication is critical. If care is taken in the communication process, the overall volume of stress will begin to dissipate. After the shock of the incident is over, questions will start flowing in through every communication path possible. A plan needs to be in place to direct all RFI through a central process to ensure consistency and accuracy. If the model is turned from inbound, reactive responses to outbound, scheduled communications, the organization is now in a position to reduce the stress of the incident.

Control the outbound communication to external parties through a designated spokesperson. Large companies and organizations have PR departments or firms under contract. These groups are trained to deal with reporters who can sometimes ask questions that would infuriate a manager whose mind is reeling from a major jolt of emotion. Do not assume that the CEO or senior manager can deal with this mission if a coworker who they know personally is on the casualty list. In the Crandall Canyon Mining disaster on August 6, 2007, in Southern Utah, the CEO of the mining company chose to be the spokesperson and was seen as defensive and dishonest when talking with the families of the fallen miners (Lavandera, 2009).

Reporters will attempt to interview employees who are in the assembly area. Use the PR group as the face of the organization and have employees refer questions to a designated spokesperson. It is recognized that employees are speaking for themselves but having a calm report is preferred to an emotional account that might not reflect what really happened or why it happened. Such a report might be stacked with emotional supposition.

Human resources is another key communication resource for employees. There will be many questions regarding employee's future work schedules, benefits, and pay continuity, if the facility is closed for any period of time. Family issues and concerns will also need to be addressed, especially if there is a fatality of a coworker.

Investors, stockholders, and other outside parties will be inquiring. Make sure lines of communication are available for them to plug into the process. Notices on web sites and product ordering sites are critical to calm customers who may be concerned about order fulfillment from a supplier who has experienced a violent incident. Postings can be updated frequently and announce when the next update will come out. Attention to these kinds of postings can reduce inbound calling.

Learn from History

If learning does not come about as a result of the event, the organization may be destined to repeat it. The entire emergency plan should be reviewed and evaluated objectively. Documentation of the entire process and incident should be reviewed by the CMT and management team to determine what changes, enhancements, or focus will need to be implemented in the future. This work has used reviews of prior incidents as the basis for recommending a plan for the organization. Most major events will generate a report that needs to be reviewed and discussed with internal and external sources to determine what could be done differently to improve the outcome.

Start with a frank review of organizational culture leading up to the incident. Try to determine whether culture was a factor. Establish whether or not current security policies and procedures were followed. Was there a planning gap or were known risks ignored? Establish whether teams and associates reacted as planned and trained. If a risk was known but the security fix was planned but not implemented due to budget constraints, which constraint may no longer exist due to the change in priority?

Try to avoid placing blame for security breaches or failures. It is not conceivable that the organization would have knowingly attracted the incident. Learn and improve as an organization as a result of the incident. Be honest with yourselves as a team and make the changes necessary to avoid reoccurrence.

Have frequent question and answer meetings with employees. Allow healing to occur through discussion. In many instances, employees will be relieved to know that they share similar feelings and concerns. Sometimes there may be a delay in symptoms presenting, so keep the channels of communication open.

Conclusion

The author's view of his life and what was important changed the day of the Olympic Park bombing in 1996. Although it does not define a person it does change a person. Over time, and with attention, the wounds heal—quickly with some and slowly with others. But as individuals and organizations, the pain and disruption fade. The results are, hopefully, a positive outcome by gaining insight and perspective to a person's life. Family and friends become more important than things and money. It is an opportunity for spiritual growth. It is probable that experience with such events can be life-changing but not necessarily life-ending.

Food for Thought

1. Do organizational policies and procedures include active shooter?
2. Who in the organization will talk to employees' families if an incident happens?
3. Who is the lead person in the organization who would be the liaison with law enforcement and fire personnel?
4. Who in the organization will be the lead person designated to address the press if they show up at the facility with questions about an incident?

References

Lavandera, E. (2009). *Frustrated family of miner clings to "one string of hope."* CNN.com. Retrieved from http://www.cnn.com/2007/US/08/09/sanchez.trapped/index.html#cnnSTCText/.

U.S. Department of Homeland Security. (2008). *Active shooter*. Retrieved from http://www.dps.mo.gov/HomelandSecurity/documents/Active%20Shooter/DHS%20ActiveShooter_Response%20Booklet.pdf/.

U.S. Department of Labor. (2009). Fatal workplace injuries in 2006: A collection of data and analysis. *U.S. Bureau of Labor Statistics, Report 1015*, 9. Retrieved from http://www.bls.gov/iif/oshwc/cfoi/cfoi2006_all.pdf/.

CYBER THREATS: AN EMERGING CONCERN

John P. Benson

INTRODUCTION

Traditional stalking can find its way into the workplace, usually with some warning, by a known perpetrator or a tangible physical threat that can be readily identified. In these situations, law enforcement can, and will likely, step in and help. The courts can be reactive and issue injunctions and restraining orders. Physical safeguards can be implemented in the workplace, like surveillance and the presence of security. Human resources and security organizations can step in and offer a plan and strategy to deal with the issue. In most instances when stalking crosses into the workplace, resolutions are reached and the problem is resolved.

Stalking when combined with technology has a different modus operandi that is often much more insidious. Below are some worrisome facts about cyber stalking.

1. Cyber stalking can originate from anywhere in the world.
2. It is often very discreet and targeted to an individual, at home and the workplace, and unless the employee is informing you, you will likely not even know it is occurring.
3. Cyber stalkers can, and often do, remain anonymous, and identifying the perpetrator is often impossible.
4. Cyber stalkers can be incredibly disruptive by employing software technology and computers to assist them in their efforts and completely overwhelm a victim with unwanted electronic contacts (e.g., automated remailers).
5. Anonymity emboldens cyber stalkers and traditional social mores that typically keep people from extraordinarily cruel and relentless behaviors often vaporize over the Internet.

6. Cyber stalkers often enlist tools on the web, like social networking sites, where they publish harassing, embarrassing, inappropriate content about the victim, whether true or false, and such information has the potential to go "viral" to huge audiences.
7. Creative cyber stalkers have the ability to enlist others, unwitting third parties, in their efforts, again, usually anonymously.
8. Cyber stalkers can invade the workplace electronically without ever setting foot inside the business where they can track and monitor efforts to stop their behavior.
9. Employees and employers rarely report incidents of cyber stalking, thereby limiting knowledge that can tell how, who, why, and what works in the detection, investigation, prosecution, control and prevention cycle.
10. Employees and employers are not well educated with respect to how evidence should be collected during a cyber stalking incident.
11. Sophisticated cyber stalkers can, create many barriers to law enforcement's ability to identify them and gather evidence.
12. Law enforcement is often ill-equipped to deal with cyber stalking from an investigative and technological perspective.
13. If the cyber stalking involves multiple jurisdictions, it may present law enforcement and prosecutorial challenges.
14. Cyber stalking can be so covert that an employer may not notice when activities have escalated from bullying to harassment (webtribution and flaming), or even to a real physical threat.

What Makes Cyber Stalking Such a Threat?

The Internet and its billions of connections is an amazing electronic world of information and communication pathways. The Internet is one of the most universal and quickly adopted and adaptive technologies. The Internet continues to expand its reach into private, business, and public lives at an astounding pace. The Internet is not just a local phenomenon, it is global in its reach. The web offers an array of tools that provide individuals the opportunity to work and live better.

If current trends hold, people will become more dependent on the Internet.

Like many tools, the web can be used to build something positive or used to harm. The Internet is subject to little regulation. Many privacy and law enforcement experts feel that the Internet is a lawless frontier. The issues presented by Internet crime should promote an increasing level of discomfort as well as an increased quest for knowledge to combat emerging threats.

In the workplace, one of the most ubiquitous tools is the computer. Many employees have desktops, or at the very least access to a desktop, and those of us who are part of the mobile workforce carry laptops from city to city, many of which contain all kinds of confidential data. Further, most of us have access to the Internet, email, and instant messaging on both computers and cell phones. Technology has migrated to "smart" phones, web-music/video appliances, and PDAs. Even without a PC, there can be the same or even greater access to the panoply of communication paths.

As a result, another pathway of potential violence is introduced into workplaces with a simple power button and a few silicon chips.

Unless companies have extremely tight security policies and knowledgeable IT/IS security staff with good monitoring tools to back them up, we leave individuals and organizations exposed. Very often employees have unfettered access to the Internet, email, instant messaging, and a wide variety of social and business networking sites. Many workers spend the majority of the workday on a computer and perform tasks of value for the employer. Not surprisingly, data suggests that nearly all employees spend a percentage of time at work using the computer for nonwork-related purposes like online shopping or personal communication.

On the other side of the keyboard are hackers, phishers, smishers, spammers, spoofers, vishers, bullies, harassers, misanthropists, haters, racists, sexual predators, and stalkers. These people prey on the everyday PC users who cannot even begin to fully comprehend the threats to which they may be exposed while surfing through any number of daily activities. Although most people learn enough to get by each day in a world of ever-changing technology, those who use technology to attack others spend whatever time is needed to learn the tools that can further illicit and illegal activities. Because Internet criminals are often very sophisticated, both employees and employers must have a stronger understanding of the potential threats they face.

Social Engineering—Old Evil, New Name— in a Data and Technology-Rich World

The unaware, the uneducated, the elderly, and the young are often victims of myriad Internet scams. Common to nearly all of these crimes is the use of some form of trickery. Such acts of deception, collectively, are often referred to as social engineering, a sterile and benign-sounding term for a very malicious act. The simplest definition for social engineering is, using pretext to create a sense of trust with another and eliciting information based on that trust. Social engineering is one of the key tools used by those engaged in victimizing others with cyber violence.

The combination of social engineering techniques and data access creates a dangerous concoction. There are many free sites where persons can be researched thoroughly and anonymously. Personal information, such as addresses, work and home telephone numbers, and even dates of birth, are readily available. Additionally, the names of relatives, coworkers, associates, and acquaintances are just a click away. Detailed professional and business information is everywhere on the web. There are countless sites that can trace an individual via genealogy or through old classmate relationships. Social and business networking sites contain vast amounts of information that individuals have posted about themselves or that others may have posted, knowingly or unknowingly, about them. The Internet is rich with information about people and businesses, and not just with information voluntarily recorded, but also with information gleaned from direct marketing companies and data aggregators. Access to others, unlike the physical world, is only limited to what exists in cyber space.

Web crawlers can look at thousands of web sites and pull information together on a single search name and deliver to the screen, in seconds, a detailed view of those near and dear and those who are unknown. Because there is an enormous amount of personal information available through Internet sources, a person who is interested in attacking or stalking can find, with little effort, private information about a potential victim.

Cyber Stalkers Are Emboldened by Anonymity

An oft used phase on the Internet is "on the internet nobody knows that you are a dog ... [and] it is impossible to tell where you are from." Disturbingly, law enforcement is challenged by a second truism, "the only ones that get caught are dumb, unsophisticated, or both" (Markoff, 2009).

The significant difference between stalking and cyber stalking is that a person can stalk another anonymously without the fear of being easily caught or creating readily observed physical evidence. A quick Internet search of the phrase "anonymous email" will generate tens of millions of hits. A similar search of the phrase "anonymous SMS," the technology of short message service that facilitates text messaging, presents over 1 million hits. Try "anonymous instant messaging" in a search engine to produce an excess of 2 million hits. The top hits on all these sites are either instructional or offer free software designed to teach and enable individuals ways to remain anonymous in cyber space. Anonymous remailers can make it virtually impossible to determine the true identity of the source of an email or other electronic communication. A number of law enforcement agencies report that they are confronting cyber stalking cases involving the use of anonymous remailers, with no success.

The anonymity of the Internet also provides new opportunities for would-be cyber stalkers. A cyber stalker's true identity can be concealed by using different ISPs or by adopting different screen names. Experienced stalkers can use technology that disguises their ISP or they use public access points (free WiFi at the library or a coffee shop) and the really smart stalkers bounce their communications from one server to the next all across the globe making tracking impossible.

Anonymity leaves a cyber stalker in an advantageous position. As stalking is very much about power over a victim, the stalker could be a total stranger, a friend across the county, a neighbor, or the coworker in the cubicle next door. The perpetrator could also be a former friend or lover, a total stranger met on a social networking site, a blog, a chat room, or some ill-behaved child who thinks playing hurtful games on the Internet is "fun." The complete inability to identify the source of bullying, harassment, or threats could be particularly ominous to a cyber stalking victim, and the veil of anonymity will likely remain as the constraints that might exist in the real world are completely absent in the cyber world.

Some perpetrators, armed with the knowledge that their identity is unknown, might be more willing to pursue the victim at work or at home, and the Internet can provide substantial information about where a person lives or works.

This combination of factors—access, anonymity, and instruction—combined with the explosion of social networking sites has created an environment where long-held social mores regarding certain types of behavior are quickly eroding. The ability to gather information about someone is easy. People, unwittingly and routinely, provide information to strangers via telephone and email. Phishers send out emails that look identical to an email from a legitimate service, like a bank, and the email solicits personal information regarding the person and his or her account. This information is used to steal from the person or it can be used to stalk and harass a person. People also share, sometimes in confidence, words, pictures, and video that may be shared on the Internet.

Thousands of times a day, people share information and find that the information is shared with a wider audience—without malice or intent. However, imagine, if someone is focused on harassing, embarrassing or hurting another, he or she might try to entice the person into making an embarrassing statement and then widely broadcast it without permission. Social networking sites are used to post everything ranging from personal secrets to information about others. Information about others is easy to share publicly, even anonymously, without permission. In many cases, humiliating material, such as video, can spread quickly.

What Is Cyber Stalking?

Cyber stalking is a form of cyber violence that can range from an attack on a company to an attack on an individual. Other than hacking attempts by those seeking personal or proprietary information from company networks, the most common form of cyber violence in the workplace is cyber bullying, harassment, and stalking.

The layperson's definition of cyber stalking is the use of the Internet, email, or other electronic communication devices to stalk another person. Physical stalking generally involves harassing or threatening behavior in which an individual engages repeatedly. The individual engages in behaviors, such as, following a person, appearing at a person's home or place of business, making harassing phone calls, leaving written messages or objects, or vandalizing a person's property.

The motivations for cyber bullying, harassment, and stalking are no different than those typically seen in physical stalking. The fact that cyber stalking does not involve physical contact may create the misperception that it is more benign than physical stalking. Further, the fact that the victim can, often, block the perpetrator electronically gives people a sense that cyber stalking is less intrusive. Although some conduct involving annoying or menacing behavior might fall short of illegal stalking, such behavior may be a precursor to physical stalking and violence and, therefore, should always be treated seriously.

The belief that virtual stalking is less damaging is not true as cyber stalkers can take advantage of the many and simple communication pathways and can launch attacks on multiple fronts. Sophisticated cyber stalkers may launch automated attacks and are able to respond to any effort to defeat the attacks by simply changing a screen name, for example. Further, because the communication is almost always nonconfrontational, impersonal, and often anonymous, many social mores quickly vaporize and the severity of the attack can be much more harsh or brutal. Simply put, someone who is unwilling to confront a victim in person or verbally by phone may have little disincentive or hesitation about sending harassing or threatening electronic communications to a victim.

The relationship between stalker and victim is usually one of the following: coworker to coworker, worker to outside relationship (dating, prior romantic, or acquaintance), or worker to stranger. Reports suggest that online bullying, harassment, and stalking occur more frequently in stranger to stranger relationships.

The U.S. criminal code defines, in relevant part, cyber stalking in 18 U.S.C. § 2261A (B) as:

to place a person … in reasonable fear of the death of, or serious bodily injury to—(i) that person; (ii) a member of the immediate family of that person; or (iii) a spouse or intimate partner of that person; uses the mail, any interactive computer service … to engage in a course of conduct that causes substantial emotional distress to that person or places that person in reasonable fear of the death of, or serious bodily injury to, any of the persons described in clauses (i) through (iii) of subparagraph (B) (2009).

Laws in the United States that address stalking, like most state laws, require that a perpetrator make a credible threat of serious injury, death, or violence against the victim or his or her family. All 50 states and the District of Columbia have enacted antiharassment and stalking laws. Law enforcement agencies estimate that electronic communications are a factor in 20 to 40 percent of all stalking cases. Forty-six states now have laws that explicitly include electronic forms of communication within stalking or harassment laws. State laws that do not include specific references to electronic communication may still apply to those who threaten or harass others online, but specific language may make the laws easier to enforce.

Cyber stalking can take place anywhere in the world and usually involves more than one of the following behaviors:

1. Gathering or purchasing online information about a person or company with the sole purpose of employing that information for the purposes outlined below.

2. Hacking web sites or networks to gather private information about a person or company.
3. Using contact information to launch a webtribution attack or send flamers (harassing) emails; usually these are not just sent to the victim, the victim is the target, but the recipients can make up a wide audience and many times these emails get forwarded to a yet wider audience.
4. Using gathered information to make unwanted solicitations or advances.
5. Using gathered information to send intimidating and threatening messages, pictures, video, or audio.
6. Using or employing malicious software ("malware") in an effort to taunt or cause distress or harm.
7. Impersonation of a person to attempt to destroy the character and reputation of an individual in a manner that instills substantial distress or fear of injury or death.
8. Impersonation of a person to engage in intimidating, threatening, or inappropriate (often illegal) conduct in their name or persona.
9. Greenmail or blackmail threats and exposure on the Internet.
10. Anonymously posting false information about a person or company as a form of intimidation or threat.
11. Encouraging or conspiring with others to engage in intimidating or threatening behaviors.

Cyber stalkers may easily ascertain information regarding people who either know or are familiar with the victim and may approach these people to obtain the victim's personal information. The cyber stalker may actively solicit information about a victim on the Internet or may employ any one of the hundreds of online investigative agencies. Technology-savvy cyber stalkers, once they have obtained certain types of user information via hacking, may secretly install key loggers and other tools on a victim's PC to enable a victim's online activities to be monitored actively. Once a cyber stalker has access to a victim's PC, the cyber stalker has achieved substantial power over the victim.

Many cyber stalkers who have access to a person's social or work network will try to involve third parties in the harassment. The cyber stalker may claim that the victim has harmed the stalker or his or her family in some way, or may post the victim's name and telephone number in an attempt to encourage others to join the assault. As most stalkers in the physical world work alone, the fact that cyber stalkers can encourage and enlist others makes this form of stalking even more of a threat.

In some circumstances, cyber stalking can evolve into physical stalking. Typically, it starts with bullying, followed by harassment, and then graduates to cyber stalking. Eventually, the activity escalates to abusive and excessive phone calls, vandalism, threatening or obscene mail, trespassing, and physical assault.

Although cyber bullying, harassment, and stalking share similar characteristics with the same offline behaviors, many perpetrators—online or offline—are motivated by a desire to exert control over their victims. As with offline stalking, most studies on the subject, and there are few, suggest that the majority of online perpetrators are men and the majority of the victims are women. Cases have also been reported involving instances of women cyber stalking men and of same-sex cyber stalking. In many cases, the cyber stalker and the victim had a prior relationship. Interestingly enough, however, there are far more instances of cyber stalking involving strangers attacking strangers. Cyber bullying and harassment do not, by definition, rise to the same level of fear and intimidation as in-person or offline bullying and harassment. Cyber bullying or harassment can include simple name calling or a perpetrator inciting a fear of events such as greenmail, or the loss of a job or relations that do not qualify under the law as a "fear of serious injury or death." Be aware, however, that bullying and harassment often escalate to stalking. Legal issues aside, a company's response to workplace bullying, harassment, or stalking should be immediate.

A cyber stalker may send repeated, threatening, or harassing messages with a simple push of a button. More sophisticated cyber stalkers use programs to send messages at regular or random intervals that eliminate the need for the stalker to be physically present at a computer terminal. Additionally, the cyber stalker can dupe other Internet users into harassing or threatening a victim by using Internet bulletin boards or chat rooms. For example, a stalker may post a controversial or enticing message on a board under the name, phone number, or email address of the victim that results in subsequent responses being sent to the victim. Each message, whether from the actual cyber stalker or others, will have the intended effect on the victim, making the cyber stalker's effort minimal. In cases such as this, the lack of direct contact between a cyber stalker and the victim can make it difficult for law enforcement to identify, locate, and arrest the offender.

The effects of cyber bullying or harassment on the victim are like those seen outside the workplace, but these effects may have a negative or severe impact on an employee's ability to perform his or her job effectively. Typical reactions include:

- Isolation from coworkers, both inside and outside the workplace;
- A decline in work attendance (if the attacks occur during working hours on company equipment);
- Overworking (avoiding nonwork environments where the threat may be focused);
- Poor work performance due to increased anxiety;
- Performance problems due to other somatic symptoms, like headaches, nausea, eating, or bowel problems;
- Sleeping at work (chronic sleep disturbance);
- Increased risk of sustaining a work-related injury;
- Increased cigarette use;
- Increased frequency of drug or alcohol abuse.

How Cyber Stalking Enters the Workplace

Cyber stalking and bullying, even outside of the workplace, can have profound impacts on the workplace. Often referred to as one of the first successful prosecutions of a cyber stalking law, prosecutors in the Los Angeles District Attorney's office obtained a six-year prison sentence in response to a guilty plea from a defendant who used the Internet to solicit the rape of a woman who rejected the defendant's romantic advances. The two met at church. The victim, who did not own a home computer, received dozens of telephone calls and personal visits to her apartment in response to Internet advertisements placed by the defendant. The defendant also engaged in email exchanges during which he impersonated the victim, providing her name, address, description, telephone number, and the code to her apartment's security system. As a result of the stress, the victim suffered physical ailments and, allegedly, lost her job because of excessive absenteeism. What if the victim had a work-related computer profile and the predator had included her work location in his attacks?

In another case, a graduate student of University of San Diego used a professor's credit card number to buy information about the professor's students via the Internet. The stalker, using computers at the university and from his home, sent more than 100 email messages to five female students that included death threats, graphic sexual descriptions, and references to the women's daily activities. Allegedly, the stalker never met any of his victims. He was arrested after authorities traced him through a local Internet provider. The stalker was found guilty of felony stalking and got one year in jail and five years of probation. The irony is that the judge ordered the defendant not to own, possess, or use a computer unless it was during the course of his employment.

A recent case that has attracted much attention, and will likely drive many legislative changes to anti-cyber-bullying, harassment, and stalking laws, involves the suicide of a 13-year-old Missouri girl who was stalked, courted, and spurned during a very short-lived online relationship on a popular social networking site. The stalker was the mother of one of the victim's school acquaintances, allegedly aided and abetted by her daughter and one of her employees. The mother/stalker set up a phony profile of a young man and then proceeded to endear the victim and then rejected her. The young girl committed suicide. The mother, allegedly, then tried to cover her tracks and had the woman who worked for her delete evidence of the false identity. What if an employee was doing something similar on company equipment or used company equipment to cover a potential crime? The mother/impersonator/stalker was convicted on three federal misdemeanor counts. (The case could not be prosecuted in Missouri at the time because there were no applicable state laws. Missouri later passed a law to address this type of behavior.) This conviction was overturned by a federal court judge because the law, under which the conviction occurred, was deemed "void-for-vagueness" (*United States v. Lori Drew,* No. CR 08-0582-GW, Decision on Defendant's F.R.CRIM.P.29(c) Motion, Filed 08/28/2009, United States District Court, Central District of California). Obviously, there are many laws that need to be passed that cover this area, especially as there are first amendment issues which have dogged legislators for years as they try to codify laws that are designed to prevent such tragedies. Missouri did pass a law related to this incident, see http://www.senate.mo.gov/08info/BTS_Web/Bill.aspx?SessionType=R&BillID=147, which updated Missouri's laws against harassment by removing the requirement in the existing laws requiring harassing communication be written or made over the telephone. The amendment now includes harassment from computers, text messages, and other electronic devices as also illegal; the law is titled "Modifies various provisions relating to stalking and harassment."

All three of these cases had a direct or indirect impact and/or connection to the workplace.

Dealing with Cyber Threats

Risk and controls, like surveillance, whether active or natural, are what keep most people from committing crime. The absence of these gating factors creates an environment where every day people do things they might not ordinarily do. For those already predisposed to engage in criminal behavior, it makes the commission of crime more likely and the crime tends to be much harsher. Traditional crime prevention techniques are not effective in the virtual world.

As much as there are those who feel the Internet has few, if any, bounds, there are many examples of instances where controls have been implemented successfully. The most sophisticated example of Internet filtering to control access and speech is the country of China that controls, to the extent it can, much of its internal Internet traffic and virtually all traffic between its borders and the outside world. China, and a few other countries like Saudi Arabia, have Internet police who constantly monitor web content and usage. Other examples of control are:

- Those that are imposed by Internet companies who basically attempt to police the activities taking place on their sites to prevent illegal activity, the loss of data, or to protect valuable assets.
- Companies that police and protect their workplace networks, data, and assets.
- Individuals who try to keep people from accessing their own machines and personal information.

There is a multibillion industry addressing security needs including companies selling hardware security appliances, firewalls, secure email, data encryption tools, and antivirus software.

Unfortunately, many cyber stalking victims do not report the conduct to law enforcement, either because they feel that the conduct is not criminal, that nothing can be done, or that law enforcement will not take them seriously or, worse still, place fault with the victim. As of now, the majority of studies indicate that significantly more than the majority of cases of cyber stalking are not reported to law enforcement.

Law Enforcement and Cyber Threats

Solve the problem by the following:

1. Report *all* incidents of cyber stalking to law enforcement. This can help them by providing more data that surrounds the patterns seen in cyber stalking incidents so that better prevention and protection techniques can be discovered.
2. Report incidents locally and to the FBI. Stalking is often multi-jurisdictional—be mindful that this can complicate the investigative and prosecutorial process.
3. *Ask* law enforcement what constitutes evidence and how it should be gathered in an ongoing investigation. This knowledge is critical because some sophisticated cyber stalkers are skilled at masking evidence, and worse

still, if they have access to company systems because an employee unwittingly downloaded a BOT or WORM, they can delete evidence in addition to presenting all manner of other threats to the organization.

4. There are many laws on the books today that can be applied effectively to cyber stalking incidents.

There is hope on the horizon. The fact that there are laws in nearly every jurisdiction in the United States to address cyber stalking means that if someone can be identified, he or she can be prosecuted. There are several initiatives under way, at both the federal and state levels, that focus solely on high-technology crimes. Although the focus is not specific to cyber stalking, what is learned about other kinds of cyber attacks may ultimately turn the tables in this area. Projects can be reviewed on the following web sites:

1. FBI Computer Crime Squads
2. National Infrastructure Protection Center in Washington, DC
3. The Justice Department's Computer Analysis and Response Teams and the Computer Crime and Intellectual Property Section within the Criminal Division of the department.

The Internet industry has made a few steps toward more realistically trying to combat and limit abusive electronic communications. Nearly all ISPs include specific language in their terms of service stating that abusive behavior is prohibited. But many times there is nothing that can be done to stop it. In some instances, these companies actually fought releasing information to authorities for cases citing an infringement of first amendment rights. If an ISP is uncooperative in cases such as this, switch to a carrier that has a track record of dealing aggressively with cyber crime.

Instances of abusive behavior should be reported to the ISPs involved, but be sure to forward any correspondence to law enforcement so better statistics can be kept and tracked. Reporting is the best way to procure resources to address the problem and to have a good handle on the size of the problem. Right now, there is not an agency that has a good grasp of the size and magnitude of this problem. When reporting to an ISP, use its web site address to which complaints of abusive or harassing electronic mail can be sent. Most often this address is "abuse@[the ISP's domain]." Additionally, ISPs, almost uniformly, have provisions in the online agreements that specifically prohibit abusive or harassing conduct through their service and provide for termination of the offender's account, if it can be identified.

Preventing Cyber Stalking

At the Company Level

At the company level, there are a number of things you can do to prevent cyber stalking. For example:

- Have well-written policies and procedures in the employee handbook concerning cyber bullying, harassment, and stalking.
- Have a policy and procedure to establish a computer response team that can look at threat prevention, evidence gathering, and post-incident analysis and review.
- Require the immediate reporting of any incident, regardless of the employee's opinion about severity, involving any bullying, harassment, or evidence of stalking.
- Require reporting of all incidents to local and federal law enforcement.
- Train employees how to properly respond to an incident.
- Have an evidence gathering policy and procedure in place.
- Unless the site is a retail establishment, do not place a picture of the office building or the site's physical address. A physical address should only be provided to those people who have reason to be on the premises.
- Make sure all listings for the company, including the telephone directory and marketing materials, do not contain the addresses and locations of any of the company's worksites.
- Implement web filtering and *block* all social networking sites and chat sites.
- Prohibit the use of instant messaging at work.
- Disable SMS/MMS on all company cell or smart phones.

- Prohibit employees and put security features in place that prevent the downloading of any program, no exception.
- Institute email filtering and filter out any email messages with threatening content or potentially unsafe attachments.
- Put key loggers in place and log all traffic from the keyboard out, review logs on a weekly basis using automated review tools.
- Log and monitor all traffic in and out of your network, review logs for suspicious activity.
- Employ data security policies and procedures that encrypt sensitive data (including UIDs and PWs).
- Use and update antivirus software.
- Use and update both hardware and software firewall solutions.

Some of these measures may sound draconian; however, good preventative measures are far less costly than an onsite stalking incident gone badly. Last, inform all employees of these policies and procedures and let them know that everything they do and see is open to company review … there is no privacy in the workplace.

At the Employee Level

Similarly, there are also a number of things that employees themselves can do. For example:

- Do not require employees to provide any more information than necessary on their signature lines (no addresses and a main line number, no direct dial numbers).
- Add a statement about the company's antibullying, harassment, and stalking policy to your privacy and confidentiality notice.
- Do not allow any first-level contact to provide a company address to any unqualified caller.
- Do not share personal information in public spaces anywhere online, nor give it to strangers, including in email or chat rooms. Do not use a real name or nickname as a screen name or user ID. Select a name that is gender and age neutral. And, do not post personal information as part of any user profiles.

- Be extremely cautious about meeting online acquaintances in person. If or when the choice is made to meet, do so in a public place and take a friend.
- Perform routine searches to see where personal information may have surfaced. If any "information" service lists personal information, contact them directly and ask to be removed. If they refuse, contact them in writing and request to be removed. If they do not remove personal information after a written request is made, file a complaint with the Federal Trade Commission (http://www .ftccomplaintassistant.gov/).
- If an individual is being targeted, he or she must be willing to change phone numbers, email addresses, or user IDs, and update both hardware and software firewall solutions.
- Collect and preserve all evidence about the case (print, store, and backup evidence; remember, if a personal PC has been hacked they many have access to that personal PC).
- Do not, under any circumstance, meet with a perpetrator to "talk" or "work it out."

Food for Thought

1. Do your policies and procedures address cyber threats and stalking specifically?
2. If you are a security organization, do you have a technical resource that can assist with these types of threats within your organization?
3. What are your policies and procedures on social networking sites from work stations at your organization?
4. Does your training in violence in the workplace include cyber threats and stalking?

Additional Resources

- CyberAngels: A Guardian Angels program. http://www .cyberangels.org/
- Department of Justice: Stalking. http://www.ovw.usdoj .gov/aboutstalking.htm
- FBI, Cyber investigations. http://www.fbi.gov/cyberinvest/ cyberhome.htm

- Federal Trade Commission: The Federal Trade Commission, the nation's consumer protection agency, collects complaints about companies, business practices, identity theft, and episodes of violence in the media. http://www.ftccomplaintassistant.gov/
- GetNetWise: Online information resource. http://www.getnetwise.org/
- High Technology Crime Investigation Association (HTCIA) is designed to encourage, promote, aid, and affect the voluntary interchange of data, information, experience, ideas, and knowledge about methods, processes, and techniques relating to investigations and security in advanced technologies. http://www.htcia.org/
- IACIS® (International Association of Computer Investigative Specialists) is an international volunteer nonprofit corporation composed of law enforcement professionals dedicated to education in the field of forensic computer science. http://www.iacis.com/
- National Center for Victims of Crime. Support guide for victims of stalking. http://www.ncvc.org/ncvc/Main.aspx
- National Institute of Justice's (NIJ's) Office of Science and Technology, the National Law Enforcement and Corrections Technology Center (NLECTC) System plays a critical role in enabling the Office of Science and Technology to carry out its critical mission to assist state, local, tribal, and federal law enforcement, corrections, and other criminal justice agencies in addressing their technology needs and challenges. http://www.justnet.org/Pages/About.aspx
- SEARCH: Online resource for justice and public safety decision makers. http://www.search.org/
- WHO@, Working to Halt Online Abuse, is a volunteer organization founded in 1997 to fight online harassment through education of the general public, education of law enforcement personnel, and empowerment of victims. http://www.haltabuse.org/
- Two reports from the U.S. Department of Justice provide detailed information on cyber stalking: Stalking and Domestic Violence: Report to Congress (http://www.ncjrs.gov/pdffiles1/ojp/186157.pdf) and Cyberstalking: A New Challenge for Law Enforcement and Industry

(http://www.justice.gov/criminal/cybercrime/
cyberstalking.htm).
- See other related National Conference of State
Legislators resources: Enacted Cyberbullying Legislation.
"State Electronic Harassment or 'Cyberstalking' Laws,"
last updated March 12, 2009. http://www.ncsl.org/
IssuesResearch/TelecommunicationsInformation
Technology/CyberstalkingLaws/tabid/13495/Default
.aspx
- See http://www.ovw.usdoj.gov/aboutstalking.htm for the
latest information from the Department of Justice on
stalking victimization in the United States.

References

Katrina Baum, Ph.D., Shannan Catalano, Ph.D., Michael Rand, Kristina
Rose (2009, Janurary 13). Stalking Victimization in the
United States, NCJ 224527, http://bjs.ojp.usdoj.gov/index.cfm?ty=
pbdetail&iid=1211.
Interstate Domestic Violence Laws. 18 CFR, Part 1, Chapter 110A,
§ 2261. Retrieved from http://codes.lp.findlaw.com/uscode/18
/I/110A/2261A/.
Markoff, J. (2009, July 16). NY Times, July 17, 2009, A5 "Web's Anonymity
Makes Cyberattack Hard to Trace, *New York Times*. Retrieved from
http://www.nytimes.com/2009/07/17/technology/17cyber.html/.
U.S. Department of Justice Office of Justice Programs Violence Against
Women Office. (2001). *Stalking and domestic violence.* Report to
Congress (NCJ 186157). Rockville, MD: U.S. Department of Justice
Programs Violence Against Women Office.

EPILOGUE: AND THE BEAT GOES ON …

As I write the final pages of this book, the notices for violent acts throughout the United States continue to stream to my email inbox. My normal process is to sort through the news blurbs to find those articles that refer to workplace violence, but the lines are beginning to blur as violence emerges in coffee shops and military bases within the United States. As a practitioner, I must avoid looking at what has happened in the past as the only barometer of what will happen in the future.

- Lakewood, Washington—Four police officers were shot while preparing for their workday in a local coffeehouse. The suspect was later found and after a brief encounter was killed by the police.
- Fort Hood, Texas—A soldier shot 12 individuals, wounding 31 others in a massive tragedy. The suspect was shot but remains alive and the details are being investigated by the FBI to determine the facts and motivations of the shooter.

As these lines blur between street violence and workplace violence. Consider the fact that these victims, police officers, soldiers, and a civilian were in their workplace and became the random victims of motivations known only to the shooters. In the case of the coffeehouse shooting, the employees and customers watched in horror as the events unfolded becoming victims of the trauma as witnesses of such a horrific incident. Are these witnesses victims of workplace violence as well as the officers?

As the facts and circumstances play out in the upcoming months, the question of emerging threats should become more and more concerning as violence begins to twist into new forms and venues. On that fateful date in July 1996 when the bombing happened in Centennial Olympic Park the reality hit that a gun in the park was not the risk, it was a bombing. I admit that the major concern on the night before the bombing was not an indiscriminate bomb that picks its victims by proximity and not as a perceived enemy of the perpetrator. It was the gun toting terrorist who was looking for an athlete or political figure to target was what was keeping him up at night. It was a targeted attack that would be directed at a particular victim or sets of victims like the Israeli team in 1972 or the Barcelona, Spain, bombing of the power grid during the 1992 games by Basque separatists.

If you looked at a list of possible threats that were considered viable prior to September 11, 2001, planes being flown into buildings was not high on the list. It was a possible scenario but not thought likely to succeed due to the high degree of coordination and sophistication needed to be successful. The concept and growth of suicide bombings using children who are obediently following a religious belief to find peace and serenity in the next life was a line of surprise and stupefying shock for those of us who are trying to delay death by living a long and healthy life. The point is that in order to find the next real threat, you must look at possible scenarios with new sets of factors when calculating a probability score. The reality when trying to cover the holes in your organization is your need to not only focus on the rearview mirror but also look forward to unknown possibilities that emerge out of the society itself. Is it possible that the line that was crossed in 1986 in Edmond, Oklahoma, is the line that cannot be retreated from and becomes a milestone to the next unthinkable act of violence?

As we move forward into 2010 and beyond, the security professionals need to put in reverse the lenses of the prevention glasses they look through and continually look for clues and cues in the headlines, blogs, and e-reports on what is happening throughout the world full of violence and think outside the overly discussed box for prevention policy. It is easy to get distracted by "it couldn't happen here" or "we are ready for anything" thinking. It is a matter of asking the hard questions, looking for real possibilities, and raising your hand with questions. The question may be are you ready for the veteran who is disillusioned with their life or job enough to carry out a violent act upon themselves or others in the workplace or the workplace of a spouse or significant other? Is the threat to our police or others who are charged with our safety randomly acted out in the workplace of others when they are customers and letting a guard down to prepare for the day's work while focusing on their laptop? Their jobs are stressful enough when they are engaged in the day-to-day risk of protecting us all.

After looking at this issue over the last year and reading countless books and articles, it is clear that the problem is going to be with us and we have to accept it, deal with it, and continue to walk forward. The security professional is often the voice of conscience and brings up the tough issues to audiences that are focused elsewhere. Even when looking at past events like Columbine and Virginia Tech, the investigators, reporters, and committees will bring new failures to light in an attempt to find fault or to bring more focus on what could have been done differently or better.

In a recent article from the Associated Press writer, Breen, T., & Sampson, Z.C. (2009, December 4) it was learned that Virginia Tech officials reportedly called their families well before an alert was sounded campus-wide before the second round of shooting at Virginia Tech. It was further reported that the Office of University President Charles Steger was locked down well before the alert was issued. New cries for resignations are sounding.

Rather than discuss the merits of the issue, I would only point out the fact that when details are not known they can create fear and panic. Lack of information can result in victims inadvertently moving into risky situations due to the failure of the communication of the incident's facts as they unfolded, which campuses around the country are trying to establish or improve. The fear then drives poor judgment that concerns oneself with self-preservation and not potentially acting on the wider issue.

This report clearly points to the Monday morning quarterbacking you can expect if an incident happens on your watch as the security manager, facility manager, or CEO. You could do 99 things right and 1 wrong, but you will be forever judged potentially in the court of public opinion by the one seeming mistake that was made under tremendous pressure in a fluid and scary situation. The context of criticism will come from families and friends of the victims that will forever be affected by the loss of their loved one.

So the point here is prevention of violence in the workplace is a basic necessity, but the complexity of that necessity is great. Denial that it could ever happen where you work or study is beyond naive and because of your reluctance to meet the issue head on will potentially end very badly. Embrace the issue as real and continue to ask what could happen so that you can stop the progression of violence in your organization in the earliest possible stage.

The scope of the problem starts at the point you are sitting or standing as you read this sentence and moves out from there. Move to the edge of your organization and examine the culture, communication, and your capabilities working with law enforcement whenever possible to integrate your solution. Think not only broadly but look through the windshield toward the road ahead as well as in the rearview mirror as to what has happened in the past. Test your paradigms.

References

Breen, T., & Sampson, Z. C. (2009, December 4). *Va. Tech report: Staff warned their families first.* Associated Press. Retrieved December 13, 2009, from http://www.yahoo.com.

C., M. (2009, November 29). Lakewood Police Shooting Kills 4 Police Officers at Lakewood Coffeehouse in Washington. *Associated Content.* Retrieved December 13, 2009, from http://www.associatedcontent.com/article/2440492/lakewood_police_shooting_kills_4_police.html?cat=8.

CNN. (2009, November 7). Officials: Fort Hood shootings suspect alive; 12 dead. Retrieved December 13, 2009, from http://www.cnn.com/2009/US/11/05/texas.fort.hood.shootings/index.html.

Thompson, A. (2009, December 3). Study reveals the angriest Americans. *LiveScience.* Retrieved December 13, 2009, from http://news.yahoo.com/s/livescience/20091203/sc_livescience/studyrevealstheangriestamericans.

APPENDICES

Author's Note

In several of the chapters and particularly in Chapters 7, 14, and 15, I speak of proactive planning. Appendices are documents readers can use to plan for prevention and recovery.

SAMPLE EMERGENCY PROCEDURES

A Company is committed to the safety, health, and security of its employees. This emergency procedures handbook has been developed to support that commitment and has been distributed to security and all floor wardens as a training and reference document. Employees needing additional information may contact security or HR.

Company emergency numbers:

- Security Extension XXXX
- Security for the Office Park at XXX-XXXX
- Corporate security at 888-XXX-XXXX
  - 911 (Emergency)
  - Security manager ext. XXXX

Accident/Injury Reporting

1. Report the accident/injury to your immediate supervisor and HR at extension XXXX.
2. The supervisor will complete an accident/incident report form.
3. HR will complete the report of first injury or incident form and send it to the insurance carrier.

First Aid

1. If an employee sustains a minor injury requiring only first aid, not medical treatment, the staff member should be treated on-site with a first-aid kit and returned to work. The first-aid kits are located in the kitchen and with the receptionist.
2. If the injury requires medical treatment from a licensed medical provider, the staff member should be transported to the nearest, approved insurance facility.
3. If the injury is life threatening or serious enough that nonmedical transport might further aggravate the injury, the staff member should be transported by ambulance.
4. Injured employees should not drive themselves to a facility for medical treatment.

Workplace Violence Policy

Violence in the workplace or threats of violence in the workplace will not be tolerated. All employees witnessing a threat or violent act must report it to security or to HR. Report should include:

- Who made the threat or committed the act and upon whom it was perpetrated.
- What was said or done; concentrate on specifics. Provide the names of any witnesses and as many details as possible.
- Where the threat was made or the act committed.
- The day and time of the incident.
- The circumstances, if any, that provoked the threat or act.
- How the person making the threat or committing the act showed aggression (screaming, shoving, physical violence, use of a weapon, language, etc.).

Armed Threat

In the event a gunman enters your building or facility and points a gun at you:

- Try to remain as calm as possible.
- Do nothing to excite the assailant.
- Do nothing to cause the assailant to take action.

- Freeze in place, wait, listen, and do what the assailant directs you to do.
- Do not hesitate in complying with the assailant's demands.
- Do not make sudden moves, scream, or panic.
- Do not move too closely to the assailant. Invading personal space may be perceived as threatening.
- Do not challenge the assailant with any kind of belligerent or defiant body language. Be submissive.
- Do not make frequent eye contact with the assailant.
- Do not become emotional. This may trigger the assailant into violent action.
  If you hear shots fired in your building or facility:
- Do not move toward the shots to see what is happening.
- If you feel it is safe to do so, close all inter-office doors leading to hallways and receptionist areas.
- If you feel there is a safe route out of the building or facility, leave as quickly as possible in the opposite direction of the gunfire. However, you will take the risk of encountering the gunman on your way out. Use great caution.
- Do not play the hero. You may cause injury or death to yourself and others.
- If you stay in the building, find a safe place to hide. If you are in an office or conference room, lock the door and overturn a desk or cabinet, if possible, and lie behind the furniture for protection. Do not stay in the center of the office, move to one side.

Biological, Chemical, or Bomb Threat

- If you open an envelope or other type of package and find an enclosed note that says you have been exposed to a chemical or biological threat, immediately and carefully put the package down and remain exactly where you are. Yell for help; don't move. Keep everyone away from the threat. Tell the person who responds to call extension XXXX to report the incident. Do not carry the object to any other location in the building. Moving will spread the threat of exposure to others. Stay in place and wait for instructions from trained professionals. If an imminent danger exists, immediately call 911. Report the issue and evacuate the premises.

If you receive a biological, chemical, or bomb threat by telephone, follow this procedure.

- If possible, while the person making the threat talks, do the following:
  - List the number (on your caller ID screen) immediately: _____
  - Write the exact language of the threat:

    _____

    _____

    _____

    _____

- Your first job is to listen. However, if the opportunity presents itself, ask the following questions:
  - What kind of substance is it? _____
  - When will it be released? _____
  - Where will it be released? _____
  - How is it going to be released? _____
  - What effect will it have? _____
  - Is the substance in one of our buildings right now?

    _____
  - Which one? _____
  - Where is it located? _____
  - What does it look like? _____
  - Did you place it? _____
  - Why? _____
  - What is your name? _____
  - Where are you calling from (number and location)?

    _____
  - What is your address? _____

    _____

    Date _____ Time _____ (a.m./p.m.)
    Received by _____ Dept. _____
    Ext. _____

Voice

☐ Loud	☐ Soft
☐ High pitch	☐ Deep
☐ Raspy	☐ Pleasant
☐ Intoxicated	☐ Other

Manner

☐ Calm
☐ Rational
☐ Coherent
☐ Deliberate
☐ Righteous
☐ Angry

☐ Irrational
☐ Incoherent
☐ Emotional
☐ Hysterical
☐ Other

Speech

☐ Fast
☐ Distinct
☐ Stuttered
☐ Slurred

☐ Slow
☐ Distorted
☐ Nasal
☐ Other

Background Noises

☐ Office machines
☐ Factory machines

☐ Animals
☐ None—quiet
☐ Street noise
☐ Airplanes

☐ Trains
☐ Bedlam (sounds of
   confusion)
☐ Voices
☐ Music
☐ Party atmosphere
☐ Mixed

Language

☐ Excellent
☐ Fair
☐ Foul

☐ Foreign
☐ Good
☐ Poor use of certain words
   and phrases

Accent

☐ Local
☐ Foreign
☐ Ethnic

☐ Regional (specify)
☐ Other

Description of Caller

Male ☐   Female ☐   Adult ☐   Juvenile ☐

1. Security will call 911.
2. Security will notify senior management and may make a PA announcement to evacuate the facility in which you are located.
3. All employees should evacuate to their designated safe area.
4. Before evacuating, make a quick check of your work area for any strange or unusual boxes, packages, envelopes, containers, packs, etc. Note: Do not handle items or allow anyone else to do so. Report them to your floor warden, security officer, or other officials investigating the incident.
5. While exiting the building, staff should stay as far away from the threat as possible.
6. Maintenance will turn off the heat or air-conditioning.
7. Do not drink from water coolers.
8. Turn off all fans and/or space heaters if in use.
9. Do not consume any food or drinks located in the building.
10. Do not remove any personal or business items from the building.
11. As much as possible, avoid contact with anything in the building (handrails, walls, furniture, door handles, etc.) during evacuation.

How to Recognize Mail Bombs

1. Mail bombs may bear restricted endorsements such as "personal," "private," "confidential," "to be opened by addressee only." These characteristics are significant when the addressee does not usually receive personal mail at the office.
2. Common words may be misspelled.
3. The package or envelope may be addressed to a title, but the title will be incorrect (e.g., functional chief, not functional director) or it may be addressed to a person by name only.
4. Mail bomb labels may have distorted handwriting or poorly typed names and addresses. The name and address may be block lettered or prepared with cut-and-paste or homemade labels to disguise the handwriting.

5. The postmark or cancellation may show a different location than the return addresses or the postmark may be from a city where the recipient does not have acquaintances.
6. Mail bombs may have excessive postage (more than normal for a mail item of its size and usually in the form of postage stamps).
7. Mail bombs may be marked with visual distractions such as "fragile," "rush—do not delay," or "handle with care."
8. Some form of special mail handling is often used such as certified, special delivery, airmail, or priority.
9. The sender may be unknown to the recipient or the style of address may be unusual. Where the name of the supposed sender is known, the return address may be fictitious or not available or there may be no return address.
10. Package bombs may be unprofessionally and excessively wrapped with several combinations of string, twine, or tape (masking, electrical, strapping).
11. Mail bombs come in many shapes. They may have protruding wires (which often may be felt through the envelope), screws, aluminum foil, or other metal parts. Mail bombs may have oil stains and/or discoloration on the envelope or package and may have a strange pungent or almond-like smell.
12. Letter bombs may be in a thick or large envelope and will probably feel rigid and appear uneven or lopsided.
13. A letter bomb will be heavier than usual for envelopes of the same size. Its weight will be distributed unevenly.
14. Mail bomb envelopes may appear to have been opened and re-glued.
15. The envelope or package may appear to contain a book.
16. A package bomb may have an irregular shape, soft spots, or bulges.
17. Package mail bombs may make a sloshing sound, but rarely will buzz or tick. Placed devices (explosives that are hidden in your business establishment) are more likely to buzz or tick.
18. Pressure or resistance may be noted when removing contents from an envelope or package.

Remember: Mail bombs can be packaged as differently and creatively as the person who assembles and sends them.

Bomb Threat Drills

1. Quickly search your area for suspicious objects and report results of the search to floor wardens.
2. Open office doors and windows, as applicable.
3. Exit building when told to do so and report to the safe area.
4. Wait until a signal is given by management and/or security before returning to the building.

Earthquake

During an Earthquake

- Take cover under a desk or table. Protect your head and neck.
- Stay away from windows or objects that could fall on you.
- Do not run outside. Falling debris may cause injury.
- Do not use elevators.

After an Earthquake

- Remain calm.
- Be prepared for aftershocks.
- Stay indoors. Do not leave your floor unless a life-threatening condition exists, or you are instructed to do so by your floor warden or safety or security personnel.
- Do not use telephones except to report fire or medical emergencies. Replace telephone receivers that have slipped off the hook.
- Assist the injured, but do not move them unless it is absolutely necessary.
- If a fire occurs, follow the fire procedure.
- Notify your supervisor of the situation, injuries, and your status. This should be done in person to keep phones free for emergency traffic.

Evacuation

- Evacuate immediately! You could be warned by the PA system, a fire alarm, a security officer, a floor warden, or a law enforcement officer. Do not remain near the threatened building! Go directly to your assigned safe area.

  [PROVIDE EVACUATION MAP HERE]

- Remain clam—keep all noise to a minimum.
- Listen for instructions over the PA system.
- Follow directions from the floor wardens, security, or law enforcement.
- Do not use elevators. Exit by using stairs.
- Do not run. Walk calmly and proceed directly to the nearest stairway or exit. Stay as far away from the threat as possible.
- Use handrails (except in cases of chemical or biological evacuation) on stairways and allow room for others to enter.
- Report to your supervisor when you arrive at your assigned evacuation area.
- Do not re-enter the building once you have evacuated, unless it is more dangerous outside. Choose the less dangerous option.
- Do not smoke either inside or outside your building during an evacuation.
- Help people with disabilities evacuate.

Fire

If a Fire Breaks Out

- Move everyone away from the area of the fire.
- Confine the fire—close all doors to the area.
- Call 911 or have another staff member assist by making the call.
- Pull the nearest alarm box. When a fire alarm sounds, staff members should leave the building through the nearest exit and reassemble at their designated safe area.

- During a fire, do not use elevators. Use the stairs to exit your building.
- Do not run. Walk calmly and proceed directly to the nearest stairway or exit. Stay as far away from the fire as possible.

Using a Fire Extinguisher

Use an extinguisher only if it can be done safely and you have someone with you and you are both able to keep an exit at your back.
- Remove the extinguisher from the wall location.
- Firmly pull the safety pin to remove it from the handle.
- Squeeze the handle to spray contents. Point the nozzle at the base of the fire and cast the spray back and forth until the fire is extinguished. Repeat the process if the fire rekindles.

If a Fire Escalates

- Before opening an internal building door, check it first. Feel the handle and door for heat. If either is warm, seek an alternate escape route. If it is normal temperature, open it slowly to prevent a backdraft from producing a sudden surge of heat or flame.
- If you cannot get out of a room through the door, block any cracks with clothes to keep out the smoke. If smoke is filling the room, crawl with your head near the floor under the smoke, because heat and smoke rise quickly. Crawl to the planned exit window.
- If a window escape becomes necessary, break the glass with a heavy object. Be sure to clear away jagged edges before exiting.
- Once you are outside the building, do not go back inside.

Medical Emergencies

In the event of a medical emergency:
1. Provide first-response care if you are trained.
2. Call 911 or have someone else call if you're able to assist the victim.

3. Provide the following information about each victim to the 911 operator:
    a. Location, number of victims
    b. Type of injury or illness
    c. State of consciousness
    d. Severity of injury:
        i. Bleeding
        ii. Respiratory injury
        iii. Head injury
4. Do not hang up until the operator instructs you to do so.
5. Do not move the victim unless the victim's life is threatened by an environmental catastrophe (e.g., fire, smoke, and explosion).
6. If the medical emergency has been caused by an accident, make the accident scene as safe and secure as possible and keep people away from the area.
7. Remain at the scene and be available to provide information or assistance.
8. If the victim is taken by ambulance, note the location of the hospital where the victim is being transported.
9. Get a contact name and phone number for the victim.
10. The most senior-level employee at the emergency location is responsible to inform management and to direct the relief efforts until that employee is relieved from responsibility.
11. In the event of serious injury or death, HR will notify the injured or deceased employee's family.
12. Contact the facility security center at XXX-XXXX.
13. Contact corporate security at 888-XXX-XXXX.

SAMPLE GENERIC PLAN AND PROCEDURE: DISASTER RECOVERY PLAN (DRP) FOR OPERATIONS/ DATA CENTER

1.1 Overview

This is limited to the recovery of the products and services defined in the technical section 1.3 of this document and reside in the XYZ Company Operations/Data Center located at 123 Main Street, Small Town, USA (The Company).

The DRP is defined as the ongoing process of planning, developing, testing, and implementing emergency recovery procedures and processes. The primary objective is to provide a plan to accomplish the following goals:

1. Minimize the economic impact of a disaster involving the operations and data center.
2. Minimize the extent of the disruption or damage and prevent its escalation.

3. Assure the efficient and effective resumption of the online services, computer operations, and communication resources in the event of a major interruption.
4. Ensure that any loss of critical processes is temporary.
5. Restore the facility or provide a replacement for it within a reasonable period of time.
6. Ensure that all legal and regulatory requirements have been observed.

The Company depends on its computer and communication resources to support essential business processes, customers, business growth, change, and the complexities of changing technology. The following list of documents and processes was used to develop the DRP needed to protect the business:

- Production servers
- Critical applications
- Backup procedures
- DRP testing plan
- Maintenance plan
- Temporary relocation plan.

Organization of the Disaster Continuity Plan

Note: In the case of a disaster, please go to Section 1.2.

This manual documents the DRP in 10 sections. It is organized to facilitate the use of the plan during a disaster. The sections are organized as follows:

- Section 1.1—*Overview*: Contains the overview of the plan, the plan scope, and the assumptions made in the plan development.
- Section 1.2—*Declaring a disaster*: Contains the steps required to declare a disaster.
- Section 1.3—*Recovery of critical Tier I products and services*: Contains the steps required to recover the products and services identified in the Matrix of Products and Services at the current site.
- Section 1.4—*Recovery of Tier II products and services*: Contains information on how to recover all other systems to the hot-site that are not mission critical, that is, email.

- Section 1.5—*Ongoing operations at hot-site*: Contains the steps required to assume ongoing operations at the hot-site after the Class 1 products and services have been successfully recovered.
- Section 1.6—*Relocation of operations to long- or short-term facility*: Contains the steps required to move out to a business recovery center.
- Section 1.7—*Establish normal operations at primary site*: Contains the steps required to assume ongoing operations at the long-term primary site.
- Section 1.8—*Vacating the hot-site*: Contains the steps needed to vacate the hot-site once the primary site has been restored.
- Section 1.9—*DRP management and maintenance*: Contains information on updating, distributing, and testing the plan.
- Section 1.10—*Supporting documentation*: Contains supporting information such as the Operations Matrix, contact lists, team information, and vendor notification procedures.

1.1.1 Scope of the DRP

This plan provides for the recovery of the products and services as outlined in the Tier Matrix and supported by the resources contained in the Operations/Data Center.

1.1.2 DRP Assumptions

This DRP is developed and maintained based on the following assumptions:
- Assumes an Operations/Data Center disaster only.
- That the plan is designed to recover from a worst-case interruption; that is, all equipment, electronic files, procedures, documentation, workspace, and the primary data center facility are not useable.
- Production applications not housed in Main Street location, not in the production domains, or not under the management of Operations are not included.
- That worst case can result in a short- or long-term outage, perhaps as long as six to eight weeks, or more. However, it is assumed that the target outage for restoration at the primary site is 10 business days.

- That the operations recovery strategy, which yields an operational site within 48 hours for primary production operations, is assumed to be valid.
- That the Tier Matrix will be used as the basis for the Systems Operation plan development.
- This project assumes that no hot backup exists. The center must be established at a hot-site location using backup tapes that are currently being stored in an off-site location.
- Data and software are only as current as the last available off-site backup. It is expected that backups will be rotated off-site within 24 hours of backup tape creation. This assumption is inclusive of all platforms.
- Those off-site backup items are in a secure environmentally protected facility sufficiently remote to Main Street to not be affected by the same interrupting event.
- That if worst-case interruption occurs (usually a day or two before the "full backup" is rotated to off-site storage), at least essential computer services *can be* restored at an alternate computer site using only backup files stored off-site.
- All critical employees are available during a disaster and can execute recovery actions.
- All company employees may or may not be able to access the building to work normal hours. The hot-site must allow for a minimum of 10 workstations at the hot-site to be brought up simultaneously with the data center.
- The hot-site facility vendor maintains the hardware configuration to support the temporary Operations/Data Center including telecom needs.
- All personnel affected by this plan are responsible for understanding their role under a disaster situation.
- At the time of a disaster, an emergency response center (ERC) will be established to manage the disaster response and will act as the clearing house for all recovery-related information, requests, and operations.
- The Operations Center, which is collocated with the existing Data Center, will be co-managed by this plan.
- Support for other affiliate products or divisions is not included in this plan and will be covered on a case-by-case basis.

- Information in this plan will be maintained on a quarterly basis and be made available and/or distributed to key individuals listed in the Recovery Personnel Directory. (Section Owner: CMT coordinator)

1.2 Declaring a Disaster

This section contains the first set of actions to be initiated following a disaster of some sort that has recently occurred at the Operations/Data Center.

Section Summary

The purpose of this section is to determine whether to make a recommendation to executive management to officially declare a disaster. To determine whether to declare a disaster, a damage assessment team is formed to investigate the damage and determine if the key revenue-generating systems (defined in Tier Matrix) can be available to our customers in 48 hours or less. If it is determined that it will take longer than 48 hours, a decision may be made to declare a disaster and begin recovery in the designated off-site Business Recovery Center located in Large Town, USA. The senior management team leads this effort. Two scenarios exist for the purposes of this step.

1. In the case of total, or near total, destruction of the Operations/Data Center, a decision and recommendation are quickly made with evaluation of the site. Damage is so overwhelming that a decision is obvious. In this scenario, the steps in Section 1.3 to move people and equipment to a hot-site can begin immediately and run concurrently with this section, if approved by the senior management team.

2. Partial destruction of The Company Data Center warrants a more detailed damage assessment. A decision is made based not on the amount of damage, but on how quickly production applications can be made available. Since production servers have a 48-hour recovery window, a decision to declare should be made if it will take longer than 48 hours to recover in place at the Operations/Data Center. If it is determined that recovery can be accomplished in less than 48 hours, The Company senior management team may, at their discretion, begin Section 1.3 as a backup plan.

If a decision is made to declare a disaster, Section 1.3 should be executed and a decision made about when the tasks in Section 1.4 should be started. If a decision is made to "Recover in Place," a plan to do so will be determined at that time. This plan does not address all the possible scenarios that a "Recovery in Place" plan might entail.

Assumptions:

- An event has occurred at the Operations/Data Center within the last 24 hours, and no decision has been made yet whether to declare a disaster and move business operations to the hot-site and Remote Operations Center (ROC).
- Access to the facilities is available.

Important information:

- Only company executive management is authorized to declare a disaster.
- Only certain people are authorized to notify the vendors and activate their recovery plans for The Company. Please see contact section of this plan for a list of vendors that must be notified, their authorization lists, and procedures to declare a disaster.
- Only the president, COO, security director, or PR team is authorized to talk to the media. Please direct all RFI from non-Company personnel to the aforementioned individuals directly or through a member of the Critical Management Team (CMT). Direct all internal RFI to the CMT—HR Manager.
- For insurance and legal purposes, good records must be kept. This includes all information collected during damage assessment, including but not limited to, damage reports, phone calls, problem logs, activity logs, and receipts for money spent.

1.3 Recovery of Critical Tier I Products and Services

The purpose of this section is to define the steps that must be taken to recover the products and services located in the Main Street Operations/Data Center in the event a disaster is officially declared and the decision is made to activate the DR hot-site.

Section Summary

Details of the steps to implement the recovery of Main Street Data Center products and services are explained in this section. The technical recovery plans for specific tasks within the project schedule are also maintained in separate documents by the technical teams. These technical recovery plans can be found online in shared files on http://www.website.com.

Important information:

- Many of the steps must occur simultaneously. First, the hot-site vendors and the tape vault vendor must be notified. Next the team leads must be notified. Once the teams are in place and the vendors configure the equipment, the restoration processes can begin. There are seven basic restoration threads that are kicked off simultaneously:

    1. Dispatch of the vaulted backup tapes to the recovery site. (Travel time will be 8–20 hours. So it is critical to notify Perpetual, the tape vault vendor, as soon as possible and get this task under way.)
    2. Recovery of the backend database
    3. Recovery of the Internet services
    4. Recovery of the custom The Company services
    5. Recovery of the networking information
    6. Recovery of the server infrastructure
    7. Recovery of the PC infrastructure.

- If a disaster is declared (see Section 1.2), The Company executive management team will notify the executive management team of the disaster. It is the responsibility of each CMT member to notify his or her department members of the pertinent information. It is the responsibility of the CMT coordinator to coordinate the recovery of the data center with the other recovery activities occurring after a disaster.
- When using the following checklist, please ensure to log the date and time that each action is taken.

The technical project steps by critical Tier I processes are as follows:

- Network information (see Section 1.10.5)
- Domain services (see Section 1.10.5)
- Internet services (see Section 1.10.5)

- Backend database (see Section 1.10.5)
- Custom The Company services (see Section 1.10.5). (Section Owner: CMT coordinator)

1.4 Recovery of Noncritical Tier II Products and Services

This section documents the steps to take to recover all of the remaining products and services documented in the noncritical Tier II services. This section can begin nearly simultaneously with recovery of critical products and services (Section 1.3). As soon as the hardware and technical resources are freed up, they will be reassigned to begin this section. Recovery of critical products and services always has priority over recovery of Tier II products and services.

Section Summary

Recovery of the Tier II products and services will need to be reviewed based on the length of time the data center will not be operational at the primary site. If it appears that the data center will not be restored in a 10-day period, consideration will need to be given to restoring the Tier II products and services in a timely manner. Because of all the possible scenarios, all of the project plans, configurations, equipment, etc. to recover Tier II must be determined in the very early stages of this effort. Very little preplanning has been done. Key decisions include:

- *Recovery location*—Based on the estimates for how long the Main Street Operations/Data Center will be unavailable, it may make more sense to recover these services in the vendor hot-site or in an alternate facility closer to Main Street.
- *Simultaneous recovery*—Depending on equipment availability (or some other resource), it may make sense to begin recovery of Tier II simultaneously rather than to faze it in over the course of the one-month recovery window. This assessment must be made before recovery begins. The damage assessment team should estimate the recovery window and document it in the recovery procedure for the services. Quicker recovery is always desired, where feasible.

Once these high-level decisions are made, detailed recovery plans for each product or service are reviewed for accuracy and current configurations and adjusted accordingly. This recovery plan should be executed after the recovery of Tier I services. If the decision is made to recover simultaneously, this plan must be adjusted accordingly.

Assumptions:

- A decision has been made to declare a disaster
- Recovery of critical Tier I products and service is occurring
- Section 1.3 tasks and resources have priority over Section 1.4.

Important information:

- Only certain people are authorized to notify the vendors and activate their recovery plans for The Company. Please see list of vendors that must be notified, their authorization lists, and procedures to declare a disaster.
- Only the president, COO, security director, or public relations is authorized to talk to the media. Please direct all RFI from non-The Company personnel to these individuals directly or through the appropriate CMT. Direct all internal RFI to the CMT lead—HR generalist.
- For insurance and legal purposes, good records must be kept. This includes all information collected during damage assessment, including, but not limited to, damage reports, phone calls, problem logs, activity logs, and receipts for money spent.

Tier II Technical Procedure

- Email (see Section 1.10.6)
- Fax to email (see Section 1.10.6)
- Additional external networks (see Section 1.10.6). (Section Owner: CMT coordinator)

1.5 Hot-Site Operations and Maintenance

Once the systems and products have been recovered and the customers notified, the switch must be made from executing the recovery processes to implementing operations and maintenance of the systems. Teams used during the recovery may be re-formed, expanded, or adjusted to fit the needs of ongoing operations based on the needs of the business. If the center is to be operational at the hot-site for more than 10 days, a rotational assignment should be developed to ensure coverage. This section documents the actions to be taken to implement ongoing operations and maintenance.

Assumptions:

- The Tier I products and services have been successfully recovered and are operational.

Important information:

- If the Tier I and II sites are different for any reason, care should be taken to ensure this process is followed at both sites.
- Since Section 1.4—Recovery of Tier II—is occurring simultaneously, care must be taken to ensure that coordination with Section 1.4 efforts is also considered.

(Section Owner: CMT coordinator)

1.6 Relocation of Critical Tier I to a Long-Term Facility

At some point, critical Tier I products and services must move from the hot-site to a more permanent location. This section documents the steps needed to move Tier I products and services from the hot-site to a long-term facility. There is a contractual time limit of six months for use of the DR partner hot-site.

When this section should start will vary depending on the nature and severity of the damage from the disaster, but it *must* be completed prior to the contractual time limits stated in the DR provider contract.

Section Summary

This section summarizes the decisions that need to be made and the steps that must be executed to move Tier I products and services out of the hot-site to a more long-term facility. It relies heavily on information and decisions made in earlier sections. For example:

- *Location*—The long-term facility may be the Main Street area or a new alternate location, depending on the detailed damage assessment reports, alternate site availability, insurance reimbursement issues, or other information that may surface during a disaster.

- *Equipment*—What equipment is salvageable from the disaster site and what equipment can be located on the open market may heavily sway decisions about Tier II recovery as well as the configuration required to support Tier I in a long-term facility.
- *Recovery*—This section makes use of the technical recovery plan(s) used in Section 1.3 where Tier I was recovered in the hot-site. Any lessons learned during the initial recovery should be fed into this plan during execution.

Assumptions:

- Tier I (Section 1.3) is currently up and running at the vendor hot-site.

Important information:

- Only certain people are authorized to notify the vendors and activate their recovery plans for The Company. Please see Vendor list of this plan for a list of vendors that must be notified, their authorization lists, and procedures to declare a disaster (unique to the organization, vendor list must be provided by the organization).
- Only the president, COO, public relations, or security director is authorized to talk to the media. Please direct all RFI from non-Company personnel to the PR team. Direct all internal RFI to The Company senior management team.
- For insurance and legal purposes, good records must be kept. This includes all information collected during damage assessment, including, but not limited to, damage reports, phone calls, problem logs, activity logs, and receipts for money spent.

(Section Owner: CMT coordinator)

1.7 Establish Normal Operations at Primary Site

Once all systems and products have been recovered at the primary site, normal operations and maintenance of the systems begins. The following actions should be taken to implement ongoing operations and maintenance.

Assumption:

- The Tier I and II products and services have been successfully restored at the primary site and are operational. (Section Owner: CMT coordinator)

1.8 Vacating the Hot-Site

Once all systems and products have been recovered at the primary site and running as normal operations, all alternate processing sites must be shut down. The following actions should be taken to implement ongoing operations and maintenance.

Assumption:

- Normal operations at the primary site for all products and services. (Section Owner: CMT coordinator)

1.9 DRP Management and Maintenance

This section provides information about the management and maintenance of this recovery plan document. This plan applies directly to The Company disaster recovery teams and indirectly to other staff members. It is essential that each staff member is aware of and supports this plan.

The objectives for DRP maintenance are:

- To maintain a plan that is adequately current at all times.
- To maintain an awareness and readiness of key personnel to effectively react to an interruption of information services and to execute recovery actions.

Roles and Responsibilities

Critical management team (CMT) coordinator:

- Keep one copy off-site in a secured location and one copy on-site in a secured location
- Coordinate all scheduled and unscheduled changes
- Distribute updated plan materials to appropriate personnel
- Formal plan review and walk-throughs once a year
- Conduct off-site tests on a scheduled basis
- Participate in planned and unplanned exercises of the plan
- Exercise the plan during an emergency.

Recovery team leads:
- Keep one copy off-site in a secured location and one copy on-site in a secured location
- Provide changes and updates to the plan as warranted
- Distribute updated plan material to appropriate personnel
- Formal plan review and walk-throughs twice a year
- Maintain an alternate team lead and keep them apprised of relevant information
- Participate in planned and unplanned exercises of the plan
- Exercise the plan during an emergency.

DRP Testing

The objective is to test the validity of the plan on a periodic basis. Plan testing is used to determine:
- The state of readiness of the recovery teams to respond and cope with a major interruption of services
- Whether the list of resources is sufficient to affect the recovery of products and services at the hot-site
- Whether the plan is current and reflects the company's current recovery needs.

The test scenario is normally developed to accommodate the objectives to be derived from the testing. There are several types of tests that can be conducted.
- *Structured walk-through*
  A disaster recovery role-play requiring participation of at least the recovery team leaders and alternates should be held annually. The test scenario will be made available in advance of the test to allow team members to review their recovery tasks in response to the test scenario. The walk-through usually requires 2–4 hours to conduct.
- *Unannounced hot-site test*
  A surprise technical test (discretely prescheduled with the hot-site) that requires that this recovery plan be executed at the hot-site facility can be used at the direction of the COO. This type of test generally involves only a small portion of the recovery team members.
- *Announced hot-site test*
  A scheduled test involving actual recovery of the Tier I products and services at the hot-site location should be held during the second quarter of the contracted period

and annually thereafter. This type of test generally involves a small portion of the recovery team members. A more thorough test can be achieved with this type of test because of the opportunity to preplan.

When to test:

- Hot-site tests should be conducted at least once each year with increasing scope as the team members become more proficient with the plan.
- The structured walk-through or tactical exercise-type tests should be held at least annually to keep the plan current. They can also be used to sustain a high level of readiness among team members.

Test evaluation:

- The CMT coordinator and CMT members will document the test results immediately after the test exercise.
- The test results will be reviewed and deficiencies remedied by the CMT members.
- The plan will then be updated as necessary.

Updating the Plan

There are two categories of maintenance for the plan (Table B-1).

1. Scheduled maintenance

    This type of maintenance is "time driven."

    - It occurs as the result of scheduled reviews of the plan. Reviews are predictable and are scheduled at quarterly intervals.

Table B-1. Maintenance Events

Event	Update Schedule	Owner
Employee contact information	Quarterly	CMT coordinator
Roles	Event driven	CMT team leads
Section information	Yearly	CMT coordinator
Technical tasks	Event driven	Technical team lead
Tier Matrix	Yearly	CMT coordinator
Equipment lists	Event driven	CMT coordinator
Configuration drawings	Event driven	Technical team leads
Customer lists	Yearly	CMT coordinator
Technical recovery plan	Event driven	IS management

- Reviews help detect required changes that may have been overlooked as the change in the environment occurs. Team leaders are required to attend scheduled reviews. Other departmental staff members will be invited to attend as needed.
- Reviews will focus on known events that have occurred between reviews to ensure that updates have, or will be, incorporated into the plan. Staff assignments are made where necessary to perform required updates.
- The CMT coordinator is responsible for the actual incorporation of changes into the plan, the distribution, and signoffs of the updated materials.

2. Unscheduled maintenance

This type of maintenance is "event driven" because certain change requirements are unpredictable. Leaders are responsible for advising the CMT coordinator of all events that may necessitate plan updates. The following are typical events that may "trigger" unscheduled maintenance:

- Changes in operating system(s) or utility software programs
- Changes in the design of production application databases
- Changes in the data communication network design (i.e., modems, adapters, and circuitry)
- Changes in off-site storage facilities and methods of cycling files and material to the facility
- Improvements or physical changes to the current Information Technology Data Center layout and structure
- Results of periodic business impact analysis, which could necessitate modification of restoration priority
- Changes in The Company business environment (i.e., acquisitions or merger, or the selling of a subsidiary)
- New application systems developed or purchased
- Discontinuance of an application system
- Transfers, promotions, and terminations of personnel (could affect call lists and team membership)
- Significant modification of basic departmental functions, data flow requirements, and application controls within an application system
- Modifications to the vendor contract due to upgrades made by the vendor to their equipment or due to requests by The Company

Table B-2. Distributing the Plan

Name	Title	Phone	Location
Mr. Boss	President	888-XXX-XXXX	Main Street
Assistant Boss	Chief operations officer	888-XXX-XXXX	Main Street
Real Boss	Chief technology officer	888-XXX-XXXX	Main Street
For Real Boss	CMT coordinator	888-XXX-XXXX	Main Street
Tech Boss	Damage assessment team leader	888-XXX-XXXX	Main Street
Cross Boss	IS manager	888-XXX-XXXX	Main Street
Critical Boss	CMT lead-operations	888-XXX-XXXX	Main Street
Super Boss	CMT facility lead	888-XXX-XXXX	Main Street
People Boss	CMT lead-HR	888-XXX-XXXX	Main Street
Talking Boss	PR officer	888-XXX-XXXX	Main Street

Audits of the Plan

Auditing should schedule a periodic, independent appraisal of the plan and provide analyses and recommendations to management. Audits should be conducted no less than once each year.

In addition,

- The COO should conduct a review process if the process is modified. A full review is not needed if contacts lists are updated.
- Random audits of the plan should be conducted.
- Plan distribution.

It is the responsibility of the CMT Coordinator to distribute the plan to the people and locations identified in Tables B-2 and B-3. The plan should be distributed each time it is updated.

1.1 Maintenance Tracking

- Any time the plan is modified the change log table (Table B-4) should be updated with the proper information.
- The CMT coordinator must be notified when the plan is updated and will ensure that the updates are distributed for review.

Table B-3. Distributing the Plan

Hardcopy Locations			
Location	**Description**	**Contact**	**Phone Number**
DR partner	Their office	Key contact	888-XXX-XXXX
Other facility	Corporate office	Key contact	888-XXX-XXXX
Crash case at vault	CMT priority materials	Key contact	888-XXX-XXXX
Local off-site location	A site in the local vicinity other than The Company	Key contact and backup	888-XXX-XXXX

Table B-4. Change Log

Change Log			
Control #	**Section(s) Modified**	**Modified by**	**Date**

- After the changes have been reviewed, the CMT coordinator will distribute the revised document(s) and obtain the required signatures on the signature page.

Signature Page

By signing this page I agree to the following terms (Table B-5):

- I have reviewed and accept the recovery plan/updates.
- I have received the final version of the plan.
- I will replace the existing document with any new versions as they are created and approved.

Table B-5. Signatures

Person	Signature	Date

SAMPLE WORKPLACE VIOLENCE POLICY[1]

Purpose

The company is concerned about the well-being and personal safety of its employees and anyone doing business with the company. The company consequently has adopted this zero-tolerance policy which strictly prohibits workplace violence. Acts of violence and/or threats of violence, whether expressed or implied toward individuals in the company workplace, are prohibited and will not be tolerated. All reports of incidents will be taken seriously and will be addressed appropriately. This policy defines prohibited conduct, as well as general procedures and potential responsive steps in the unfortunate event that workplace violence occurs despite these preventive measures.

---

[1] The policies provided are samples only and do not constitute and are not a substitution for consultation with legal counsel. The law in this area constantly changes and must be reviewed before implementing any policy of this regard. These sample policies should not be implemented or executed except on advice of counsel.

Scope

This prohibition against threats and acts of violence (including domestic violence) applies to all persons involved in the operation of the company, including, but not limited to, company personnel, contract and temporary workers, and anyone else on company property.

Definition of Workplace Violence

Workplace violence is any conduct that is severe, offensive, or intimidating enough to make an individual reasonably fear for his/her personal safety or the safety of family, friends, or property. Examples of workplace violence include, but are not limited to, threats or acts of violence or behavior that causes a reasonable fear or intimidation response and that occurs:

- On company premises, no matter what the relationship is between the company and the perpetrator or victim of the behavior; or
- Off company premises, where the perpetrator is someone who is acting as an employee or representative of the company at the time, where the victim is an employee who is exposed to the conduct because of work for the company, or where there is a reasonable basis for believing that violence may occur against the targeted employee or others in the workplace.

Examples of conduct that may be considered threats or acts of violence under this policy include, but are not limited to, the following:

- Threatening physical or aggressive contact directed toward another individual or engaging in behavior that causes a reasonable fear of such contact.
- Threatening an individual or his/her family, friends, associates, or property with physical harm or behavior that causes a reasonable fear of such harm.
- Intentional destruction or threat of destruction of the company's or another's property.
- Harassing or threatening physical, verbal, written, or electronic communications, including verbal statements, phone calls, emails, letters, faxes, web site materials,

diagrams or drawings, gestures, and any other form of communication that causes a reasonable fear or intimidation response in others.

- Stalking is defined as a pattern of conduct over a period of time, however short, which evidences a continuity of purpose and includes physical presence, telephone calls, emails, and any other type of correspondence sent by any means.
- Veiled threats of physical harm or intimidation or like statements, in any form, that lead to a reasonable fear of harm or an intimidation response.
- Communicating an endorsement of the inappropriate use of firearms or weapons of any kind.
- Possessing weapons of any type, whether licensed or not, and particularly firearms. The only exception is local, state, and federal law enforcement officers acting in the line of duty. Weapons include, but are not limited to:
  - any firearm, loaded or unloaded, assembled or disassembled, including pellet, "BB," and stun guns;
  - knives (and other similar instruments) other than those present in the workplace for approved work purposes or for the specific purpose of food preparation and service;
  - any switchblade knife;
  - brass knuckles, metal knuckles, and similar weapons;
  - bows, crossbows, and arrows;
  - explosives and explosive devices, including fireworks, ammunition, and/or incendiary devices;
  - throwing stars, nunchakus, clubs, saps, and any other item commonly used as, or primarily intended for use as, a weapon;
  - self-defense chemical sprays (Mace, pepper spray) in canisters or containers larger than 2 ounces;
  - any object that has been modified to serve as, or has been employed as, a dangerous weapon.
- Domestic violence is defined as a pattern of coercive tactics carried out by an abuser against an intimate partner (the victim) with the goal of establishing and maintaining power and control over the victim. These coercive tactics can be physical, psychological, sexual, economic, and/or emotional. Where the abuser's tactics include any

of the above-described conduct on company premises, this policy applies. Where such tactics include any of the above-described behaviors off company premises, this policy applies where the abuser is someone who is acting as an employee or representative of the company at the time, where the victim is an employee who is exposed to the conduct because of work for the company, or where there is a reasonable basis for believing that violence may occur against the victim or others in the workplace. The term "intimate partner" includes people who are legally married to each other, people who were once married to each other, people who have had a child together, people who live together or who have lived together, and people who have or have had a dating or sexual relationship, including same-sex couples.

No-Violence Policy

Any employee who commits workplace violence will be subject to disciplinary action up to and including termination of employment and will be directed to stay away from company property. Violators may also be subject to criminal prosecution.

Additionally, where an employee is convicted of a crime of violence or threat of violence under any criminal code provision, the company reserves the right to determine whether the conduct involved may adversely affect the legitimate business interests of the company, and as a result may implement corrective action up to and including discharge. Any employee convicted of such a crime must report the conviction to the company absent a court order to the contrary. Failure to do so is a violation of this policy and subjects the employee to disciplinary action, including termination from employment.

Procedures for Reporting

In the event that an employee believes that a threat or act of violence has been made against that employee or others, the employee should report the details immediately to his/her supervisor, site manager, and/or security and human resources at [**insert applicable telephone #s**].

Another option for reporting concerns (either anonymously or using your name and contact information) is the [**company hot-line, at ___**].

A 911 call may be appropriate first, in the good judgment of the employees or managers involved. Under this policy, decisions may have to be made quickly to prevent a threat from being carried out, a violent act from occurring, or a life-threatening situation from developing. Nothing in this policy is intended to prevent quick action to stop or reduce the risk of harm to anyone, including requesting immediate assistance from law enforcement or emergency response resources.

Failure to report any threats or acts of violence in violation of this policy is itself a violation of this policy, and may subject any employees involved to discipline, up to and including discharge.

Retaliation against anyone for reporting an actual or suspected violation of this policy in good faith will not be tolerated and will subject the individual engaging in the retaliation to discipline, up to and including termination. Any complaints about retaliation may be reported in the same manner as violations of this policy are to be reported.

What to Expect from [the Company]

All reported incidents of violence and threats of violence will be taken seriously and investigated. The company will decide whether its workplace violence policy has been violated and whether preventive or corrective action is appropriate. The company may consult with law enforcement authorities or other resources as it deems appropriate, and may require a fitness for duty examination or other professional assessment through providers chosen by the company to determine whether a perpetrator presents a threat to himself or herself or others in the workplace. If a violation of this policy occurs, the company will take appropriate preventive and corrective action, up to and including termination.

Threat response team (TRT)—At the corporate level, the company has created a TRT that consists of senior management staff appointed by the CEO or COO. Each company facility will have a site TRT. The membership of the site TRT will consist of the following: senior site management, director of corporate security/facilities and/or manager of corporate security, senior site HR representative, and the manager of the affected department. Outside support services, such as local public safety officials, EAP, threat specialists, and local municipal officials, will be involved as dictated by each situation. If warranted, corporate security and/or human resources will notify members of the site or the corporate TRT concerning any given situation. In such circumstances, this team will evaluate the current situation or incident for assessment and planning purposes.

Company Expectations of Targeted Employees

Stay Away Orders

The company reserves the right to seek stay away orders against any person who violates this policy to the fullest extent allowed by law. In such situations, the company has an interest in assisting any employee who reports proceedings to obtain a stay away order, including one that may apply to the workplace. Employees of the company who are targeted by the perpetrator may be asked to work with the company to obtain such an order against that individual. Likewise, employees who have previously sought a stay away order against a perpetrator and/or are protected by an existing stay away order *must immediately*:

- Notify the company of the existence of any such order and provide a copy of the order
- Notify the company of any violations or attempted violations of the order
- Notify the company of any changes to the order
- Notify the company of the order being lifted.

Confidentiality and Safety

These provisions on workplace violence are intended to protect the safety of all employees, and are in no way intended to infringe on an employee's privacy. The primary goal of these guidelines is to encourage an open, ongoing dialogue with the affected employee, and those within the company who need to know, so that the company can take reasonable steps to protect workplace safety. The company's goal is to handle all situations with the utmost sensitivity to the particular situation, while meeting the goal of workplace safety and security.

Avoiding Endangerment

Unfortunately, victims of violence sometimes choose to be uncooperative with their employers' attempts to protect them and other employees. For instance, victims may decide not to tell their employers about threatened or actual domestic violence that may follow the employee into the workplace, or they may engage in behaviors that either provoke or continue the threat of such violence. These behaviors can include simply not reporting a known threat or act of violence that poses a threat in the company's workplace or by sending "mixed messages" to the perpetrator about whether to stay away, provoking behaviors designed to agitate the perpetrator, or inappropriate contact with the perpetrator when a stay away order is in place. These behaviors by the victim endanger not only the victim, but also others in the workplace. In such situations, the company reserves the right to take corrective action against the uncooperative victim, up to and including termination. This aspect of the company's policy is not designed to punish the victim, but is necessary to protect all employees from the increased threat posed by endangering behavior.

Search Policy

The company reserves the right to conduct workplace inspections at any time, with or without notice, for purposes of enforcing this policy, including searching:
- Outer clothing, packages, handbags, briefcases, backpacks, lunch bags, boxes, and/or other containers being taken in or out of the company's buildings, or to or from the company's grounds
- Vehicles parked on company property (owned, leased, or occupied), or company-owned vehicles
- All workstations, computer files, book shelves, lockers, desks, credenzas, file cabinets, store rooms, and other areas.

Any refusal to permit an inspection upon request may result in disciplinary action, up to and including termination of employment. The discovery of any violation of any other company policy as a result of such a search may also result in disciplinary action, up to and including termination of employment. Any illegal activity discovered during an inspection is subject to referral to the appropriate law enforcement authorities.

SELECTION OF A BACKGROUND SCREENING PROVIDER

There are over 2,500 companies in the United States that advertise they do screening services of some sort. What steps should you take in the selection of a provider/screening partner?

1. Discuss your risk model internally and with legal counsel to make sure you are addressing the risk for your particular organization.

2. Consider a steering or planning committee composed of HR, legal, functional or operational management, senior management, and corporate or organizational security. If you have a labor relations function, they might be helpful also.

3. Create a matrix of the types of searches your organization needs to be complete to mitigate your concerns.
   a. Identity verification
   b. Criminal checks
   c. Civil checks
   d. Driving history

    e. Credit history

    f. Past employers

    g. Education verification

    h. Professional licenses and certifications

    i. References

4. Consider a family of searches (i.e. criminal plus employment verification) based on the job responsibilities and level of access in the company to people, records, trade secrets, funds, or proprietary information.

5. Consider checking social web sites as background information.

6. The company you select does not have to do all the checks mentioned. You may want to do references and checking of social sites in-house.

7. Ask for a performance trial from your potential provider against known results.

8. Negotiate service-level agreements tied to performance and penalties if violated.

9. Rescreen any employee who moves into a higher, more robust position since the risk increases as the individual moves up in the organization.

10. Consider ongoing monitoring for drivers.

11. Consider the use of drug screening, especially in manufacturing and construction jobs.

12. RFPs are important for capability and not just pricing.

EARLY WARNING SIGNS OF VIOLENCE FROM AN INTERNAL SOURCE

An employee may be exhibiting warning signs that may be a precursor to a violent individual who is escalating toward violence. Taken separately, these may not be significant but look for clusters of behavior. (Baron (1993)). *Violence in the workplace.*

Does an employee in the organization (including contractors, vendors, volunteers, and consultants) display any of the following behaviors?

1. Does he or she have attendance problems?
2. Do the activities of the associate have impact on supervisor/managers' time?
3. Is there a pattern of decreased productivity for this individual?
4. Is there an inconsistent work pattern with this associate?
5. Does the individual have poor on-the-job relationships with coworkers or associates?
6. Does he or she have trouble concentrating on the tasks at hand?

7. Are there violations of safety rules with an individual who is trained and has demonstrated compliance in the past?
8. Has this associate developed poor health and/or show poor hygiene in a depreciating pattern?
9. Is unusual/changed behavior starting to be manifested by the individual that seems inconsistent with past behavior?
10. Does this person have any fascination with guns or firearms?
11. Is there evidence of possible drug or alcohol use or abuse in this individual?
12. Has there been evidence of serious stress in the employee's personal life recently or developing over time?
13. Does the employee tend to continually blame others and make excuses for his or her behaviors?
14. Has this individual developed a case of unshakable depression?

Reference

Baron (1993). *Violence in the workplace.*

CHECKLIST FOR VIOLENCE ATTRACTING CONDITIONS

Below is a checklist of conditions in your business that might attract violence. Assess your risk answering the questions below. National Victim Assistance Academy (2002).

- Does your organization have contact with the public?
- Is there an exchange of money at your organization or business?
- Are there deliveries of passengers, goods, and services?
- Does your organization have a mobile place of business (i.e., lunch wagon or a police cruiser)?
- Does your organization work with unstable or chemically dependent persons?
- Does your organization require workers to work alone or in small numbers?
- Does your organization require persons to work at night or work late hours?
- Does your organization require persons to work in a high crime area?

- Does your organization require the guarding of valuable property or items?
- Is your location in a community-based setting or a standalone building in a remote area?

Reference

National Victim Assistance Academy. (2002). *Foundations in victimology and victims' rights and services.* Retrieved August 30, 2009, from www.ojp.usdoj.gov/ovc/assist/nvaa2002.

WAYS TO DIFFUSE FRUSTRATION IN THE WORKPLACE

- Provide email address boxes or internal company blogs where questions can be asked and answered. Post answers to questions back to all in a generic manner so as not to break a confidence with a source.
- Additional EAP resources may be sourced and made known to the workforce.
- Allow and facilitate company meetings in both large and small forums down to the work team level to discuss the realities of the company's economic dilemmas.
- Try not to hide from the tough discussions or appear defensive. Avoidance or defensiveness will only confirm the appearance of uncaring corporate executives who are lining their pockets at the expense of the rank and file.
- Remember to communicate. If there is one area that is relatively inexpensive yet often overlooked it is this simple factor. Communication will be absolutely critical to changing or improving a corporate culture.

CLEAR

To change an organization's culture from one that breeds violence to one that is healthy, be CLEAR.

C—Communication—Is this a priority in the organization? Does the organization remember to communicate? Remember correction is good, but training is better. Communicate.

L—Learn to listen; to learn—Does leadership really listen to employees or is lip service being paid to the concerns of the people?

E—Evaluate and examine—Are policies, procedures, strategies, and tactics up-to-date and current with the organization's current posture?

A—Accountability needs to be established—Where in the business are initiatives placed for change? Is it high enough to make it relevant?

R—Response to issues—How quick are the responses to concerns or questions from employees?

WAYS TO AVOID THE COST OF VIOLENCE IN THE WORKPLACE

The checklist below demonstrates the ways violence in the workplace can be avoided through a proactive budget.

1. Has the organization completed a risk analysis of the potential for violence in the workplace?
2. Does the organization have a pre-employment and an ongoing background screening program for our employees and contractors?
3. Has the business negotiated security into its lease paying attention to lighting, fencing, and access systems?
4. Is the organization a good neighbor in its building, complex, or area with neighbors creating interlocking security and safety systems wherever possible?
5. Does the business participate in professional and local crime prevention associations?

6. Who at the local police department is someone with whom we could counsel?
7. If the organization does not have a security organization, is a reputable security consultant known who could create a security plan including preventing violence in the workplace?

RESPONDING TO ACTIVE SHOOTERS

Guidelines

In general, how you respond to an active shooter will be dictated by the specific circumstances of the encounter. If you find yourself involved in an active shooter situation, try to remain calm and call 911 as soon as possible.

If an active shooter is outside your building or inside the building you are in, you should:

- Try to remain calm.
- Try to warn other employees and visitors to take immediate shelter.
- Proceed to a room that can be locked or barricaded.
- Lock and barricade doors or windows.
- Turn off lights.
- Close blinds.
- Turn off any devices that emit sound.
- Keep yourself out of sight, stay away from windows, and take adequate cover/protection, that is, concrete walls, thick desks, and filing cabinets.
- Silence cell phones.
- Have one person call 911 and provide the following information.

"This is XYZ Corporation (give your exact location)—we have an active shooter here, gunshots fired."

If possible, include other crucial information.

- If you were able to see the offender(s), give a description of the person's(s') sex, race, clothing, type of weapon(s), location last observed, direction of travel, and identity—if known.
- If you observed any victims, give a description of the location and number of victims.
- If you observed any suspicious devices (improvised explosive devices), provide the location observed and a description.
- If you heard any explosions, provide a description and location.
- Wait patiently until a uniformed police officer, or a manager known to you, provides an "all clear."
- Unfamiliar voices may be an active shooter trying to lure you from safety; do not respond to voice commands until you can verify with certainty that they are being issued by a police officer or company official.
- Attempts to rescue people should only be attempted if it can be accomplished without further endangering the persons inside a secured area.
- Depending on circumstances, consideration may also be given to exiting ground floor windows as safely and quietly as possible.

If an active shooter enters your office or work area, you should:

- Try to remain calm.
- Try not to do anything that will provoke the active shooter.
- If there is no possibility of escape or hiding, only as a last resort when your life is in imminent danger should you make a personal choice to attempt to negotiate with or overpower the assailant(s).
- Call 911, if possible, and provide the information listed in the first guideline.
- If the active shooter(s) leaves the area, barricade the room or proceed to a safer location.

If you are in an outside area and encounter an active shooter, you should:

- Try to remain calm.
- Move away from the active shooter or the sounds of gunshot(s) and/or explosion(s).
- Look for appropriate locations for cover/protection, that is, brick walls, retaining walls, large trees, parked vehicles, or any other object that may stop bullet penetration.
- Try to warn other employees and visitors to take immediate shelter.
- Call 911 and provide the information listed in the first guideline.

What to Expect from Responding Police Officers

The objectives of responding police officers are:
- Immediately engage or contain the active shooter(s) to stop life-threatening behavior.
- Identify threats such as improvised explosive devices.
- Identify victims to facilitate medical care, interviews, and counseling.
- Investigation of the incident.

Police officers responding to an active shooter are trained to proceed immediately to the area in which shots were last heard to stop the shooting as quickly as possible. The first responding officers may be in teams; they may be dressed in normal patrol uniforms, or they may be wearing external ballistic vests and Kevlar helmets or other tactical gear. The officers may be armed with rifles, shotguns, or handguns. Do exactly as the officers instruct; do not initiate any interaction with the officers. The first responding officers will be focused on identifying and stopping the active shooter, and initially they may need to treat everyone present as a potential suspect. Their second objective is creating a safe environment for medical assistance to be brought in to aid the injured. Do not interfere with the officers' activities.

SAMPLE WORKPLACE WEAPONS POLICY

Policy Statement

To ensure a safe environment for employees and customers, our establishment, **[Employer Name]** prohibits the wearing, transporting, storage, or presence of firearms or other dangerous weapons in our facilities or on our property. Any employee in possession of a firearm or other weapon while on our facilities/property or while otherwise fulfilling job responsibilities may face disciplinary action including termination. A client or visitor who violates this policy may be removed from the property and reported to police authorities. Possession of a valid concealed weapons permit authorized by the State of Minnesota is *not* an exemption under this policy.

Definition

Firearms or other dangerous weapons means:
- Any device from which a projectile may be fired by an explosive
- Any simulated firearm operated by gas or compressed air

- Slingshot
- Sand club
- Metal knuckles
- Any spring blade knife
- Any knife which opens or is ejected open by an outward, downward thrust or movement
- Any instrument that can be used as a club and poses a reasonable risk of injury.

Exemptions

This policy does not apply to:
- Any law enforcement personnel engaged in official duties
- Any security personnel engaged in official duties
- Any person engaged in military activities sponsored by the federal or state government while engaged in official duties.

Notification

"No Firearms or Other Dangerous Weapons" signs shall be conspicuously posted within all **[Employer Name]** facilities and in parking areas and grounds surrounding our facilities. These signs will clearly indicate that firearms and other weapons are not to be carried onto our property or into our facilities.

Reporting

Staff or security personnel will request any visitor found in possession of a firearm or other dangerous weapon to remove it from the facility and local law enforcement authorities will be notified promptly.

Special Instructions for Employees

Any employee concerned about personal safety may request an escort (e.g., to a parking lot off premises) or other appropriate intervention by security personnel. Educational materials will be made available on request regarding the magnitude of the workplace violence problem in the United States and the role of firearms and other dangerous weapons in this violence. Training will be provided to employees on this and other workplace violence prevention measures that **[Employer Name]** has implemented.

Reference

Minnesota Department of Labor & Industry (2009). Retrieved from http://www.dli.mn.gov/WSC/PDF/vguideape.pdf.

SAMPLE WORKPLACE VIOLENCE PREVENTION POLICY

Agency/Facility/Campus/Unit_____
Date_____

Mission

Employees are our most valued asset. The strategic goal of the (name of organization) is to improve the quality of our employees' working environment. In that regard safety and security are of the utmost importance. To the extent reasonably possible, (name of organization) will provide a work environment where employees will not be subjected to acts of physical assault or threats of bodily harm while performing their official duties, wherever those duties are performed. *There shall be zero tolerance of such threats or acts of violence.*

Policy on Violence

(Name of organization) views aggressive and/or violent behavior as disruptive and contrary to the development and maintenance of a safe, productive, and supportive work environment. Such behavior is actively discouraged. Employees who exhibit such behavior will be held accountable under the policy and work rules, as well as local, state, and federal law.

All threats and acts of aggression or violent behavior should be taken seriously and addressed immediately. Such threats or acts include, but are not limited to:

- Harming or threatening to harm any employee or guest
- Damaging or threatening to damage property or the property of any employee or guest
- Possessing a dangerous weapon or incendiary device on property without prior authorization (law enforcement officers and employees who carry weapons in the performance of their duties are considered authorized)
- Engaging in stalking behavior of any employee.

Accountability

All personnel are responsible for notifying their immediate managers, or, in the absence of their manager, another member of the management team, of any threats that they have witnessed, received, or have been told that another person has witnessed or received. Even without an actual threat, personnel should also report any behavior they have witnessed which they regard as threatening or violent, when that behavior is job related or might be carried out on a state-controlled site, or is connected to state employment. Employees are responsible for making this report regardless of the relationship between the aggressor and the individual to whom the threat or threatening behavior was directed.

Directive

Any person who makes substantial threats, exhibits threatening behavior, or engages in violent acts against employees, visitors, guests, or other individuals while on (name of organization) property shall be removed from the premises as quickly as safety permits, and shall remain off DOR premises pending the outcome of an investigation. Employees are not to remove individuals from the premises.

Assistance must be requested from the Capitol Police or local authorities. DOR will initiate an appropriate response which may include, but is not limited to, suspension and/or termination of any business relationship, reassignment of job duties, suspension or termination of employment, and/or criminal prosecution of the person or persons involved.

Employees and managers should work together to identify and report situations or locations where there is a potential for physical assault or threat of bodily harm. Managers may keep files on persons and locations where past specific behavior indicates the existence of anger and hostility; where a significant enforcement action is being taken; or where other behaviors, experiences, attitudes, etc., indicate a potential problem.

Employees should record specific incidents, behaviors, or conversations that may indicate a potential for violence. Documentation should be forwarded to their manager. In instances where their manager is the source of potential violence, documentation should be forwarded to the next level of management with a copy to the safety officer.

Managers must carefully review and assess information provided by employees or other sources. Appropriate precautions should be taken based on the specific situation. For example, if a problem situation or location is identified, it should be communicated to other employees who are likely to become involved in the situation or come in contact with the location.

Individuals who apply for or obtain a protective or restraining order which lists those specific locations that areas being protected, must provide to their manager and the safety officer with a copy of the petition and declaration used to seek the order, a copy of any temporary protective restraining order which subsequently is granted, and a copy of any protective or restraining order that is made permanent.

The safety officer will monitor and evaluate the violence reports in the department on an ongoing basis and will submit annual program reports to the secretary.

INDEX